Telepathic T

"An extraordinary compendium that unveils a hidden dimension of human experience, revealing the uncanny reality of mind-to-mind communication and psychic phenomena across cultures and throughout history. Daniel Bourke's meticulous research and storytelling offer compelling evidence for these mysterious abilities—so often dismissed by conventional science, yet woven deeply into the fabric of our collective memory. Overflowing with rare anecdotes and astonishing premonitions, *Telepathic Tales* is a captivating journey into the unexplained powers of the human mind. Examined through the lens of contemporary psychic research, these tales shed light on the universal human experience of extrasensory perception that conventional science often overlooks."

DAVID JAY BROWN, AUTHOR OF *DREAMING WIDE AWAKE* AND *THE ILLUSTRATED FIELD GUIDE TO DMT ENTITIES*

"In *Telepathic Tales*, Daniel Bourke gathers an impressive, convincing, and entertaining body of evidence from folklore and legend around the world that attests to the global ubiquity of what we call the paranormal. His wide research argues that precognition, bilocation, clairvoyance, and other realities still denied by Western science are a common human experience, one that readers of this engaging book can share."

GARY LACHMAN, AUTHOR OF *DREAMING AHEAD OF TIME* AND *TOUCHED BY THE PRESENCE*

"In *Telepathic Tales*, Daniel Bourke takes the reader on a multicultural voyage of discovery through the history of vivid case studies of such paranormal experiences as precognitive visitations, mysterious dreams, and glimpses of the afterlife. This is an enjoyable book that encompasses the full range of psychic experiences dating back to the birth of civilization and as far away as Peru, Iran, Sweden, and Japan. By presenting numerous accounts from modern Western parapsychologists all the way back to ancient times, Bourke has given the reader a different and personal way to consider not only the meaning of ESP, but also the reason for our very existence."

MARC J. SEIFER, PH.D., AUTHOR OF *WHERE DOES MIND END?*

"*Telepathic Tales* is a visionary collection of testimonies confirming the very real possibility that precognition exists within all of us. Read it for the compelling data it is and discover the power of transcending time in your own mind."

THERESA CHEUNG, SUNDAY TIMES BESTSELLING AUTHOR OF *THE DREAM DICTIONARY FROM A TO Z* AND COAUTHOR OF *THE PREMONITION CODE*

"Are you open to knowing that our minds are much more intertwined than the narratives of conventional science tell us? That you are not just an individual but part of the collective human organism? Through the collective human mind, you are enmeshed not only with other people, but also with the plants and animals of our natural world. In *Telepathic Tales* you will find compelling evidence of our interconnectedness. Read this book and connect!"

BERNARD BEITMAN, M.D., AUTHOR OF *MEANINGFUL COINCIDENCES* AND *LIFE-CHANGING SYNCHRONICITIES*

"A veritable treasure trove of anomalous human experiences from disparate cultures and centuries that, collectively, remind us how deeply connected we are. Bourke's painstaking archival work is reminiscent of a botanist collecting and cataloging specimens to ultimately enrich the field. The materialist paradigm will be sorely challenged by these many, many voices that speak of transcendent—yet surprisingly ordinary and intimate—knowledge from across the arc of human history."

PATRICIA PEARSON, AUTHOR OF *OPENING HEAVEN'S DOOR*

"Bourke has mastered the art of portraying—in a well-documented way—a wide range of cases of telepathy, premonition, and death-related phenomena across the centuries and in different cultures and traditions expressed by these extrasensory abilities reported since the dawn of time. They all point to our true nature as spiritual beings—with consciousness as the fundamental essence of reality. *Telepathic Tales* is an important contribution to the elaboration of a post-materialist philosophy. I highly recommend this outstanding book."

EVELYN ELSAESSER, AUTHOR OF *SPONTANEOUS CONTACTS WITH THE DECEASED*

Telepathic Tales

Precognition and Clairvoyance
in Legend, Lyric, and Lore

A Sacred Planet Book

Daniel Bourke

Destiny Books
Rochester, Vermont

Destiny Books
One Park Street
Rochester, Vermont 05767
www.DestinyBooks.com

Destiny Books is a division of Inner Traditions International

Sacred Planet Books are curated by Richard Grossinger, Inner Traditions editorial board member and cofounder and former publisher of North Atlantic Books. The Sacred Planet collection, published under the umbrella of the Inner Traditions family of imprints, includes works on the themes of consciousness, cosmology, alternative medicine, dreams, climate, permaculture, alchemy, shamanic studies, oracles, astrology, crystals, hyperobjects, locutions, and subtle bodies.

Copyright © 2025 by Daniel Bourke

All rights reserved. No part of this book may be reproduced or utilized in any form or by any means, electronic or mechanical, including photocopying, recording, or any information storage and retrieval system, without permission in writing from the publisher. No part of this book may be used or reproduced to train artificial intelligence technologies or systems.

Cataloging-in-Publication Data for this title is available from the Library of Congress

ISBN 979-8-88850-173-3 (print)
ISBN 979-8-88850-174-0 (ebook)

Printed and bound in the United States by Lake Book Manufacturing, LLC

10 9 8 7 6 5 4 3 2 1

Text design and layout by Kenleigh Manseau
This book was typeset in Garamond Premier Pro with Big Caslon CC and Classico URW used as display typefaces

To send correspondence to the author of this book, mail a first-class letter to the author c/o Inner Traditions • Bear & Company, One Park Street, Rochester, VT 05767, and we will forward the communication, or contact the author directly at **daniel_bourke_89@hotmail.com**.

Scan the QR code and save 25% at InnerTraditions.com. Browse over 2,000 titles on spirituality, the occult, ancient mysteries, new science, holistic health, and natural medicine.

*For Laura, Barry, Laurence, and Jack
With Love Forever*

To the anthropologist we say, the evidence we adduce is your own evidence, that of books of travel in all lands and countries. If you may argue from it, so may we. Some of it is evidence to unusual facts, more of it is evidence to singular beliefs, which we think not necessarily without foundation.

ANDREW LANG, THE MAKING OF RELIGION

Contents

Foreword by Gregory Shushan, Ph.D.   ix

Acknowledgments   xiii

Introduction
Death, Life, and the Magic in the Mind   1

■■■

1   **I Knew You Were Coming**   4
*Vardogers and Strange Knowledge
of a Visitor's Arrival*

2   **I Knew You Were in Trouble**   49
*Historical and Cross-Cultural Visions
of a Distant Crisis*

3   **A Date with Destiny**   75
*Nearing-Death Awareness in
Legend, Lyric, and Lore*

4   **Discoveries at the Deathbed**   110
Veridical Visions and Dreams of the Dying

5	Revenants, Wraiths, and Disinterested Shades	127
	Vampires, Zombies, and Mysterious Knowledge of a Distant Death	
6	Treasure, Tombs, and Visionary Boons	146
	Cross-Cultural ESP Involving Mysterious Knowledge of an Item's Location	
7	I Knew the Cure	172
	Sacred Healing, Other Worlds, and the Origins of Botanical Knowledge	
8	I Know What You Dreamed	206
	Shared Visions, Double Revelations, and Ultimate Truth	

■■■

Epilogue	
The Magic in the Mind	235
Notes	237
Bibliography	263
Index	297

Foreword

Gregory Shushan, Ph.D.

Throughout history and around the world, people have reported extraordinary experiences of clairvoyance, telepathy, and related unusual phenomena. Sometimes these experiences are spontaneous, at other times they are deliberately sought and brought about by ritual activity. They can occur in dreams and in visionary trance states, as well as in fully waking moments. Sometimes they are dramatic—such as individuals "appearing" to someone before they have actually arrived (known as a *vardoger* in Scandinavian folklore)—though at other times they are simply feelings, vague premonitions, or even hunches. The types of information acquired through such apparently "paranormal" means range from the mundane to the profound: forewarnings of deaths, medical information that will facilitate healing, the location of missing objects, and revelations of metaphysical realities.

Accounts of such experiences are not confined to "insider" literature written only by true believers. Indeed, the majority of the accounts in the present book have been culled from the works of Western scholars: anthropologists, historians, folklorists, classicists, and so on. While scholars are only as reliable as their sources, the fact that these experiences have been reported from so many diverse and often unconnected cultures has profound implications. It suggests one of two things: people around the world invent similar kinds of stories about supernatural phenomena or people around the world genuinely have these kinds of experiences.

Even among some of Bourke's sources—the very people who have reported the accounts—there is skepticism as to their reality. While there is no true consensus, the sources being products of their times (many date back to over a hundred years ago or more), most of the scholars place Western modes of thought, reason, and religion above those of the individuals they studied. With rare exceptions, few took the logical step of examining the reported phenomena in light of contemporary accounts from psychical research—a field that blossomed in the nineteenth century and has never gone away.

One might argue that evaluating truth claims is not the remit of the anthropologist or historian of religions, but an equally valid argument is that unless one is prepared to take seriously the extraordinary experiences within a given society, only a partial and indeed incomplete understanding of that society is possible. In other words, the refusal to engage with extraordinary phenomena as universal human phenomena is to impose Western scholarly assumptions and disciplinary dogmas on the societies themselves. This is not only a value judgment, but it also creates an artificial gulf between culture and extraordinary experience, and implicitly adopts the stance that such accounts are invented and therefore untrue. And yet those same scholars accept more or less without question what their sources say about the facts of history, or what their Indigenous informants tell them about their kinship systems, diet, taboos, rituals, crafts, food production, burial practices, and so on.

Herein lies the importance of this, Bourke's second book, *Telepathic Tales*. In presenting accounts from such a range of sources, the author demonstrates that these are indeed panhuman phenomena. As such, they require explanation. His chapter on the vardoger phenomenon, for example, raises the kinds of questions addressed by the sociologist David Hufford in his work on sleep paralysis, most notably in his classic study

The Terror that Comes in the Night.[1] Hufford was the first to identify the cross-cultural occurrence of reports in which an individual describes being held down by an ominous presence, a weight on the chest, waking in a state of terror and being unable to move or even scream (and in a terrified state). The experience seems incredibly, confusingly real to those who have them. Hufford discovered that while sleep paralysis is found around the world, the identity of the malignant presence is culturally determined: in Newfoundland it is the Old Hag, in Cambodia an angry ghost, in the United States extraterrestrial aliens, and so on.

This demonstrates the profound impact of extraordinary experiences upon human beliefs in the supernatural; but while this particular phenomenon is proven to have a mundane psychological explanation, what of the veridical accounts found in the present book, of those who dream of events that later come to pass, or those who see apparitions of individuals not known to have died, among so many other types of "unexplained" phenomena? Does the sheer weight of these accumulated accounts lend them more credence? Of course, they might all be dismissed by skeptics as simply "anecdotal" in the sense that they are not consistently replicable under controlled scientific laboratory experiments. That, however, does nothing to explain the existence of the accounts across time and across cultures in the first place.

Aside from its importance for these types of philosophical questions, the range of phenomena—many of which have been underrepresented in discussions of the paranormal—as well as the varieties of cultures makes for fascinating and engaging reading. As with his previous book, *Apparitions at the Moment of Death*, readers will marvel at the depth and breadth of Bourke's research and his command of the sources.

Among the numerous accounts reviewed are those involving such famous individuals as Charles Dickens, Mark Twain, Daniel Defoe, Carl Jung, and the famous medium Eileen J. Garrett—not to mention the numerous saints, shamans, and other holy figures of different religious traditions, from Rumi to Saint Anthony to Chaitanya

Mahaprabhu. Perhaps the majority, however, involve everyday people who at least initially find their unbidden, spontaneous experience bewildering. This again emphasizes both the diversity of contexts for the reporting of such experiences and the author's skill in hunting them down. In one section alone we are swept along by accounts from Native Americans, ancient Chinese, Aboriginal Australians, medieval Italians, nineteenth-century psychical researchers, Indigenous Africans, ancient Greeks, early Celtic Irish, medieval Japanese, and church fathers of the Middle East, to name but a few!

The vast scope of this rich work is truly astonishing and provides the foundations for a world's history of the diverse forms of telepathy, clairvoyance, and precognition. Daniel Bourke has not only done a service to researchers in compiling so many accounts from such an impressively wide range of sources, he has also produced an entertaining and highly readable book.

Gregory Shushan, Ph.D.
San Francisco, California

Gregory Shushan, Ph.D., is the leading authority on near-death experiences and afterlife beliefs across cultures and throughout history. He is an award-winning author affiliated with Birmingham Newman University, University of Winchester, Marian University, and the Parapsychology Foundation. A former researcher at the University of Oxford and University of Wales, he lives in San Francisco.

Acknowledgments

Firstly, a huge thanks to my editors Dorona Zierler and Sharon Reed, without whom this book would be so much less than it is. I'm grateful to everyone at Inner Traditions for seeing the value in this project. To Gregory Shushan for his wonderful foreword and the added context and balance it brings to the proceedings. My thanks also go to Aaron Davis for the colorful cover art.

I would also and especially like to thank you, the reader, for taking an interest in this work, and I hope it offers something of the same strange sense of mystery and magic that I felt while compiling it! And of course, to my mother, father, and two brothers. With love always and forever.

INTRODUCTION

Death, Life, and the Magic in the Mind

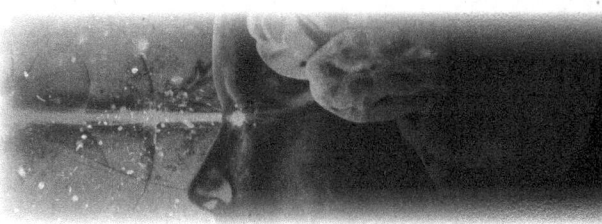

> *Despite all the technology and the animal experimentation, we are no closer now to grasping the neural basis of experience than we were a hundred years ago. Currently, we lack even a back-of-the-envelope theory about what the behavior of individual cells contributes to consciousness. This in itself is no scandal. It is a scandal if we allow the hype to obscure the fact that we are in the dark.*
>
> — ALVA NOË

In all ages, certain people have claimed knowledge not only of ordinary things; they have also claimed secret knowledge of extraordinary things. According to the records of all lands, information about distant events in space and time has, by some magical means, become mysteriously known to the suitably receptive individual. Despite our prevailing ideas regarding the "location" and reach of the mind and consciousness itself, we are still in the early stages. Neuroscience is mere decades into its existence, and the hard problem of squaring the experience of consciousness with the material machinations of the physical brain is as great a challenge as ever. There is much room for discovery, and little room for philosophical biases in assessing anomalous facts. Indeed, although unknown to many, there exists a mysteriously persistent body of knowledge that speaks to something more, some further fascinating frontier.

If the evidence and collected attestation of the folklorists, the anthropologists and ethnologists, the historians, and the parapsychologists are to be believed, the mind reaches out far and wide beyond arm's length and, at times, breezes by the restraints and limitations we may have hastily placed upon it. Here, a great variety of those sources will be brought to bear, at most upon their reality and, at the very least, upon the questions of ubiquity and belief regarding these seemingly "extrasensory" capacities—and they have long been recorded.

In these pages, we will encounter examples ranging from Greek seer Iamos—who announced the death of Hercules at the moment of its occurrence to the legendary twins Castor and Pollux—to the far-reaching visions of the shaman in his ecstatic trance, who might warn his tribe of approaching danger or inform them regarding the location of game or lost items. Whether from within or without the Abrahamic religions, their saints, too, commonly claimed or were ascribed often indistinguishable abilities such as thought reading, consorting with dead martyrs, bilocation, and myriad others. The witches, wizards, and heroes of romance, too, were privy to secret things: strange and accurate knowledge of their own oncoming deaths and the deaths of others, intimations regarding the well-being of loved ones, and so on.

While many illustrious witnesses to these strange and wondrous events fill historical and legendary volumes, the folklorists, gathering their tales from as far apart as the plains of Peru, the haunted highlands of Scotland, or the snowy taiga forests of the northern latitudes, have recorded the same among the ordinary people of all continents. In our own age, too, our contemporaries continue to be moved by the same magic.

While esteemed classicists, psychologists, parapsychologists, and other serious scholars who dared to approach these psychical topics in the late nineteenth century and beyond, concerned with presenting their best academic face in a climate highly skeptical of their work, largely dismissed the testimony of the past, we are under no such constraints here and bring some much-needed historical and cross-cultural volume to the conversation. The reader, then, can decide their ultimate value. It is this magic in the mind that will be the subject of the following chapters.

ONE

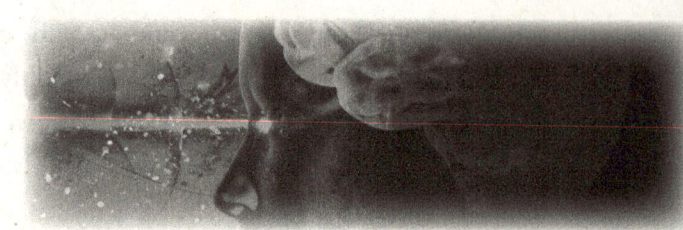

I Knew You Were Coming

Vardogers and Strange Knowledge of a Visitor's Arrival

> *Witches have red eyes, and cannot see far, but they have a keen scent like the beasts, and are aware when human beings draw near.*
>
> — JACOB GRIMM

In the 1970s a rural Finnish woman offered the following memorate to Leea Virtanen, former professor of Finnish and comparative folk poetry studies:

> My mother had the gift of knowing in advance when visitors were coming and who they would be. She had this gift all her life. Occasionally, she has been mistaken, but then it has turned out that the person intended to come, but was prevented.[1]

Some decades earlier, in his autobiography, English writer Osbert Sitwell stated, rather unceremoniously, regarding his time at boarding school, that:

I knew beforehand when my mother, or my brother or sister, was coming to see me. Infallibly, invariably, and without being informed of it, I became aware the previous day, and even when it appeared most unlikely that such a visit was impending, and equally I could tell if suddenly it had to be postponed.[2*]

While a couple of anecdotes may not impress, such experiences are surprisingly common and involve the seeming reception of knowledge regarding the approach of someone to one's own location at a time when this couldn't have been conventionally known. This, as we'll see, might be a visitor known to the informant, a loved one, a stranger, an animal, or even entire armies, and may become known by way of a dream, a vision, a footstep, a voice, a scent, or a sound. While there is no agreed-upon terminology to describe what seems to present as "clairvoyant" or "telepathic" experiences, they are nevertheless widely found. Renowned novelist Charles Dickens wrote in his journal of just such a thing, a dream regarding which he made it clear that "all the circumstances" were "exactly told." Dickens saw a lady in a red shawl who identified herself as "Miss Napier." Dickens wondered in the morning why on earth he would dream such a thing, noting he had never heard of a Miss Napier. That same night, however, the identical lady in the red shawl turned up in his retiring room, and her name was Miss Napier. She had been traveling to see him with two others known to him.[3]

Vardøger (vard-deh-ay'-grr) or, roughly, "spiritual predecessor," is the Norwegian term most closely related to these experiences, and unlike the numerous strange and seemingly "extrasensory" phenomena that have been so well described over the past half century, these mysterious vardogers and especially their relatives have gone mostly untouched.[4] They have certainly been acknowledged to some degree; how much

---

*Sitwell had considered this to be a form of "intuition" and believed, based upon his lifetime of experiences, that one might have "intimations of the future." While his father had always called him superstitious, Sitwell stated that he eventually admitted that he had the same gift when he was younger but that "it dies as one grows older."

they have been historically and cross-culturally represented, however, remains significantly and conspicuously unexplored. These phenomena themselves, as it happens, are found not just among a variety of folkloric sources, but literary, allegorical, anecdotal, anthropological, and legendary sources on every continent. Here, we hope, for the first time, to give a much firmer indication in this regard. Furthermore, the extent to which these mysterious accounts have been neglected warrants the relatively bulky presentation that will be our first and longest chapter here, the first port of call in our explorations of these "telepathic tales."

WORLD OF VISIONS AND VARDOGERS

While these are phenomena most commonly associated with Norse and some Scottish sources, such visions, dreams, and intimations are to be found in impressive abundance much further afield, for example, among Africans, Polynesians, Siberians, and the First Peoples spanning the entirety of the Americas. Even those spread liberally throughout the present chapter are only indicative of a much greater trove of accounts that have rarely, if ever, been related to their more recognized northern European counterparts.

Award-winning American folklorist Barre Toelken was himself greatly impressed with such incidents—which fell under the category of "moccasin telegraph," as it is often referred to among the Navajo Indians—and gave numerous examples. One of a particularly striking character from 1956 had the author driving over three hundred miles from Salt Lake City to a reserve in Blanding, Utah. When he arrived, Toelken found an old Navajo woman preparing food. Upon speaking to her regarding his arrival, she said, "Of course, that's why I cooked up all this food!" Toelken expressed great disbelief, noting this woman had no way to know they were coming—no electricity, phone, or even windows. The rather measured folklorist had "no doubt" these things happened, although he made clear the difficulty in explaining them.[5] While again, singular stories may not impress, Toelken observed that these anecdotes are common and that, while surprise was often the reaction of outsiders, for the Navajo themselves, it was rather taken for granted.

According to Danish polar explorer, author, and anthropologist Peter Freuchen, when he visited an old friend called Manasse in Ikamiut, a settlement in western Greenland, he was, upon his arrival, "greeted with a smile" before Manasse noted that "he had known we were coming because his last few dreams had told him of our arrival."[6]

English ethnologist and folklorist Charles Hill-Tout, who worked primarily in British Columbia, heard of an elk man and his wife who lived among the Canadian Salish and Dene Indians "long ago." Their daughter left home to seek an old aunt who lived somewhere far to the south. She had not, however, traveled long before her aunt, who was a very wise woman, learned in a dream that her niece was on her way to seek her out.[7]

Strange Connections

Something of interest here is the extent to which these events are often incidentally referenced, presented dispassionately by those recording them, and divorced from any "vardoger-specific" or otherwise strange or spiritual/psychical context. The social scientists, in fact, have independently recorded innumerable examples and often express great surprise at their occurrence. Like Toelken, Elmer Miller, anthropologist and former chair of the Anthropology Department at Temple University, Pennsylvania, gave multiple anecdotes of this kind. While in the Gran Chaco region of South America on August 11, 1960, Miller pointed out very briefly in his chapter notes that a practicing pastor of the Toba people, Acosta, had a vision of their coming the night before he and another of his colleagues set out to visit him. In relation to this vision, Elmer wrote that, "Despite more than a year in this cultural milieu, I was perplexed."[8]

Considering how little has been written on these prophetic intuitions, it is unsurprising that ethnologists, folklorists, and, as we'll see, hagiographers (the biographers of the saints) rarely make the connection between their own records and those of the relatively more established visions and vardogers of the north. Nevertheless, they persist. In another diary entry, Miller writes of a man, Jose, who dreamed that Miller's daughters were coming to visit, which the author later confirmed to Jose by presenting photographs upon their actual arrival.[9] He also wrote seven years earlier in his diary that while visiting a man named Jose Braunstein, another named Valentin Moreno arrived "because he dreamed Braunstein would have a visitor" and says nothing more.[10]

These are by no means unprecedented reports among academically oriented travelers to those particular regions. Psychotherapist Bradford Keeney, after arriving at Curuguaty, a village in Paraguay, heard from a great shaman there that he had dreamed he was on the way and had informed the community that they might be prepared for his arrival.[11]

Mystery Across the Americas

Among the Sibundoy of southwestern Colombia it is particularly strongly believed that people can dream of a visitor's coming before they arrive. One Sibundoy gave an example, which echoed Sitwell's and, like Toelken, later referred to their ubiquity. "I dreamed of so and so," the informant's father used to say, "and then truly the next day in the evening that person would arrive. And so it was true." The Sibundoy, indeed, have a saying, *genti-mi muscu-chi-mi, caya-ndi chi genti chaya-ngapa ca*, which McDowell gives as meaning "You are made to dream a person, the next day that person will arrive."[12]

Anthropologist Philip DeVita wrote that after looking for a man of the New Mexico Mescalero people, an Apache tribesman named Bernard, he finally met his wife, who told him that Bernard was already waiting for him. "You're late" were Bernard's first words to the author. "How could I be late when I didn't know I was coming here?" DeVita replied, further stating, "I, thinking only of telephones, denied having been called." Bernard shrugged and said he had dreamed specifically that someone had arrived on the reservation with whom he was going to record some of the things he knew about his people. As it happened, this was DeVita's plan for the day.[13] These were not new ideas in the Americas and were certainly not some solely imported belief. As early as 1681, Spanish missionaries found that among the inhabitants of what is now New Mexico, peyote cactus was used to induce visions in which "a person could tell just what persons might be on the way from New Spain to New Mexico."[14]

Shifting scenes for a moment for something related, Presbyterian minister and missionary George Schwab had an instance of the "seeing eye" among a Liberian tribe in which there were rumors circulating of an approaching party of foreigners bringing harm to them. Acting upon this rumor, one of their seers applied a certain medicine to his eye and had an "oracular vision in which he saw the *palaver* [war] coming," and they did really arrive.[15] Worlds away, too, American humorist and folklorist Charles Leland, in 1893, was given surprisingly similar information regarding certain Sibyls, witches, and fortune tellers who were then famed in Florence, Italy. One of these was personally known to him. They were renowned for many skills, which, as was the case with so many shamans and medicine men, were apparently often expressed "by virtue of certain plants." Of most interest here is that, using their divination, "they would predict the coming of people."[16]

Returning to the Americas, though, when pioneering German-American anthropologist Franz Boas visited the dwelling of a Kwakiutl Indian on the Pacific Northwest Coast, that man, named Ai'x'agdda'lagdlis, seemed to know he would be arriving. "This was my dream last night," he said, "that you should come into my house here, friends."[17]

In a more legendary Seneca Indian tale from New York State, an old man crossing a clearing heard a cry above him and saw a human leg writhing and bleeding among the clouds. That night, the man, confused as to the meaning of this, dreamed of its interpretation. He now somehow knew the stone giants, common figures in Seneca and some Iroquois folktales, would be coming the following day. That morning, he took some friends to a high mountain and heard the war songs of the marching giants as they arrived.[18] However fantastical might be their mythical records, the Seneca invariably report the same things in more grounded memorates too. When a certain man arrived home, his mother-in-law told him that she dreamed he would arrive and that she and her daughter were already waiting for him.[19]

As with the Seneca, these ideas may be as much found in the myths of the California Indians as they are in their more sober anecdotes. In the midst of a Mewan Indian creation myth, we read of a Captain Ho'-ho the Buzzard who, at one point, tells his people, "I dreamed that a north Indian is coming—the son of Yi'-yi." He then tells those with him to watch, and they did. "After a while," they saw him coming, and he reached their village shortly thereafter.[20]

Among the Grand Canyon–based Havasupai Indians, we read in a retold version of one of their tales that a young boy spends the night with three girls who lie to him, telling him they are single and virgins. In the middle of the night, however, he wakes up from a dream in which he learns they are the wives of a man named Blackbird, and that Blackbird was, at that very moment, coming to find him. As soon as he finished exclaiming this, Blackbird arrived.[21]

Howling Fox, a native man of the Pawnee Indians of Oklahoma, dreamed of a certain woman, who told him, "I want to speak to you [...] Tomorrow remain on the grounds and I will be there to talk to you." The next morning, he went to the grounds, and in the evening, when the men had all gone home, he sat still waiting. Soon he saw the woman from his dream coming toward him from the west.[22]

Despite proclaiming his general disbelief, ethnologist Daniel Brinton also relayed examples that he admitted to being "outside the realms of chance." According to Captain Jonathon Carver, he, in 1767, was among certain Indians whose chief had been specifically consulted as to when the relief, which they then relied upon, would arrive. After the "usual preliminaries," presumably some form of induced vision, this chief announced that the next day, exactly when the sun reached its zenith, a canoe would arrive. According to Brinton, "At the appointed hour the whole village, together with the incredulous Englishman, was on the beach, and sure enough, at the minute specified, a canoe swung round a distant point of land, and rapidly approaching the shore brought the expected news."[23]

The chief, the medicine man, the magician, the wise person, the witch—his or her clairvoyance is expected. When the shaman dreams, his literal soul, or some aspect of it, is widely believed to leave the body and view the actual surrounding landscape. These out-of-body experiences are taken very seriously; in many cases, only visions that later proved true were enough for the specialist to retain their reputation. This can be spoken to more broadly with reference to, for example, the Chorote Indians of Paraguay. When a Chorote shaman is said to have "dreamed of a man far away," it is stipulated that "he had not only dreamed it; since he was a shaman, he had [literally] seen him."[24]

As it relates to the present subject, such clairvoyance is ubiquitous. Some of the shamans of northeastern Asia are said to "look around in a dream" and accurately predict the coming of visitors in this way. In one example, Scabby-One, a Chukchi shaman native to eastern Siberia, said to his wife, "Place me near the rear wall and give me my drum, I shall beat it for a while, I shall look around in a dream." After a while, he said to his wife, "Have plenty of food cooked today. Guests are coming."[25] Something similar comes from the Naskapi of Lake Saint John in Canada, when one of them stepped outside camp and felt a sudden feeling of fear. He told others to pick up and beat their drums. "Yes! He is coming. I know it," he said. He soon discovered, using his "inner power," that a cannibal was coming in their direction, after which he directed his power against him. The man was later found dead. "His drum spoke the truth."[26]

Easter Island, Australia, Siberia, and Beyond

Some nine thousand kilometers away, according to English archaeologist and anthropologist Katherine Routledge, the Indigenous people of Easter Island were powerfully attuned to their dreams, noting that they might relay information such as regarding someone coming home with "all the assurances of a wireless message."[27]

Belgian-French explorer Alexandra David-Neel had an experience in Tibet in which her porter was two months late in returning from an errand. She dreamed that he arrived "in a somewhat unusual fashion, wearing a sun hat of a foreign shape. He had never worn such a hat." The next morning, the man, Wangdu, arrived, and as David-Neel noted, "exactly as I had seen him in my dream." This case, in fact, exactly resembles the typical vardoger in that, after the dream, the apparition of Wangdu was also seen, and then seen to disappear ahead of his actual arrival.[28] The very same was true of something recorded in a history of Inverness County in Nova Scotia. A young girl saw a vision of a certain man, seemingly dead, in the house where she was staying that night. The following evening, that very man arrived at the house. She ran to her mother, saying, "Oh, mamma, that is the dead man I saw last night." The man, according to the tale, died within the hour.[29]

In County Kildare, Ireland, one Bishop Ibor of Moville was in the process of describing to his brothers a vision in which he thought he had seen the Blessed Virgin, Mary; however, when Brigid, the saint who was perhaps held in the most affection among saints in Ireland, entered his chamber after traveling to Kildare, Ibor exclaimed, "This is the woman I saw!"[30]

South African journalist Lawrence George Green noted rather in passing, regarding the Sahara Desert, that "Centuries before wireless telegraphy came to the Sahara, there were men in the great trading centres, Timbuktu and Kano, Cairo and Khartoum, who announced when a caravan would arrive." Green noted that even in his own time there, there was "usually a wise old man who will predict the day and the hour when new faces will be seen under the palms."[31]

While the specialist may induce these experiences in order to attain the relevant information, as did the New Mexicans with peyote or Brinton's "usual preliminaries," we have seen that by no means are they solely capable of such things. Ethnologist and anthropologist Craighill Handy, in fact, observed among the Polynesians that "since the soul was believed to be capable of wandering off by itself when the physical body was asleep," therefore was "every man in his sleeping hours at least a clairvoyant and seer."[32] This tallies with anecdotes given much later, and indeed, just as had the Chuckchi shaman with his drum, certain of our more recent informants have attempted such things themselves. American doctor of botany Louisa Rhine gave the case of a woman from Indiana who was headed for Indianapolis when it dawned on her that she had not telegraphed ahead and there would be no one there to meet her. This woman specifically "decided to try telepathy" and repeated to herself, "Meet the two a.m. train." When she arrived, her husband was there to meet her, and when she asked how he knew she was going to be arriving, he said, "I don't know. I was sound asleep when something kept telling me to meet the two a.m. train from St. Louis. So I got up and called the station and was told there was a two a.m. train from St. Louis—so I met it."[33]

None of this, of course, is to diminish the place of the specialist, as certainly spontaneous cases generally seem to be rarer events in an individual's life than those of the former. Coming back to Rhine's account, though, we see the impact and believability of the dream in that it spurred the man to action. A Jewish tale is similar in this way and positions the legendary Rabbi Judah the Pious in the midst of a vision that "so and so" was coming to see him. Then he said to his students, "I smell the fire of hell. A Gentile is coming, who will ask for me. Tell him I am not at home and he cannot see me." When the man arrived, as the vision had suggested, his pupils told him that Judah was not home.[34]

Returning to Africa, when anthropologist Rosalind Shaw was studying migrant Temne diviners in Kono, Sierra Leone, a Temne diamond digger who showed her around told her that he was helping her with her work "because," as Shaw explained it, "he had 'dreamed' me before I arrived."[35] While the stipulation was made that she had a different face in the dream, the rest was implied to be intact, and the belief, possibility, and/or reality of such things are made clear.

On the other side of the globe, recorder of traditions and folklore Janet Mathews gave an instance from an Aboriginal Australian community in which, one evening by the fire, a man named Barker overheard an old man saying "um-um" and a moment later, "er-er." Barker tells us that these sounds were often an indication "that a message had been received." The old man turned to another and said, "Billy will be here tomorrow." The following afternoon, he arrived.[36]

Returning to Siberia, we read, according to explorer Vladimir Arseniev, that a certain shaman invited two others from distant places due to the sudden illness of a young man. They arrived so quickly that it seemed they must have set out before any messenger could have physically arrived. According to Russian anthropologist Sergei Shirokogorov "the Tungus speak about such cases as a common thing and do it when they have no time for sending a messenger."[37] Unlike the likes of Brinton, it is clear Shirokogorov took these accounts rather seriously, suggesting the experiences may be taken as a starting point for investigation. He then gave an account in which a small Tungus boy "saw" his grandfather's uncle kill his father. The boy predicted that the murderer would return after three days, which occurred exactly as it was laid out.[38]

Among the Yakuts, a Turkic ethnic group who mainly live in the Republic of Sakha on the Russian landmass, one named Omogon dreamed that a particular man seemed to have come to town. "Let eight horsemen try to find the man and bring him here," were his orders. Accordingly, the man was found.[39] Farther west, an old tale from Alaska has a woman dreaming that her older brothers came into the shelter where she had been staying. Suddenly she hears a noise, and there are her older brothers, who have just arrived.[40]

Louis Golomb noted that then modern-day Muslim curer-magicians in Thailand would "frequently inform their visitors that the latter's unheralded arrival has already been foreshadowed in one of the magician's dreams or visions."* Occurrences of this kind are considered to be one of the nontherapeutic miracles that would be cited "over and over

---

*Of interest here is that Golomb makes a direct comparison between these arrival visions and those of the ancient pagan rulers of Indonesia, who were said to have "dreamed of the coming of Islamic holy men to their shores." This is one of only a few comparative references to these phenomena in the literature.

again" as an indicator of the individual's supernatural power, perhaps lending truth to our later ideas regarding their common implementation in the lives of the saints.[41]

Described in *The Atlantic Monthly* of July 1866 was a case in which a party of voyagers were fatigued and in danger, depreciating from their original ten to a mere three along the plains near the Mackenzie River in northwestern Canada. When those last three were similarly ready to turn home, they were met by some warriors of the very group they were looking for. They had apparently been sent by their medicine man to intercept the travelers; their arms and attire were "minutely described." When the one of the warriors was asked to explain this extraordinary occurrence, he could apparently offer no other explanation than that he saw them coming and heard them talk on their journey.[42]

Thirty-eight years earlier, in 1828, something similar came about regarding the rescue of a vessel from Quebec bound for Liverpool, although it was spontaneous and did not involve any specialists. A certain shipmate of the captain relayed to him a dream. "Captain," he said, "we shall be relieved this very day." When asked what reason he had for saying so, he replied, as the captain went on to note, "that he had dreamed that he was on board a bark, and that she was coming to our rescue. He described her appearance and rig; and, to our utter astonishment, when your vessel hove in sight, she corresponded exactly to his description of her."[43]

From the pioneer times of California, a certain Englishman, Lusk, had come into the service of one Captain Sam Jackson of the Bark of Blue Bell ship. After some time together, Lusk told the captain, "I dreamed of you before you came here; I longed to be in your service."[44] British geologist and surgeon John Beaumont noted similar occurrences regarding "those who have second sight." The author tells us of a man who could look into the fire and know which stranger would be coming to his house the next day, or even very shortly on that same day.[45]

Almost two hundred years later, an account also given as an

example of second sight came in the words of a hospital surgeon regarding a patient of theirs. We read of a man confined to his bed and increasingly attacked by "mental derangements." Among a number of clairvoyant feats, he told his sister, "There is a handsome man and an old woman coming to see you this afternoon." A coach soon arrived, bringing her brother and a nurse for her father from eleven miles away.[46] Something of notable similarity may be found among a collection of beliefs and superstitions from Utah. A certain Mrs. G had been bedridden for years when she dreamed of a white-haired man coming to visit her. One morning, she noticed the very same man from her dream coming up the walkway.[47]

While the majority of accounts of interest here involve the visitor arriving soon after or coincidentally with the vision, there are many cases where longer time frames are involved. This is brought out in "The Poor Widow's Son," an old Armenian folktale. After twenty years away from home, a father returns without telling anyone, only to see his wife embracing another as he approaches where his house used to be. He overhears the woman, who happened to be speaking about him; she told the other person the following: "Last night I dreamed in my dream that he had come home."[48]

The same was true in a much older account involving a monk, one of the founders of the Cistercian order, Stephen Harding. He is said to have been at the bedside of one of his dying brethren in the south of France when a vision came upon him. He told the abbot that he saw a multitude of men washing their clothes in a fountain of pure water near the church of Citeaux. According to the tale, "The dream was taken to mean that a multitude would come to Citeaux to wash their stained garments white by repentance." The author notes that the monastery was very rarely visited, let alone by more than one man, yet in the year 1113, a large number of men entered the cloister, begged to be admitted as novices, and wished to change their clothes for the cowl of Saint Benedict.[49]

The stories, then, share striking similarities, and their collectors and experiencers return remarkably similar sentiments and idiosyncrasies, however far apart they might be collected. The social scientists, the folklorists, and the collectors of curious anecdotes record the same strange phenomenon among specialists and laymen alike.

FOOD FOR THOUGHT

Long ago, English poet and topographer George Waldron spoke to a "prevalent superstition" as it then existed on the Isle of Man. He mentions certain sorts of "friendly demons" who "give notice of any stranger's approach." He himself, while visiting a friend, noted with the same cool yet intrigued mindset as had Toelken that:

> As difficult as I found it to bring myself to give any faith to this, I have frequently been very much surprised, when on visiting a friend, I have found the table ready spread, and everything in order to receive me, and been told by the person to whom I went, that he had knowledge of my coming or some other guest by these good-natured intelligences. [. . .] That this is a fact, [Waldron continued] I am positively convinced by many proofs, but how or wherefore it should be so, has frequently given me much matter of Reflection.[50]

Perhaps unbeknownst to Waldron, who had expressed the same surprise as would the ethnologists, the anthropologists, and others, the fact that some external intelligence might be involved in the relaying of this information speaks strongly to the vardoger itself; the idea in Norse folklore being that the individual has a companion spirit who goes ahead and warns of their arrival. In Norway, in fact, it was customary to open the door for a guest twice: once for the guest and once for their companion spirit.[51] It becomes clear just how old this particular idea is, not just in general but specifically in relation to these account types, in, for example, Virgil's ancient *Aeneid*. There, as we'll see, a "household god" gave knowledge of the visitors coming. This is very much the case, too, regarding the tutelary spirit of the shaman and, as we'll see, other culturally particular messengers. Waldron picked up on something else, however. In speaking again to the real-world effects of these experiences, a distinctly large number of stories involve the subsequent preparation of food for the visitor whose arrival became mysteriously known. R. H. Molton, living in Yorkshire, England, took a job in Newcastle-upon-Tyne. One day, missing his wife, he decided on the "spur of the moment" to get a train home. He and his neighbors had no telephones then, but when he arrived home, Molton noted, in his own words, that his wife "had a meal ready for me and was waiting to greet me," before going on to explain to him that she simply "had a feeling" he was coming home.[52]

While again, it is in the context of the vardoger that such visions and apparitions of coming visitors have most commonly been explored, most treatments simply report and reprint the same half-dozen accounts or so. Just as Toelken had found among the Navajo, psychiatrist Nils-Olof Jacobson, in one of those accounts, noted that in rural Sweden, such phenomena were not universally regarded as exceptional. Jacobson had a case from there in which the informant's father was heard driving into the coach house, seen helping the coachman ungird the horses, but never came in. The informant found it rather natural to say, "Now they've come the first time, we can put on water for tea, for they'll be here in fifteen minutes," before noting, "I was never afraid of this, it was completely natural."[53]

Researcher John Spencer gave the case of Wiers Jensen, an Oslo University student who "often found his meal ready for him" at his boarding house, and importantly, this was the case "no matter what time he arrived." His landlady had apparently become accustomed to seeing his vardoger prior to his arrival and knew therefore when to begin cooking.[54] Similarly, Olof Jonsson, a Swedish-American engineer and claimed psychic, noted that his great-grandfather was "generally quite surprised" that his wife, who he claims was clairvoyant in certain situations, could so often have his meal "in order and served when he came, in spite of the fact that he arrived at times not agreed upon."[55]

Canadian actor, novelist, and playwright Chris Humphreys, in the "author's notes" section of his fictional book *The Fetch*, wrote, "My grandfather was psychic. He did walk into a building in Oslo and terrify the elevator operator, who swore he'd taken him up five minutes before—his first experience of vardogr."[56] The same basic phenomena are recorded from much earlier Swedish sources too. According to a fairy tale, after one of two sisters from the parish of Nasinge, not too far from Oslo, went missing, one of them dreamed of the absent other. "Make your bed tomorrow night in the barn," she told her sister, "past which the trolls and I shall pass, and I will give you a handsome dower." The next night, the girl made her bed in that barn and left the door open to see if her sister would come, which she did, just as the dream foretold.[57]

Motifs Represent Real Events

The dizzyingly numerous motifs of the folklorist are not merely arbitrary categories helpful in the organization of tales; they are often representative of phenomena reported among greatly disparate cultures as literal happenings. The extent to which these motifs are often representative of actual and ongoing wondrous events sometimes seems lost, even on the folklorist. They are consistently experienced and expressed by individuals unfamiliar with the related categories or traditions, and in this way, they unconsciously make their own contributions *to* those traditions. Thus, famed author Mark Twain, while lecturing, saw a lady well known to him enter the room. Later, having met him at supper, this woman told Twain that she had not been present and had been unable to arrive on time. Lang, having relayed this incident in an issue of *The Illustrated London News*, made the point that this was what Norwegians would call a vardoger and that Twain himself had no acquaintance with the phenomenon.[58]

Comparable was the case of the wife of David Leiter. Leiter, writing in the *Journal for Scientific Exploration*, decried the lack of work in this area and honed in wonderfully on how, while far less "flashy" or psychologically impactful than the near-death experience and other more popularized phenomena, some of those who experience this vardoger "are forever convinced that a purely materialistic worldview is untenable." Leiter himself, having come home to his wife as usual, saw that she was in the kitchen preparing supper, a scenario that had occurred "thousands of times before" during their twenty-year marriage. Leiter was surprised, however, when she said, "What are you doing coming in again?" Upon questioning, she told her husband she had seen him come in about ten minutes before. While Leiter was dumbfounded, she became increasingly agitated and had their son corroborate her claim. Leiter concluded with the intriguing observation that, "For several years following this first experience, neither I, my wife, nor our son, had any idea that such a thing had ever happened to anyone else, much less knowing that the phenomenon actually had a name."[59]

Classicist and pioneering parapsychologist Frederic Myers, too, in his meticulous work, gave no notice to the vardoger of the north when he gave Victorian examples of "cases where a man's coming is unexpected, so that there is a real coincidence in the fact that his phantom is seen in the place to which he is going, shortly before he arrives there in flesh and blood."[60] Even for people descended from those lands, however, such things are often long forgotten. When American author Brad Steiger asked a minister of Norwegian descent if he knew of the vardoger, he replied in the negative. When Steiger described it, however, he nodded emphatically and observed that he never thought of them as spooky or even noteworthy enough to have a name of their own.[61]

While the phenomenon might profoundly affect some, then, it seems that for others, it was nothing quite so strange. Tallying with the observations made by the likes of Toelken and Jacobson among the Navajo and rural Swedes, respectively, philologist and lexicographer

William Craigie, having collected numerous accounts from Norway, wrote that the vardoger "is not a thing which excites much surprise or anxiety among those to whom the idea is familiar; it is one of the recognized facts of ordinary life, even though its occurrence may be somewhat unusual." Indeed, one of his informants, a teacher in the town of Drammen, having heard her husband's characteristic steps, told her children, "Go to bed, children; it was only papa's vardogr and now we know for certain that he will be home for tomorrow." This despite him not being expected for days. He arrived an hour later.[62]

In another Norwegian account from 1936, the wife of a man named Gudbrand Molandssveen, a rail worker, "often heard him coming back at night, even though he was not yet there." Indeed, she was so used to this phenomenon that "whenever she heard his vardoger, she would get up and fix some food for him."[63] Again, given by Eric Dodds, was the case of George Eady of South Wales. He wrote similarly in 1962 that "there had always existed a sort of telepathy between us" (he and his mother), further noting, "I many times descended upon her without notice, when I have been living many miles away, and found that she has been expecting me and has ordered extra provisions, etc.; but having been accustomed to this sort of thing since childhood I have never considered it to be remarkable."[64]

Varsels, Etiäinens, and Forerunners

English-born author and editor William Sabine gave an account in which one of his Swedish pupils in London told him that, as a child, she and her family would hear their grandfather enter the house and take off his riding boots a half hour before the actual event took place.[65] She specifically referred to this as a *varsel*. With a wider coverage than just sounds or apparitions, varsel, in fact, is a rather helpful term for us here in that, according to an old Swedish encyclopedia, they are "Mental experiences which appear to be a presage of future occurrences, or to be a witness to some contemporary or recent event which has not been cognized by any hitherto known forms of mental impressions."[66] Varsel experiences can take the form of vague presentiments or true dreams or of hallucinations."

Once again, in rural Finland, such things were very well known. The *etiäinen* was the name given and similarly involved the individual's companion spirit, variously announcing their arrival ahead of time.[67] Indeed, Leea Virtanen's previously referenced Finnish sample contained "many instances of a percipient knowing when visitors are coming."[68] While the etiäinen goes unmentioned, Virtanen called these and related intimations "simultaneous informatory experiences." In one of those, a young girl saw her brother in a waking vision wearing light-colored summer clothes and was so impressed with its meaning that he was returning home that she urged her mother to prepare a meal as he would soon be home.[69]

Across the Atlantic, another author, Pearl Rainwater, wrote that her North Dakotan grandmother of Norwegian heritage "often had this strange way of getting ready for visitors," noting that she would suddenly spring up, stoke the fire, and set out cookies and drinks. "I just heard footsteps," would be her explanation, with the visitor seemingly arriving soon thereafter.[70] An English woman from the samples collected by folklorist Gillian Bennett told the author the following: "I've got up some mornings and thought, I must do so-and-so, because somebody might come. And they have come, you know. You know, tidy the kitchen or whatever. And I've thought, Isn't it a good job I did it? They did come! Or I've made a batch of scones for unexpected visitors, and they have come!"[71]

We find the very same idea in a much older Hungarian folktale. A woman tells her lover, who had just arrived, "My dear, while you have been away, I had a dream. I dreamt that you would be coming home about this time of night, and therefore I've prepared all these savory things so I could serve you with your favorite dishes as soon as you came." It seems in this case the woman drew on the belief in order to lie to her husband, nevertheless suggesting both the extent to which such things are believed possible and might not necessarily evoke surprise.[72]

From a collection of folklore on Canada's Edward Island, where such happenings were particularly well known and fell under the category of a *forerunner*, we find something alike. The granddaughter of a Miss Macmillan tells that her grandfather was an engineer and was often away for days at a time. His wife, however, "would always know when he was going to return, though she never received any message from him." Furthermore, she too would have a cup of tea, and some food prepared just before his arrival.[73] Again, from New Brunswick, Canada, author William Savage gave a much earlier reference to the "Dubois House," a building that entertained occasional travelers who happened to be passing through the region. One woman there, Miss Adely, while concerned as to whether or not her father would be coming along, was told by her Aunt Patty, "I'd a dream about him last night that makes me think he's comin'." Moments later, her father was standing at the door.[74]

Similarly relayed, from as far removed as thirteenth-century France, was the tale of a paralytic woman believed to have the gift of prophecy. It was said that when any of the abbots or monks of the Cistercian order came to her house, "it was revealed to her by God [a turn of phrase we will meet with often] before they came," after which she would stipulate the day they would come and have her servants "prepare all that was necessary beforehand, and so it turned out."[75]

Indian scholar and environmentalist Vandana Shiva wrote that her mother would somehow "always know which day I was coming and have the special food I liked cooked for me." Shiva continued, "She did the same for my brother and sister, who were at different schools. She had some uncanny way of knowing what we were up to."[76]

ANTIQUITY, FARTHER EAST, AND NOTHING NEW UNDER THE SUN

The great Irish hero Cú Chulainn, in *The Wasting Sickness of Cú Chulainn*, experiences a spiritual illness in which he dreams of two women, with one of them dressed in a green mantle. One year later, he recalls his vision and returns to where he had it, and the woman in the green mantle soon appears to him.[77]

If the particularly notable extent to which these accounts happen to turn up in Irish legend and myth speaks to their archaic pedigree, so too, of course, would those from antiquity. After his troops were routed by Caesar, Gnaeus Pompeius Magnus, a general and statesman of the Roman Republic, escaped and wandered his way through Tempe and northern Thessaly and down to the sea. He rested in a fisherman's hut and, in the morning, took to the waves. He soon saw a merchant ship in which there was a Roman who, "though not intimately acquainted with Pompey, nevertheless knew him by sight." This man, Peticius, had dreamed of Pompey the previous night and was just telling this to his men when he turned around and recognized Pompey, whose appearance even matched the previous night's vision.[78]

As previously alluded to, in Virgil's *Aenied*, that man notes at one point while at sea that "In a dream my household gods instructed me that Dardanus (a son of Zeus), the founder of our race, had come from Hesperia, and thither we must bend our course," which they proceeded to do.[79] Irish religious scholar Eric Dodds was adamant that the extraordinarily influential Augustine of Hippo deserved a "more honorable place in the history of psychical research." Augustine, in his *Literal Commentary on Genesis*, gives us something of notable similarity from late antiquity regarding a priest who would commonly visit a certain "hysterical" patient after a twelve-mile journey; this patient would "habitually recognize the moment at which the priest was setting out to visit him and would describe exactly all the stages of his journey."[80]

Plutarch, too, relays an incident in the life of Roman statesman Cicero, which is given as the reason why he took so readily with friendship to a certain young man, later to be the emperor Octavius. He dreamed of a temple door opening and saw the young man emerge. As relayed by Plutarch, it was "by such a dream" that "Cicero had impressed upon him the appearance of the youth, and retained it distinctly, but did not know him." The very next day, however, he met the man from his dream coming toward him.[81] If this vision seems to be implicated in the very coming to power of Octavius, there is another much clearer example regarding the manner in which, in the third century, Demetrius, bishop of Alexandria, came to his own position. Bishop Julian, while on his deathbed, had a vision of a man "coming to him with a present of grapes." Just as Julian was waking, a man—indeed, Demetrius himself, a peasant—came from the country, bringing grapes. He was "accordingly" made bishop, suggesting the important role of the vision itself.[82]

Similarly, in a Japanese tale, a certain villager from Shinano Province in Central Japan dreamed that "Kannon" would come the next day at noon to bathe, giving details as to that person's clothing. Taking action based upon this vision, the man told everyone he knew, and a crowd gathered to welcome this man, who arrived exactly when the dream had told the villager and attired in the same manner as in the dream.[83]

These tales are old and found in numbers in the East and Far East. In a thousand-year-old Chinese myth, *Mazu, Goddess of the Sea*, one Lin Moniang had a dream that a certain merchant ship would beach on the shore, so she climbed a mountain in an attempt to guide them to safety.[84] From a collection of Eastern romances, the following, entitled *Story of the Unlucky Shoayb* and set in Baghdad, has an example of this kind. When the story's protagonist, Nassar, reaches a hermitage where he wishes to meet a certain hermit, he sees the man asleep. Beside the sleeping man, whom he had decided, against his best judgment, to awaken, he found a slip of paper that contained the words, "Fortunate youth! On the bank of the river of life no tree grows which is not blown down by the wind of Fate. In a vision I was informed that you would come hither."[85]

Within the pages of *History of an Armenian State*, we read that a holy man from there, Giwt, was come upon by a prince. Giwt was not at all surprised by the prince's arrival, as he was "apprised of his coming through a vision."[86] Once more, we note the extent to which the individual specifically cites a visionary experience, as opposed to other more "terrestrial" explanations often later posited. There are most certainly known, impressive, and at times elaborate means by which the isolated tribe, for example, might contact others distantly—smoke signals, mirrors, drums, the passing on of information by long-range coordinated vocalizations. Generally, however, those suggesting these as explanations for every incident of this kind ignore the contradictory explanations of the informants themselves.

The two explanations, of course, are not mutually exclusive. A vision of this kind is linked to the construction of Khandzta, a medieval Georgian monastery founded by Gregory of Khandzta in 782 CE. In those days, there lived an ancient hermit called Khuedios. This man had a waking vision in which, on that "sacred spot," he saw a cloud of light in the form of a church issuing a powerful scent. Soon, Khuedios heard a voice state, "On this place a church will be built by the hands of Gregory the priest, the man of God, and the perfume of his prayers and those of his disciples will mount to God like a sweet incense." While, for the reader, this vision may not necessarily imply that Gregory is in fact on his way to carry this out, Khuedios, apparently "accustomed to visions from God," started to "wait for the holy man who had been announced," apparently sure of the meaning. Then, according to the tale, Gregory arrived in Khandzta, where Khuedios lived, and they met accordingly.[87]

In a letter to clinical psychologist Sally Rhine Feather, a North Carolina woman claimed, "I also sometimes know that I will have a visitor on a given day without them calling or telling me they are coming by." While suggesting that this could rather simply be true, the author also suggests that representative scientific experiments would need to be carried out in order to establish its reality.[88] With that said, not only aren't we adhering so carefully to the "truth" of these accounts here, we might also suggest simply that there is something very powerful in the realization this chapter presents us with: that these very same claims and beliefs have been made and held in all ages and times from an impressive variety of unconnected sources and continue to be.

Prompted through Prophecy

Shifting scenes once more in this spirit, in the tenth century, Emperor Ming of the later Han Dynasty not only had the same kind of vision but was, like the English woman from Bennett's sample and others, similarly moved enough to prepare for the arrival of those incoming. He saw a man the color of gold, over ten feet tall, approaching. His state minister, "possessed of enlightenment," told him this was a sign that a sage would arrive from a foreign land. When priests from India arrived with relics and texts for his enjoyment, he "joyfully recognized these men as those he had been expecting."[89]

As we have seen on the North American continent, in Ireland, and beyond, such ideas and claims, as it happens, are also very old in India. In the ancient *Panchatantra*, a collection of verse, fables, and prose dated to 200 BCE (although the tales are likely far older), we read of a merchant's related dream. A Jain monk appears to him and tells him, "Tomorrow morning I will come to your house in this same form." After pondering whether or not this dream would prove true, the following morning, while his barber was working on his wife's nails, the Jain monk suddenly appeared.[90]

Among the Vaishnava, devotees of Krishna or Vishnu, we read of a certain Vaishnava called Misra who dreamed that a god came to him and said, "Misra! Don't worry. Nimai Pandita has just arrived near here. He will teach you both the practice of perfection and the goal of life." The next morning, Misra saw him sitting on a bench in front of his house.[91] According to the Indian scholar Bidpai, in his collection of tales, which has been related to Aesop and influenced some early modern European literature, a certain king dreams eight dreams. Having initially been told these portended ill, another wise man, Kibariun, cheers him up and tells him that seven of the dreams indicated that a king was going to send messengers bearing him valuable presents. In just a few days, "the messengers arrive with the presents, as Kibariun had predicted."[92]

Clearly, then, as we have noted regarding the preparation of food or the subsequent establishment of structures, that one might be moved to action under the impression of these visions and intimations—something later keyed in on by researchers in reference to their seriousness—is no new idea and will be a continuing theme here. Perhaps the most ancient form of this sort of vision in the more general sense, as is the case with the majority of "supernatural" phenomena still encountered, is related to Enkidu, one of Mesopotamian mythology's most legendary figures. As described by an ancient Mesopotamian epic, he decides to travel to Uruk and challenge his friend Gilgamesh. Gilgamesh, however, is said to have been "apprised by duplicate dreams" of his arrival.[93]

According to Slavic legend, Nicon, a famed reformer and founder of the Orthodox faith, was to visit then-reigning Tsar Alexei Mikhailovich (1645–1676) to convert him from the old ways and prepare him for certain teachings. Mikhailovich, however, was "warned in a dream" that Nicon was coming, and so he shut himself up in a guarded castle. The reality of this vision was apparently an "old belief."[94] Such visions are, perhaps predictably, to be found among the great Norse sagas too. Brynhild of Teutonic legend had a vision of Gudrun coming toward her, and on the next day, Gudrun arrived in a gold-decked chariot.[95]

In *The Destruction of Da Derga's Hostel*, an Irish tale belonging to the Ulster Cycle of mythology, a man dreams of a naked stranger coming along the road with a sling in his hand. This dream was "fulfilled the next day" with the arrival of the legendary Irish High King, Conaire.[96] Similarly, though from among the Micmac Indians of the Northeastern Woodlands, we find a dream that involved a man learning that at a "certain hour the next day," a particular king and one of his servants would visit. "At the hour indicated in the dream," the king arrived.[97]

VOICES INCOMING

At certain times, too, it seems to be a voice that announces the arrivals, and we have another ancient example of this in the apocryphal Assumption of the Virgin. At one point in the text, John hears a voice, construing it as the Holy Ghost, which tells him, "This voice which you heard signifies the coming of your brethren the apostles and of the holy powers, which is to be; for today they are coming here," which was soon fulfilled "as had been said."[98] Something alike came in the apocryphal Acts of John (10: 17–22), in which, at the time certain men were looking for Peter, a voice ascribed to the Holy Spirit tells him, "Simon, three men are looking for you. So, get up and go downstairs. Do not hesitate to go with them, for I have sent them."[99] It is similarly said that Saint Patrick, having spent years in slavery in County Antrim, had a dream in which a voice told him a ship would be waiting to take him to his own country. He found this ship and was able to return to his family.[100]

By no means relegated to the religious texts or the lives of the saints, in the seminal *Phantasms of the Living*, the Victorian authors recorded a small number of these "arrival cases," as they called them, including one from 1885 in which a Mr. Stevenson, sitting by the fire, heard a voice say, "David is coming." A couple of minutes later, his brother David arrived, and this was "quite unexpected."[101] These same accounts, of course, were collected entirely apart from their parapsychological counterparts. From Portugal in 1902, a man named Rua Luiz Barboza to whom, while returning home having felt there was something wrong, even hearing his name called twice, something related occurred. "My son had an intuitive feeling that I was coming," he explained, "and declared that I should return on a Wednesday, which was in fact the day of my arrival home."[102]

At times, both voice and vision are combined. On the night the Welsh saint Cadoc was born in the early fifth century, his father dreamed of a "venerable-looking priest" entering his castle and heard a voice say that this man would be the guide and teacher of his son. Later, "the arrival of the priest at the castle accorded exactly with the dream."[103] Author Michael Wells was told about something similar in the life of a Latin American pastor. In a Catholic family, a couple must have their parents' approval before marriage, so he had to go and visit them. When he arrived, however, the woman's mother, despite having never met the man, recognized him and accepted his conditions upon the authority of a dream. The previous night, as it happened, she "had a vision in which she saw the young man's face." She also heard a voice tell her, "Do not turn this man away!"[104]

IRELAND—MESSENGERS, HERMITS, AND SAINTS

These accounts are found with particular ease among Ireland's hagiographical and other records and often involve a third party, such as the Holy Spirit, Mary, an angel, or God, relaying the news of the visitor. These ideas were not exclusive to the lives of the saints, however, and we can perhaps speculate that, at least in some accounts like those of the following, the messenger may have been nonspecific and later attributed to Mary if historical knowledge was not unfamiliar to the experiencer. As we have already seen, and as will be expanded upon in a later chapter, the ill man or woman, in fact, when coming closer to death and therefore to the clairvoyant powers one might attain in the otherworld, often became privy to such information. In a rural region south of Naples, Italy, for example, a man confined to bed for three years had a vision in which the "blessed virgin" appeared in his chamber and told him, "Tomorrow thou shalt see my children of the house of Mater Domina. Confess, repent of thy sins, and Jesus will pardon thee!" The tale suggests that this man "knew nothing of the approaching mission. They arrived, however, the following day.[105] Similarly, Irish Jesuit Henry Fitzsimon recorded that in 1580, the Virgin Mary appeared to a certain Mrs. Bealing who lived near Dublin, warning her that soldiers were about to search her house and that she should hide a priest she was keeping.[106]

The incredibly influential and visionary Irish monk Fursey, while assisting in the building of a monastery in France, was once "warned in a dream of the approach of a youthful pilgrim from Rome." He duly "went forth to meet him and bid him welcome."[107]

Something alike was said of Moling, a saint of County Kerry in Ireland. When, in the early Middle Ages, he was on his way to Cluain

Cain Maedoc, it was "revealed to Maedoc [Saint Aiden] that a noble unknown guest had come to him." He said, "Leave off for us the order there, for on his way to us is one whom it is not meet to delay."[108] Bearchán, a sixth-century Irish saint famed as a prophet, had a related vision in which it was revealed to him that his death would come when three kings came uninvited to his house. Accordingly, "three such guests did indeed come."[109]

Gaelic folklorist, scholar, and minister Robert Kirk, long ago, in his 1691 treatise *The Secret Commonwealth of Elves, Fauns, and Fairies*, referred to these kinds of accounts. He called these visitors *co-walkers* or *reflexes* and noted that such a thing, referred to even then as something "old," was "often seen of old to enter a house, by which the people knew that the Person of that Likeness was to visit them in a few days."[110] Perhaps Kirk, referring even then to what he had considered to be an ancient phenomenon, was aware of even older cases from those regions, such as the following: Seemingly written in seventh-century Ireland was the *Altus Prosator*, a greatly venerated Latin hymn traditionally ascribed to Saint Columba. In the preface to this hymn, it is noted that while Columba was at Iona off the western coast of Scotland, "it was revealed to him that guests had arrived," all seven of whom had come from Rome.[111]

Coming to Wales's patron saint, David, he, on his way to Jerusalem, was visited by an "Angel of God" in a dream, this being told him—that "three Catholics from the bounds of the West are coming to thee. Receive them with honour." David is said to have "greatly rejoiced" at these words, and he soon after "received the holy strangers with marked distinction."[112]

Like those medicine men we have seen so specifically enlisted, Benedict the Moor, a sixteenth-century Sicilian Franciscan friar, was said, if somewhat more vaguely, to have mysteriously attained information of this kind on more than one occasion. While the son of one Augustin Benacollto was lying ill in Spain, Benedict declared that intelligence of his recovery would be arriving, which occurred five days after the prophecy. He also told one Lucretia Navaretti that her husband would soon return to his own country, "which was verified by the event."[113] The *Orlando Furioso*, a greatly influential Italian chivalric romance first published in 1532, has a surprisingly similar reference. After one of the lead protagonists, Rogero, is shipwrecked while sailing to Africa, a certain hermit with whom he ends up staying is "warned in a dream of his coming."[114]

It is clear that, like so many extrasensory phenomena recognized by parapsychologists, these accounts gather in numbers around the lives of mystics and saints, some surely true, others undoubtedly embellished, though importantly, often drawn from established and therefore believable traditions. When one of the earlier Irish monastic saints, Brendan the Voyager, arrived on the Island of September, a hermit named Festivus said that "he had been warned in a dream of his visit" and that this was why he chose to wait there.[115] The same was true upon Brendan's return to the shores of Kerry. People from all over the province of Munster had gathered. "How did you know we were returning?" Brendan asked them. "Ah," came the reply of one named Nanno, "we just thought 'twas time you were home, and I had a dreaming!"[116]

Dermott O'Duivna, a warrior-hunter of the Gaelic Fianna, once dreamed that a fair young woman came to him and stood above him. "He wakened," goes the tale, "and it was as he had dreamed." The same woman had just arrived.[117] Of interesting relation, it is said more generally of Rusticula, also called Marcia, French abbess of Saint-Jean d'Arles from 575 until her death, that while she was on the road between towns, as she approached, this would be variously revealed to certain people in those towns before her arrival.[118]

According to Byzantine monk and chronicler Theophanes the Confessor, when the abbot Theodosius sent important relics, including those of Saint Stephen, to Chalcedon, an ancient maritime town of Bithynia in Asia Minor, the arrival was revealed to the Eastern Roman empress, Pulcheria, in a dream. She saw Stephen himself, who stated, "Behold, your prayer has been heard, your request is fulfilled, and I have come to Chalcedon." She arose, and found the relics had just arrived.[119]

SHAMANS, FAMILIARS, ANGELS, AND VISITORS

Clearly, then, other than voices, visions, apparitions, or intimations, a third party commonly offers the relevant information. We saw Waldron allude to this happening on the Isle of Man, when he noted that "friendly demons" might offer such notice to the individual. The same was true in the lives of both the saints and the shamans, in which their own particular messengers were involved. Far beyond that tiny island's confines, Waldron's words bear out.

In traditional cultures, the guardian spirit is the more common herald of the relevant information. American anthropologist Leslie Spier noted that among the Sinkaietk in Washington "one with a strong guardian spirit could easily see the power of anyone who was spiritually weaker, and could observe at any distance a person who was on the way to visit him or who was hurt."[120] In these cases, the shaman's familiar plays the same role in imparting this information as might the Christian's Virgin Mary, Holy Spirit, and so on, a theme that will persist through these pages. Something related comes from the Chinese marvel tale "The Fisherman and His Friend." When one Mr. Hsu arrives at a village called Wu-Chen, the landlord who owns the inn he stays at seems to know who he is, with Hsu wondering "how he came to know it."[121] While the man ran off, multiple people there told him that "a few nights before they had seen their guardian deity in a vision, and he had informed them that Mr. Hsu would shortly arrive."

Ronald Rose, in his work among Australian Aboriginals, similarly explained that the totem is an "appropriate mediating vehicle" for tribal natives but that the Christian might find the angel performing a similar function, of which there are many others unrelated to this chapter's very particular focus.[122] Remaining among the Aboriginals of Australia and recalling the use of peyote in sixteenth-century New Mexico, we read that, according to anthropologist Katie Parker, who lived among the Euahlayi people, the tribesmen there might be warned by their totems while they are ingesting an "intoxicating drink" of the coming of another group or tribe.[123]

As is so often the case with the more allegorical or legendary events demonstrably indistinguishable from common extrasensory phenomena, these kinds of dreams are frequently and rather unceremoniously found implemented in longer tales and poems. Rarely, again, is the connection made between these accounts and, for example, their better-known Norse analogues. Returning to the North American continent and the Blackfoot Indians, historically of southern Canada into Montana, a tale from long ago, *Lodge Boy and Thrown Away*, has a man and his wife living in a grass lodge. One morning, the sun informs the man in a dream that a visitor will arrive and how they should be treated. While the man was out hunting as usual, the stranger came to his lodge, just as he had been told.[124]

The Dead Know More

While, as will later be investigated, the shaman, the medicine man, or even the Christian mystic might historically be consulted in relation to the location of another, often missing, person, the Unitarian minister, psychical researcher, and author Minot Savage had a similar experience of his own in the early twentieth century that also involved a third party. In the presence of a medium, a woman went into a trance and received the information, ostensibly from her deceased husband, that her friend, who was meant to have been coming the next Monday, would be arriving on Saturday instead. Entirely disbelieving this, as she had just received a letter confirming it would be Monday, the woman disregarded the message. That Friday, however, she got a note that her friend had changed plans and would be arriving on Saturday after all.[125]

Of particular intrigue, whether known or unknown to Savage, is that historically and traditionally, the dead also often play the role of familiar or messenger. The English-American anthropologist Edith Turner recorded something related in Zambia. While tending to a very sick woman in her hut, this patient, Manyosa, told her that her throat had been cut while she slept. She then had this dream that her dead sister, Mwendiana, visited her and told her, "Nessy my daughter is coming to see you." The very next day, according to Manyosa, this woman came just as her dream suggested.[126]

In a Texan folktale, an early settler named Josiah Wilbarger lies near death after having been shot down in an ambush. His sister, whom he hadn't known had died the previous day, appears to him. "Brother Josiah," she said, "you are too weak to go on by yourself. Remain here, and friends will come to take care of you before the sun sets tomorrow." The woman soon disappeared, and the people she had specified arrived at that time.[127]

Holy Messengers

Returning again to Ireland, the messenger theme continues. According to a late-fifteenth-century Gaelic manuscript, the *Book of Lismore*, on a certain day, the horse of Oengus, son of Cremthann, died. When Oengus slept that night, an angel came to him in a vision and told him, "Ciarán the son of the wright will come and will bring thy horse for thee to life." This was later exactly fulfilled, for at the angel's word, Ciarán came and healed his horse.[128]

The ability of the saint to become aware of the day another will die is something found widely. Berach, the celebrated sixth-century saint of Termonbarry (of questionable historicity), predicted the death of Aedh, son of Eochaid Tirmcarna, who was king of Connaught at that time, sixty years in advance. When this was fulfilled, Cu-Allaid, son of Diarmait, set off to acquaint Berach with this news; however, it had already been "revealed to Berach that Cu-Allaid was coming on this errand," and Berach then sent someone to intercept him, which they did.[129]

Remaining among the fruitful ancient Irish texts, we read that when Maine Morgor of Irish mythology set out for his wedding, another had a dream of his coming. King Conchobar, sleeping at Emain, a mythical island paradise, dreamed that a woman came to him with numerous warnings. One of those was that "Main Morgor, son of Ailell and of Maeve, is coming this very night." Rather than wait, however, Conchubar set out and intercepted Maine and his men in battle before they arrived.[130] Comparably, seventh-century Celtic Saint Gohban was once told in a "vision of the night" that "barbarians more savage than the Vandals were coming out of the North," soon after which they swept over the district.[131] Similarly, when Bairre, bishop of Cork and abbot of a monastery in what is now the city of Cork, Ireland, set out to visit his tutor Eolang, God is said to have "revealed to Eolang" that Bairre was coming.[132]

These visions, so distinctly like those we have seen attained by the shaman, are ascribed to saints around the globe and their etiology is often similarly described. Much removed, one Mor Yuhanon bar Abdun, former patriarch of Antioch (a major city of ancient Syria) and head of the Syriac Orthodox Church from 1004 until his death in 1033, having retreated to pray at the Monastery of Mor Barsoum, and eventually relocating permanently to the "Black Mountain," had his own mysterious intimation. At the time of this vision, a certain disciple was himself coming to the monastery. One day before his arrival, "God revealed" this to Bar Abdun, saying, "Tomorrow will arrive a saintly man who will become the leader of the church of God." The man arrived the next day.[133]

When a woman was being led to the dwelling of the fourth-century Christian monk and hermit Macarius of Egypt in order that she might be healed of a certain illness, it is recorded that to Macarius, "God had revealed that she was to come."[134] Again and again, the messenger varies; the message, however, remains the same. In a medieval Japanese tale, a holy man dreamed that he met a golden Jizo, a bodhisattva, who addressed him as follows: "Tomorrow at dawn you will know me without fail in the first person you see as you walk down that lane." As he was going down that lane in the morning to preach, a layman came and told him, "I am Ki no Mochikata." Recognizing this as the man he was told would arrive, he broke down in tears. "Trusting profoundly in my dream," he said, "I have met you, sir."[135]

From the eighth-century Japanese *Nihongi*, a man named Kumano no Takakuraji dreams that the god Amaterasu Oho-kami tells him that he will be sending the Yata-garasu, a certain large-headed crow, and it will be his guide through the land. "Then," goes the tale, "there did indeed appear the Yata-garasu flying down from the void." As the man explains, "The coming of this crow is in due accordance with my auspicious dream."[136]

The *Sejarah Melayu*, a renowned literary and historical Malayan work, presents a certain ruler's conversion as related to a similar vision. The Prophet appears to him in a dream and, among other things, tells him of the imminent arrival of a teacher from Jeddah. That same afternoon, a religious teacher arrives as his dream had foretold, and convinced by this event, both the ruler and his court embrace Islam.[137]

Mystical Figures Bring Healing

The thirteenth-century poet, scholar, and mystic Rumi tells the story of a king whose lover falls ill very soon after they meet. The king is visited in a dream by a saint who assures him that a certain sage will soon arrive to diagnose the girl's illness, which is fulfilled thereafter.[138]*

In a particular Persian *mathnawi*, a kind of poem, too, a prince sees a vision in which an unnamed ancient informs him that a certain physician will arrive soon who can help his sick lover. The next day, this same person arrived.[140]

On whatever continent these accounts are found, in fact, it is somewhat striking how often they relate to the visit of one, often a saint, who might bring healing to the recipient of the vision or someone nearby. Thus, the "Indian St. Francis," Chaitanya Mahaprabhu, a fifteenth-century Indian saint, is said to have given sight to a blind man who was "warned in a dream of his advent."[141]

Ruadan, or Rowan, was an Irish Christian abbot who founded the

---

*The Islamic saint's expression of extrasensory skills was not at all unusual or unexpected. Rumi gives a tale in which a man, about to give a poor woodcutter some coins, finds that this man "was a saint" who at once "read his thoughts."[139]

monastery of Lorrha. While sleeping, he was visited by an angel who told him he must heal a certain queen of Cualann. When he sent a young man to her for this purpose, this was revealed to the queen "through a vision of sleep," in which Ruadan said to her, "I will send a young man to you on a day like this. His appearance will be like mine, and he will heal thee." This was all soon fulfilled with the man's arrival.[142]

Once more from the apocryphal Acts of John, regarding the travels of John the Evangelist, Lycomedes "had a vision telling him of the arrival of John from Miletus and promising him healing."[143] A Chinese example has a poor man lying down weary and worn beside the temple of a certain field god and having a dream. The god came to him and told him, "Tomorrow the Eight Immortals will pass along this road. Cast yourself down before them and plead to them!" The man awoke and waited all day for his dream to come true until, at last, eight figures, whom he recognized as the eight immortals, came down the road.[144]

Relating to the history of Yu Huang—or the Jade Emperor, a Chinese deity—a certain emperor in 1012 dreamed just as auspiciously. "In a dream," he told his men, "I had a visit from an Immortal, who brought me a letter from Yu Huang." This letter spoke of a certain man, T'ai Tsu, and said, "I am going to send him in person to visit you." Just "a little while after," and "according to Yu Huang's promise," this man arrived.[145]

SYMBOLS AND STRANGERS

Dreams in Classical Tales

As we have seen to some extent, as with many things of the otherworld, such visions are often presented allegorically to the visionary. The biblical figure and, later, saint, Joseph, was ascribed numerous such experiences. On one of those occasions, said to have shown his "glory and dignity," he saw the sun, the moon, and eleven stars descend to adore him. Accordingly, "this vision was fulfilled" when his father and eleven brothers came into Egypt to pay him homage.[146]

King Adrastus, Greek mythology's king of Argos, once called upon the legendary Greek seer Amphiarus, renowned for his capacity to foresee and foretell, to tell the king the meaning of a dream that troubled him. He dreamed that a lion and a bear came to Argos and married his daughters. Amphiarus told him that the following day he should go to the city's north gate, where he would see the lion and the bear of his dream. Adrastus did so and saw two young men coming toward him in fine garments and with painted shields. On one shield was a lion, and on the other, a bear. Adrastus then "knew that these princes were sent to him by the gods [. . .] according to his dream."[147]

Regarding a shared vision of an arrival, with a nod to chapter 8 on shared experiences, and again symbolic, in Heliodorus of Emesa's ancient Greek novel, *Aethiopica*, when a girl is presented to King Hydaspes, the king says that he dreamed "that a daughter [. . .] had been born to me this very day [. . .] identical in appearance to the person I see before me." Likewise, the queen, away from the court at the time, later understood the meaning of her own earlier dream of the birth of a daughter to her, which, upon her arrival home, she then knew was related to the girl's coming.[148]

In *The Story of the Finding of Cashel*, an early medieval tale that speaks to the founding of Cashel in County Tipperary, Ireland, a similar vision is found. A certain swineherd, staying at Clais Duirdress north of Cashel, learns in a prophetic vision of the coming of Patrick to Ireland, which, at the end of the legend, is fulfilled accordingly. The swineherd and one other "saw a cleric in his white chasuble, with two chanting choirs about him, symbolizing the coming of Patrick."[149]

We read in the twelfth-to-thirteenth-century Icelandic *Sturlunga Saga* of a related vision dreamed by Sturla himself, which combines many of the previous elements. Sturla dreamed that his father came to him and told him, "You have probably heard about the arrival of a ship in Eyjafjör and that there is a black bear on board, which our kinsman Bödvar of Stað owns, and that this animal is said to be rather savage." When Sturla asked one Þórð Hitnesing for his thoughts, he very readily assumed its meaning, stating in fact that he "knew very well" its meaning, that Þorgils Böðvarsson had either arrived or was sailing there at that moment. He arrived, indeed, less than a day later.[150]

In a Mongolian tale, with its similarly symbolic presentation, it was only after the visitor arrived that the meaning became clear. In 1196, Yesiigei, the father of a boy named Temiijin, sets out to find his son a wife. On the way, he makes a stop at the camp of a wise Onggirat chief named Deiscechen. "Now, friend Yesiigei, last night I had a strange dream," he began. "A white falcon, with the sun and the moon in its claws, came down from heaven and perched on my hand. It was a fine omen, as I understand now that you come to us with your son with you. My dream was to announce that you came, you of the clan Kiyat."[151]

The same was true of another abbot, this time farther east on that side of the world. In the *Genkō Shakusho*, the first Japanese Buddhist history, we read that the day before the priest Jitsuhan's arrival at Daigoji (in Kyoto before 1346), Genkaku, the abbot of a certain monastery, dreamed of a blue dragon arising from the pond in the garden, lifting up its head, and spouting clear water from its mouth. Understanding immediately the meaning of the dream, the abbot ordered his pupils to clean the monastery in order to graciously receive the venerable pupil, who actually arrived.[152]

In a Papuan myth translated from the Trans–New Guinea language of Toaripi, a girl named Moro is taken inshore by two fish. She makes her way up the beach, leaving a trail of mixed footprints of pigs, wallabies, cassowaries, turtles, and crocodiles behind. That same night, this coming is represented symbolically to the beach's guardian, Evara, who dreams that a log floated ashore and came to rest on his beach. He immediately listens to his dream and finds the woman there.[153]

For a more general reference to the phenomenon, and once more among the Indigenous Australians, this time the Wakelbura, if a man dreamed of seeing a kangaroo, he should expect a person of the Banbe people to arrive the following day.[154] The Wakelbura, in fact, associated different totems, respectively, with the coming of certain people. The same is true among New Zealand's northernmost Maoris. If they dream of a friend on a journey but his face is hidden in a culturally relevant manner, "it is a good sign of your friend being near his home."[155] One senses here a more typical and general traditional folkloric belief, perhaps a later development representative of important and actual previous experiences.

Deirdre, the tragic heroine of Ireland's Ulster Cycle, had many prophetic dreams. Just as the mythological former king Fergus mac Róich was arriving at her home, she proclaimed that she knew before the others that he would be coming "because of a vision I saw last night."

> "Three birds I saw coming to us from Emain Macha [an ancient ceremonial monument near Armagh, Northern Ireland], and three drops of honey in their mouths, and they left them with us, and three drops of our blood they brought away with them."
>
> "What meaning do you put on that, Queen?" said one named Naoise, the nephew of our previously mentioned King Conchobar.
>
> "It is," said Deirdre, "Fergus that is coming to us with a message of peace from Conchubar, for honey is not sweeter than a message of peace sent by a lying man." She then told one of her people to go down and greet him, which they soon did.[156]

Again, from ancient Ireland, when Mochuda, abbot of Rahan, County Offaly, and subsequently founder and first abbot of Lismore, County Waterford, was traveling to Ard Finain sometime between the fifth and sixth centuries, the wife of that place's king became aware of this in a symbolic vision. She saw a flock of birds coming to where they were, and one of them landed on the king. When she told him this, he said, "It is Mochuda who will be journeying hither, and the flock is his train, and he himself is the bird that settled on me." Mochuda arrived shortly after.[157]

We still find such symbolic intimations of the visitor's arrival in more recent serious surveys as well. In another experience from rural

Finland, a man born in 1907 saw a vision of his father and uncle appearing to be riding into his yard on a sleigh. Based on this, his mother said that those two men would be arriving in half an hour. When they arrived thirty minutes later, they were dressed and appeared just as they had in the vision.[158]

CANOES, INVADERS, AND HOSTILE NEIGHBORS

The arrival of foreigners to indigenous shores that had been either predicted or visualized ahead of time by vision or dream is a common story. Whichever of those tales are true, their ubiquity speaks strongly to how ingrained the belief is in the possibility itself, and furthermore, they too have their later analogues. Long ago, and told again among the Micmac Indians, was the dream of a woman who, long before the arrival of the French, saw an island floating toward the land with trees upon it and creatures dressed in skins. This island from her dreams appeared the next day, and she found that the trees represented masts and the creatures were men who spoke a strange tongue.[159]

Munei, a medicine man of the East African Akamba, a Bantu ethnic group primarily of Kenya, was once incredibly moved by his own dream, so much so that in the dead of night he summoned the village elders and told them:

> Mark well my words, ye came to me for rain and the rain came, I then slept and while I slept God (Mulungu), by means of a dream ordered me to tell you a message and that I should then die and the message is this— that after a time a new kind of people will come into this land and you will know them by their red faces and red ears and when those people come you must listen to their words and obey them.

Immediately after delivering this prophecy, Munei died. Many years later, when the first Europeans appeared, the elders met together and discussed the matter, saying, "Truly these are the reddish people Munei told us of."[160]

Whether told in earnest or something more approaching jest, one can readily imagine the impact such a vision might have upon the belief that such things are possible in the first place. Furthermore, the reality of the characters, deities, or other elements perceived in the vision would therefore also allow the stories to gain greater traction within a community. A certain *Kabaka*, or king of the Kingdom of Buganda, a Bantu kingdom within Uganda, heard a similar dream. When Russell Train, founder chairman emeritus of the World Wildlife Fund, and some colleagues came to those shores, the Kabaka's mother told him that she "dreamed a dream a few nights ago, and in her dream she saw a white man on this lake in a boat coming this way, and the next morning she told the Kabaka, and, lo! you have come."[161]

Precognition as Battle Strategy

Such dreams and visions, then, whether incubated or spontaneously acquired, had important implications for intertribal warfare. On one occasion on the Southern Plains, for example, a group of Apache Indians were not at all surprised when an enemy Comanche appeared, for one of them had dreamed that they would come and were already prepared to bring him in when he arrived.[162] According to some of their journals, Jesuit missionaries were often "astounded" at the skills of "dream trackers," who would actively travel in their dreams in order to locate war parties. If the information proved inaccurate, the dreamer might even be driven out of the village.[163] The Shoshone Indians, too, "had men with power to predict the arrival of enemies."[164]

Among the far northern Yuit of the Russian Chukchi Peninsula and on Saint Lawrence Island in Alaska, their shamans were greatly valued because, with their skills, "the strength of an enemy approaching the village or camp could be ascertained before their actual arrival."[165]

Among the Sambia of Papua New Guinea's Eastern Highlands, shamans were indeed "critical in warfare" and were therefore rather numerous. When American anthropologist Gilbert Herdt asked a war leader why this was so, the reply was that "shaman's dreams foretell raids."[166] Remaining in Polynesia, and returning to the messenger theme, a certain king of the Malayan Archipelago once saw the "prophet of God" in a dream, who told him that the next day a ship would arrive at his coast and that he should comply with the directions of the men who should land from it, which all came exactly to pass.[167] Something of this kind can be found in yet another Micmac Indian story. Once, in a large settlement north of the mouth of a river, a war party of Mohawks was approaching stealthily, planning an attack. A certain Micmac named Ababejit was warned in a symbolic dream of their intentions and location. He dreamed of a flock of pigeons setting upon the wigwam and completely covering the top of it. Knowing the meaning of this, the arrival of the Mohawks confirmed the information.[168]

An incident even more alike was given long before by Plutarch. While the Spartans lay encamped at Tegea, a former settlement in ancient Greece, Pelopidas, an important Theban statesman and general in Greece, dreamed that the ghost of another, Scedasus, appeared to him and told him that the Spartans were then coming to Leuctra, a village of ancient Boeotia in Greece. Pelopidas sent certain persons to "examine the truth of the matter," and "everything agreed with his dream." Using this information, Pelopidas advanced to intercept them.[169]

These "interceptions" are surprisingly common. Returning to the North American continent, the Mohawk Indian, Island Woman, dreams that a war party is coming from the river Susquehanna. The warriors go out, intercept the party, and destroy the raiders before they can attack.[170] The Pawnee Indian, Handsome Boy, whose rather elaborate adventures will feature multiple times in this volume, dreamed of a mysterious being who came with a message. "In about three more days you are to see hard times," was the warning. "You are to have a hard time with some enemies who are coming this way." Three days later, the being comes once more in a dream and tells him he must head east and that he will "meet the enemies who are coming," whom he soon intercepts as predicted.[171]

Like those shamans we have met with from the South American rainforests or the first people of the frozen north, the ancient druids too were said to be able to see over great distances by supernatural means, and again, symbolic visions are also widely found. Indeed, some of the earliest Gaelic texts commonly combine the two. In a dream, Eochaid, then High King of Ireland, saw a flock of black birds come from the depths of the sea and fight with all the people of Ireland. Having relayed this to his wizard, he was told that this flock represented warriors that were at that very moment coming across the ocean by the thousands.[172]

The Boons of Belief

As we approach the end of our chapter, it should be noted that, without doubt, in many traditional societies, while the waking and visionary worlds overlap, generalizations in this area are outdated and rarely helpful. While it has been easy to disregard the seriousness with which dreams are taken in certain parts, they are often founded upon actual and repeated *veridical* experiences. The Semai people, for example, an ethnic group from the Malay Peninsula, Southeast Asia, believed in the prophetic potential of the dream; however, they were very discerning in this regard. Anthropologist Robert Dentan found that they were "hesitant about interpreting their dreams until after the prediction indicated in the dream has come true."[173] These are common procedures in Malaysia too. The Temiar people generally categorize their dreams as "true" or "untrue." True dreams are those that were subsequently proved correct.[174]

Likewise, among the Wyandot Indians of the Northeastern Woodlands, only the dreamers whose dreams had been "found several times true" were accredited.[175] Austrian-born American anthropologist Robert Lowie noted something related among the Crow Indians of Montana: that they "did not confuse an everyday dream with a revelation. It was only those dreams that were intrinsically stirring or proved harbingers of good fortune that stood as more or less equivalent to visions."[176] The utility of the dream as a tool in warfare would clearly be subjected to such distinction. Furthermore, the idea that some visionary experience that occurs during sleep must therefore be a dream may, in itself, be untrue. This is important to keep in mind.

ANIMALS AND ARRIVALS

Worthy of short and final note here is that the arrival vision may as much pertain to an animal as to a person in both the tales and the memorates too. By far the most comprehensive work in this area and subjects related to this chapter in general was carried out over five years by English biologist and author Rupert Sheldrake. In his seminal *Dogs That Know When Their Owners Are Coming Home*, Sheldrake, among 585 other reports, gave the case of his Norwegian informant, Kate, who would find her husband greeting her with a hot cup of tea whenever she arrived home. This, despite the fact that she had a highly variable schedule. Apparently, Tiki, the family dog, "rushes to the window and stands on the windowsill," and this is the signal to the man that Kate is on the way home.[177]

Similar to this was the case of Peter Edwards, whose Irish setters would almost always wait for him at the gate shortly before his arrival, despite Peter's "irregular hours." They would know he was coming home "regardless of which way the wind is blowing or what vehicle he returns in.[178] Another of his informants who worked on an airliner had a dog, Rusty, who would, according to them, always "jump around and bark at the same time I landed and then sit quietly watching the front door until I got home. This, again, despite there being "no routine" to her comings and goings.[179]

Sheldrake, entirely convinced of the "telepathic" nature of these occurrences and interpreting data in order to push back against exclusive explanations involving routine, scent, and hearing, posits an evolutionary explanation and suggests the influence of so-called "morphic fields," fields of influence that link social groups of animals and people over long distances.[180] In legend and lore, the same things occur. There, however, it is most often the individual who envisions the arrival of the animal. An old Indian folktale collected in 1923, for example, has a king dreaming that a horse has come to the local market. In order to "test the truthfulness" of the dream, the king went to the marketplace and found that very horse standing there.[181]

A shaman of great skill among the Yamana of southern Argentina, Chile, and beyond dreamed of two whales approaching their shore, both pregnant, and noting that soon they would be in sight. And indeed, "that same evening," the tide washed up two pregnant whales.[182] A related and final vision was implemented in a ballad from Cheshire, England, in relation to a legend of Saint John's Church there. Ethelred, king of Wessex from 865 until his death in 871, dreamed a dream "sent by the power divine" in which a voice like music seemed to say, "Arise! where though, O king, Shalt see a milk white hind at bay, They pious work begin!" The following day, and in accordance with the dream, "Ethelred a white hind saw."[183]

NEW LIFE FOR THE VARDOGER

Despite earlier speculations to the contrary, the vardoger, or more broadly, the seemingly extrasensory intimation of a visitor's arrival that later proves accurate, is a widely recorded kind of experience across cultures and through time. The vardoger is most commonly related to the apparitional form of another before their arrival; however, we have seen that sounds alone are enough to warrant this moniker. With that said, therefore, it could be that every kind of information related to this chapter might be similarly named. That is to say, they are all outright vardogers. Much work remains to be done in this area. In any case though, it is clear that the experience of accurately anticipating a visitor's arrival, whether induced or spontaneous, is a widely known and remembered reality. Medicine men, shamans, mystics, and saints, separated by oceans and lifetimes are attributed these capacities, as are the unsuspecting ordinary men and women whose words have been recorded by the folklorists and others. While the messenger varies, the mysterious vardoger and its visionary relatives, it seems, lives on. As a Norwegian man of letters and law told William Craigie, when quizzed on the subject: "I know about it; but that can't be anything that is peculiar to Norway. It must exist in other countries," he said. "We are all made alike."[184] These were prescient words, and words to be kept close at hand as we further explore this strange and pervasive magic in the mind.

TWO

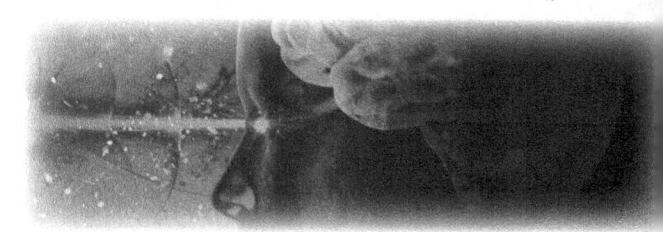

I Knew You Were in Trouble

Historical and Cross-Cultural Visions of a Distant Crisis

> *The unconscious helps by communicating things to us, or making figurative allusions. It has other ways, too, of informing us of things which by all logic we could not possibly know.*
>
> CARL GUSTAV JUNG

Nurse Arlene Centerwall, in the *Journal of Christian Nursing*, described a "strange premonition" in which, while tending to the family of one patient in a Montreal hospital in 1997, something very unusual happened.[1] Just as one of the family members was asking her about their father, Centerwall suddenly heard a "small voice" within her exclaiming (regarding a patient in another part of the hospital) "Mrs. Belanger is hemorrhaging!" Arlene immediately grabbed a disbelieving nurse and rushed to Belanger's room, where they found blood pooling around her legs. The woman was indeed hemorrhaging, and they quickly resolved the issue. "How in the world did you know?" another nurse asked Arlene. "I don't know how I knew, except that I heard a still, small voice inside me, and I believed it," she said. "Obviously," Centerwall later concluded, "it was the Holy Spirit."

Coming to the work of Janine de Peyer, a therapist who seemed to have developed inexplicable rapports with some of her patients, one of those told her of a dream in which she had awoken to the sounds of her own husband groaning and found him on the toilet, losing blood.* De Peyer, however, on that very same night, had herself awoken to find her husband groaning on the toilet and losing a lot of blood—something that had never happened to him before and was soon resolved. "This convergence," wrote de Peyer, "brought the feeling of boundarilessness between us to a new pitch. I said nothing on that day of my own experience, but I silently wondered if I had somehow emitted to Jordan my life-threatening situation."[2] De Peyer, who has experienced numerous comparable dreams, explains that "The preponderance" of such reports "can no longer be dismissed as coincidence or magical thinking."[3]

The French astronomer and author Camille Flammarion related something similar in which Dr. Aimé Guinard, a hospital surgeon living in Paris in 1891, was awake one night with toothache. He passed the time meditating upon the subject of an article he was writing about the surgical removal of stomach cancer. When he arrived at his dentist the following morning, he was greeted with the words, "How strange! I dreamed of you all last night." Guinard's dentist, whom he had no friend in common with and had known for only six months, dreamed, in his own words, that he "had a cancer in the stomach, and I was possessed with the idea that you were going to open my abdomen in order to cure it."[4]

Before we move on to perhaps the most common kinds of extrasensory experiences reported, those involving strange and accurate knowledge of a distant death, here we consider their relatively forgot-

---

*The nonverbal and potentially telepathic interactions between therapists and their patients are indeed a real and surprisingly persistent phenomenon reported and compiled sporadically over the past century or so. See, *Where Are You, My Beloved? On Absence, Loss, and the Enigma of Telepathic Dreams* by Ofra Eshel or the works of Jan Ehrenwald more generally.

ten cousins: veridical dreams, visions, and other intimations of general distant unrest, troubles, illness, and crises primarily unrelated to death. Like the vardoger, these kinds of experiences have gone greatly underexplored from a cross-cultural and even historical perspective. The speculation has commonly been that such "calls" might have an evolutionary origin. While the question does not concern us here, it seems reasonable on its face that if such a capacity were to emerge, particularly in widely separated rural communities, it would be selected for.

Sigmund Freud, himself rather skeptical throughout his life of such phenomena, nevertheless increasingly dabbled in those more occult subjects and was entirely in agreement. Freud wrote that telepathy "may be the original archaic method by which individuals understood one another and which has been pushed into the background in the course of phylogenetic (evolutionary) development by the better method of communication by means of signs apprehended by the sense organs. But such older methods may have persisted in the background and may still manifest themselves under certain conditions."[5]

Like the vardoger accounts, these experiences often impel the individual to action, and such visions may therefore greatly impact the individual and his or her worldview, as was the case in the following account given by the inventor of electroencephalography, Hans Berger. Berger had been serving a year in the German military in 1892 when he was thrown from a horse in an accident.[6] That day, Berger received a telegram from his father, rather inconspicuously checking in. Berger's father, in fact, had never sent him a telegram before, but his older sister apparently had a feeling something was wrong with him. While not as eventful or dramatic as many of the other accounts, for Berger, this uncanny encounter influenced a lifetime of research. Berger went on to attempt to develop a device in Austria to track the electrical currents in the brain that might somehow have enabled his sister to become aware of his near-fatal collision with a horse-drawn cannon, which prompted her to send an alarmed and inquiring telegram. Berger, in fact, "hoped to reveal the energy responsible for telepathy."[7]

Carl Jung, in one of his own numerous related experiences, told of something similar. At one time, while riding a train returning home from Bollingen, Switzerland, during the Second World War, Jung found himself "overpowered by the image of someone drowning." Upon reaching his destination, he discovered his youngest grandson had nearly drowned, and in his own words, "at exactly the time I had been assailed by that memory in the train." "The unconscious," wrote Jung matter-of-factly, "had given me a hint."[8] Jung, unlike Freud, found nothing particularly objectionable in such experiences as they present. Freud, however, had himself set out to explore psychical phenomena, at least through a psychoanalytic lens, after a certain patient's dreams accurately discovered a rather idiosyncratic pregnancy. The man dreamed his second wife had twins and found out later that, in fact, his daughter had, that same night, given birth to twins a month before their due date.[9]

Psychiatrist Nils-Olof Jacobson made note of just how commonly these impressions were connected not just with death, as most popularly they are, "but also with accidents or sudden illness of a close friend or relative." In one of many cases that came to him, an informant dreamed one evening that her mother's flashlight went out as she was descending the stairs to the cellar, before she tripped and ended up lying still with an "ugly wound" on her leg. A couple of weeks later, when she traveled to her mother's, she saw the bandage on that same leg and found that every detail of the incident matched the dream.[10]

A UBIQUITOUS BELIEF

Persuasive Visions

Such experiences, of course, and in keeping with our theme here, have a much older pedigree. One of the most ancient accounts in which a distant crisis was said to have been mysteriously witnessed in this way brings us to the account of fourth-century Neoplatonist philosopher and mystic Sosipatra. While, again, scholars have expressed great skepticism as to whether such old tales might qualify as evidence for "telepathy," here we are under no such constraints. Furthermore, restrictions of this kind have seemingly hidden from our attention the true ubiquity of such beliefs and experiences, at the very least in a historical/parapsychological context. As Swiss classicist Georg Luck noted, "Whenever a magician makes grandiose claims, charges a fee, and then produces certain special effects, we ought to be suspicious. But there also seem to be cases that are above suspicion."[11] Such sentiments might only be magnified when the account is placed in the kind of continuum that will run through these pages.

Luck, in suggesting certain accounts were above suspicion, was in fact referring to Sosipatra. The account tells that she, in the midst of a discourse on the nature of the soul, suddenly became silent and, after a time, cried out. "What is this? Behold my kinsman Philometer riding in a carriage! The carriage has been overturned in a rough place in the road and both his legs are in danger," before further noting his wounds and that he was being carried home at that very moment.[12] The vision turned out to be exactly accurate, and this convinced many of Sosipatra's omnipresence and power.

That such visions might bolster the reputation of the mystic is a common refrain. Moving greatly in time, if not so greatly in space, to Turkey and a collection of translated tales from there, we read of just such a mystic, a renowned sheikh, known to be able to leave his body. Often, he would go to the governor, tell him that such and such a caravan was in difficulties, and insist on help being sent to it without delay. Inquiries were frequently made as to the accuracy of his inspirations, and people say that the sheikh was always right.[13]

Magical Dreams across the Globe

Despite the cultural disparities, the general notion that one might discover a distant crisis by various magical means is widely held and comes out in the legends, lyric, and lore of all places and times. In a Zulu tale, we read that one night a boy dreamed of his sister being eaten by cannibals near a certain place, which he recognized. When he woke up, he went to hunt in the direction of which he had dreamed and found a crowd of cannibals under a tree in which his sister was indeed hiding.[14]

Perhaps as far distant as one might imagine, we find numerous similar crisis visions in returning to the Lenape. In "The Doom of Toad Face," after a Lenape had a run-in with a bear and climbed a tree for safety, a rescue party arrived led by a man named Roaring-Wings. "I dreamed you were out there needing help," he said, before noting, as if such intimations were a common thing, that "As usual my dream came true."[15]

In returning to the Havasupai Indians and a retold version of one of their tales, "Wolf's Boy," this boy's father dreams, as he apparently commonly does, of his son, who is not at home. He spoke to another named Crow, telling him, "I want you to go down and see my boy. I dreamed that he was crying." Crow started out and found him surrounded by many other Indians who were about to kill him.[16] Similarly, in Texas, and returning to a folktale involving an early settler, we find Josiah Wilbarger having been shot through the neck in the desert while away from home with two comrades. Having seen him fall, they thought he was dead and retreated. Back at home, Mrs. Hornsby woke up with a start and shook her husband awake. "Wilbarger is alive!" she said. "I have seen him in a dream. He is naked; he is wounded and scalped; but he is alive." No one believed her; however, she went on to describe his exact location, and the man was later found.[17]

Symbolic Crises

In the Russian tale "Ivan the Peasant's Son and the Thumb-Sized Man," we read that in the courtyard of a certain king, there was a pillar with three rings: one of gold, one of silver, and one of copper. One night, the king dreamed that a horse was tied to the golden ring; every hair on the horse's body was silver, and on his brow was a glistening moon. His interpreter told him that this was not a dream, stating, "For last night the twelve-headed dragon came to your kingdom on that horse and wanted to steal your daughter."[18] Like the vardoger accounts, the king here apparently perceived the crisis in an allegorical fashion, as do people today and as might the medicine man or the mystic in all parts. Among the Copper Eskimos, for example, such a man, Ilatsiak, claimed that his tutelary spirit often visited him in his sleep and would warn him when others were in danger. Whenever he dreamed of small knives, he knew this meant specifically that certain children were ill.[19]

Also of a symbolic character, in an old Chinese folktale, a man named Bai awoke from a rather elaborate dream in which warriors in golden armor knocked out a tiger's teeth. He had the particular impression that the dream related to his son, and he sent another son to deliver a message of warning. As it turned out, the man's son was missing his front teeth and had lost them when he fell off a horse. According to the tale, in a clarification often invoked in modern accounts, the date of the accident was the same as the date of his father's dream.[20] Likewise comes an account from Nam Xuong, Vietnam. One Truong Singh dreams that a girl in a blue dress asks him to save her. This was "about the time" that she had actually jumped into a river, unknown to Singh. The next morning, a fisherman offers him a turtle with a blue shell, which, in fact, rather than eating, he "saves" by returning it to the ocean.[21]

An Indian tale involves one King Ashoka who, at one point, dreams of two vultures about to tear out the eyes of his son, Kunala. Eventually Kunala was found and brought to him, and the king's dream had been accurate; his son's eyes had indeed been torn out—the man then declaring, "Behold the realization of my bad dreams; in sooth, this is Kunala, whose eyes have been torn out."[22]

More obscurely, in a tale from Kerala, a state on the Malabar Coast of India, Othenan, a soldier of great repute and a legendary figure in north Kerala, had a dream in which someone stood before him and told him, "Go to Kadathanad at once. Your little brother's life is in danger. Save him!" Othenan, seemingly not initially possessing the assurance that so often characterizes these cases, assumes it was merely a bad dream. Having returned to sleep, he felt like he had been hit on the head, which forced him to take the vision rather more seriously as he set out immediately for Kadathanad, arriving within hours. His brother, as it turned out, had been buried alive in a tomb, and Othenan went to where he was confined. He called him by his name. "Oh! Is that my brother?" Kunjan asked from the tomb. "Yes," replied Othenan. And then Othenan said, "Stand away from the door!" With one kick, he broke the door of the tomb. He embraced his brother before killing those responsible.[23]

Mystical Aid

It was in fact exactly these kinds of visions, whether bestowed upon the ancient Sosipatra or upon Carl Jung, Hans Berger, or the innumerable unnamed men and women filling the pages of the folklorist, that might similarly mark a potential shaman, mystic, or saint. Just as we have seen, the medicine man and/or the shaman often claimed the capacity to attain distant information, whether from where they were or by induced out-of-body travel, often with the aid of certain brews, spirit guides, and various other techniques. We could find such general references regarding these capacities on any continent; others, however, are more pertinent here.

The Parintintin Indians of the western Amazon in Brazil, for example, a culture with a highly developed system of dream interpretation and entirely in line with the kinds of experiences still being collected, believe one can pick up on another's longing for them in a dream.[24] Conversely, and rather than spontaneously, the specialist might be enlisted to incubate a dream specifically to attain such information. In something of a representative manner here, the Menominee Indians of Wisconsin and Michigan might use the *tshi'saqkan*, a wigwam built with four posts and wrapped with bark, in which he could fast and dream, "so as to enable him to see at any distance where game was to be found, and where his enemies were in hiding."[25]

In speaking to the similarity of skills between specialists in traditional cultures and those, for example, practiced during the Middle Ages, we can refer to the Italian chronicler De Voragine's popular *The Golden Legend*. There we meet Placidus, a very young monk who fell into a river while drawing water. He was pulled and submerged by the current. According to the legend, "Saint Benedict, sitting in his cell, immediately knew this by an inner vision." He then called an accomplice and ordered him to go and rescue Placidus. This man, Maurus, hurried on his errand before reaching the youth and pulling him out by the hair.[26] We find something similar in another Japanese tale. A certain man, Taicho, dreams of a god, who tells him, "Gyoja has bound me with a spell," he complained, "and he's left me at the bottom of the ravine. I'm suffering horribly. Please, Your Grace, use your power to free me and heal my pain." Taicho awoke, went where the dream indicated, and found the god trapped exactly as the dream had told him.[27]

In something of a reversal, and returning to his work, South African journalist and writer Lawrence George Green, convinced of telepathy though mystified by its process, noted that "many great events are supposed to have become known by telepathy" among South Africans. He gave the case of a king as recorded by Mr. R. C. A. Samuelson, an interpreter working in South Africa at the time. The king dreamed that his rival, Masumpa, had surrendered and that there was peace in Basutoland (a former British crown colony). When Samuelson was told the dream, "There was no reason to suppose that Masumpa was on the point of surrender." The news, however, soon came, and according to Samuelson, "the strange thing about the dream was that it was dreamt before the King or any of them knew of the surrender of Masumpa."[28]

PRISONERS AND WAR

Historically, such crisis visions were primarily between those with the strongest bonds. We therefore "shouldn't be surprised," wrote Sally Rhine Feather, Ph.D., "to find that ESP sometimes fills that gap when normal communication channels are slow or unavailable."[29] We could find many hundreds of these cases (though primarily related to deaths) spread throughout the relevant literature of the past half century and beyond; our main interests here, of course, being those of more obscure origin.

Related to the Turkic Koroghlu epic cycle of oral traditions dealing with Koroghlu and his band of warriors, we read in one of those unedited versions of three famous champions and some companions setting out to meet Koroghlu himself. On the way, however, they come into some trouble. Having attempted to pillage the caravan of another champion, Bamas Bezirgan, they are held at bay until one of the previously mentioned companions, Ayvas, overcomes him. When Bamas returns to his king, his men are dispatched, and the men who had set out to find Koroghlu are captured at night and thrown in a dungeon.[30] Importantly here, Koroghlu was "warned in a dream of the misfortune of his companions" and had set out to help them even before a letter that had been sent with intelligence arrived, a qualification that has, historically, been of great importance to the parapsychologist.

More ancient still, Pliny wrote in his natural histories of an incident in which a woman dreamed of a remedy for rabies, a particular wild rose called Cynorrhodon. Her son was attending to military duties at the time. According to Pliny, "by chance it happened that the soldier, after being bitten by a dog, was beginning to show a horror of water when a letter arrived from the mother, who begged him to obey the heavenly warning."[31]

Cicero records that when the Romans were prosecuting the Macedonian war, Roman politician Publius Vatinius dreamed that two handsome men on horseback appeared to him and announced outright that Perseus, the King of Macedon, had been taken prisoner. Letters containing official intelligence were soon received, which showed that the king had been captured on the same day as the vision.[32] Similarly, in a metrical romance from as far as the Philippines, a woman named Blancaflor is sentenced to exposure on the Durano River for refusing a king's advances. Floristo, the king's son, who secretly loved her, was "warned in a dream" of Blancaflor's peril, took action, and arrived in force to save her.[33]

In Portugal's national epic, *The Lusiads*, telling, among other tales, of the voyage of explorer Vasco da Gama to India in the sixteenth century, just such a warning was implemented. Da Gama was "warned in a dream by Mercury" that his enemies were preparing to cut his boat's cables and took action accordingly.[34] In an Armenian tale, this time relating to their own national epic, *Daredevils of Sassoun*, at the very moment the caliph of Baghdad was being "pressed sorely" at war and crying out for help, a woman sleeping in Baghdad dreamed accurately that this man was "in great trouble" and similarly divined some of his later intentions.[35]

Across the depth and breadth of its mystical and magical literature, Turkey is a land filled with such magic. Warren and Uysal, in their own collection of Turkish folktales, gave something alike in "The Early Life of Hasan Bey." Bey, having been gravely wounded at war, was brought to a fountain to have his wounds washed. According to the tale, at this very time, another man, sleeping somewhere in another town, awoke from a terrible dream. "I dreamed," he said, "that Hasan Bey was in great distress." He dressed himself, rang a bell, and called together his five hundred friends in the square before his mansion before riding to Hasan Bey's aid.[36]

In Arthurian legend, when Joseph of Arimathea is thrown into prison after preaching the gospel in Britain, Mordrain, the Eastern King, in Sarras, is "notified" of this "by a dream" and makes a military expedition for his release.[37]

Returning to the Seneca Indians, one named Grandmother Twylah magically learned, while her son Bob was in the navy, that a fire had broken out on the ship while he was playing with the band. "One day," as she told it, "I had a vision of him on a ship at sea with sirens sounding all around him. I could see that there was trouble."[38]

Fairy tales, romance, and allegory, then, replete with the strange and the magical as they are, hold numerous examples of the kind essentially indistinguishable from the more sober and seemingly extrasensory memorates of the folklorist and the parapsychologist. In the midst of the 1801 siege of Cairo, which took place during the French Revolutionary Wars between French and British forces and Ottoman forces, the learned Shaykh Alaysh dreamed that he saw two certain individuals fighting violently, so he hastened to the place he had dreamed of to break them up. When he arrived, he found the sultan and the czar fighting exactly as the dream had suggested.[39] Worlds apart, John Dee, court adviser to Elizabeth I and famed occultist, is said to have once had a similar clairvoyant vision, "showing him his house had been broken into by a mob." While it took some months to receive the intelligence, as he was not at home, a letter came from his brother confirming the details.[40]

In a story related to a fire, and collected in Norrland, Sweden, in the late nineteenth century, the informant's father had journeyed to a great market in Sjalaerad, as was his yearly habit. On one of those nights, however, he appeared to two members of his family when they thought he was still away. He appeared to the informant's mother and told her "he had been saved from mortal danger." As later found, he had appeared in this manner at the very time he was being pulled from the window of a flame-engulfed house where he had been staying.[41]

Botanist and parapsychologist Louisa Rhine described a case in 1981 in which the informant told Rhine that "something had happened to my brother." She was sure he was hurt. The informant's mother then traveled ninety miles and found him in a hospital, banged up, and bandaged in San Francisco.[42] These are the kinds of accounts collected in the hundreds by Western parapsychologists and others. Unembellished and to the point. Similarly, though in northern Peru, a woman named Flor told the author that she dreamed her daughter needed her and that she was in fact dying. Later, following the dream's instructions, she finds her daughter and discovers she has been barely surviving on a handful of corn a day.[43]

LOST AND FOUND

The missing person, whether mysteriously waylaid by the lure of the fairy, the song of the siren, or some other supernatural entity, as they so commonly are in the tales, or finding themselves lost in more mundane recent cases, is often in circumstances around which such visions seem to cluster. Maria Leach, an American writer and editor of books on folklore, relayed an example from 1763. A young child, Sarah, had gone missing. People from miles apart took up the search through the mountain forests for her. A couple of days later, a man from twenty miles south came to the parents' house. "Call in all the searchers," he said, "and I will find the child." He had dreamed of her sleeping under pine boughs by a brook, guarded by a bear. The child was later found exactly there.[44]

American cultural anthropologist Alfred Boeldeke noted that the Indians near Chuc Rurras in Peru would induce clairvoyance using a hallucinogenic brew of sorts in order to discover the location of tribesmen whenever they failed to turn up. After carrying out his ritual, one clairvoyant said, "The others would never reach us, and suggested that we should stop and force our way through the jungle. Before nightfall we should meet the other party. One of the men would have an injured leg and another a hurt back." The Indians then insisted on following this advice, and accordingly, "everything worked out as had been foretold."[45]

Among the Colombian Cuna, if a hunter is considered lost or does not return from a hunt, his relatives consult a *nele*, a clairvoyant, who, on the basis of dreams, discovers and describes the whereabouts of the missing person.[46] Considering once more just how widely it was believed that the shaman might "look around in his dreams" and quite literally visualize the landscape around him to assist the community, we should not be surprised to find expressions of this belief as it relates to instances of crisis among so many tales of the Native Americans. According to another Seneca legend, for example, a man named Gaga had been traveling and, needing food, he intermittently stole from other hunters. At a certain camp, one of those hunters told his brothers that he dreamed of this man and that he was stealing their food. He said, "Let us follow the direction given by the dream." Doing this, they found Gaga sleeping where it had been indicated, and, taking pity on the man, they simply stole his food in return.[47]

In an example from the work of American anthropologist Melville Jacobs, two Coos Indian children once vanished. The following morning, a dream came to their father and told him, "You will go down the bay to La' Xai. A rock is standing out from the land with bushes all over the top of it." Further noting, "there you will find your children," who had apparently been kidnapped. His wife told him, "Oh sometimes a dream is indeed (true). You had better go to there!" He set out with some companions and found everything "just like his dream had told him."[48]

In "Pitch Woman," a story from an Athabascan-speaking woman from Canada's unforgiving northwestern climes, we read that so-called pitch women often travel in pairs at night and sometimes steal children. At one point, after the son of a wealthy old man is stolen, the father dreams of a man who tells him his son is alive and where he can be found. The boy was later retrieved.[49]

Among the Kalapuya, Native Americans traditionally of the Willamette Valley of present-day western Oregon, it was said that a shaman "knows everything through his dreams." That he "sends out his dream-power when he wants to know what people are doing at some different place." Furthermore, if someone didn't return from an outing, then the people would say to a shaman, "Try (to see) what has become of that person. He has not gotten back. Maybe he will die." The Kalapuya shaman then, having attempted to discover the relevant information in a dream, might say, "Oh he is living. He is quite all right. He did not die."[50] The general clairvoyance of such specialists allows us to reasonably assume their familiarity with visions of distant crises, even in cases where no such tales are referenced. Consider, for example, the elders of the ancient Huichol of Mexico and the United States who would actively follow the progress of those on their "peyote pilgrimage" in their dreams. In these dreams, the elders "usually predicted where they are on the pilgrimage and what has happened to them."[51]

Likewise, during a curing session among the Aguaruna Jivaro of Peru, the shaman is called upon at one point "to see events in a distant location." One attendee asks, "How are the grandchildren I left behind in Shimpiyacu?" The reply was, "All right. They're fine." The reasonable assumption, of course, being that if they weren't fine, this would also have been known.[52] The same capacities were ascribed to mystics in all lands. In a related Jewish example, before going to sleep one night, a certain rabbi specifically wished to learn the location of a missing girl, and in his dream he "learned the truth."[53]

Among the Finno-Karelians, a *tietäjä* is a seer of sorts with supernatural skills. According to some of those Finns living in Canada, Kuuvalon Jussi was one such specialist. When a certain boy got injured in the woods after his drunk father managed to startle their horses in the forest between Creighton and Sudbury, his mother brought him to see this man. He told them of a dream he had, which included all the details of exactly how the young boy had been injured. According to Salo, "there can be little doubt of the strength of belief involved in this case."[54]

When Brooklyn-born Brant Secunda was traveling in Mexico in search of adventure, specifically to a village five days from Ixtlan, where he had previously been, he passed out, lost and dehydrated. Soon after, he was attended by some Mexican Huichol Indians. They told him that a shaman from their village had a dream about him and sent them out to find him.[55] Similarly, among the Seri or Comcaac people indigenous to the Mexican state of Sonoro, a woman named Loreto Marcos, while in the desert gathering fruit, takes a fall and loses it all. It is said that a certain Juan Mata "saw this happen in a dream."[56]

Ordinary and Extraordinary Mystics

Again, we may easily transition between accounts coming from the layman and the specialist, the spontaneous and the induced. The same discoveries and knowledge actively sought by specialists, often under the influence of some magical brew, are still made by ordinary people. This comes out not only in more recent folklore, but in the old tales also. According to another collection of folklore from Texas, when a group of men near Bastrop were attacked, only two came back, and they assumed the rest had been killed. A woman from town, however, dreamed of one of the missing men, saying that he was scalped and calling for help and that he was "by a creek bed, washing his head and seriously sick." A search party found him there soon after.[57]

In the second book of the *Jātaka*, a large body of literature native to India concerned with the previous births of Gautama Buddha and some of the oldest classes of Buddhist literature, we read something interesting. According to this particular tale, when King Assaka lost his wife and was in the deepest grief and pain, even having her embalmed, oiled, and placed under his bed, a certain ascetic who lived at the foot of the distant Himalayas "saw this king lamenting," using his "heavenly vision," and "straightaway resolved to help him."[58]

In a Bengali household tale, "The Goddess Itu," there once dwelled a Brahman with his two daughters and wife in a certain village. This man banishes his two children to the forest for eating some of his food. While assuming they have died, one night their father dreams that the goddess Itu appears to him and says, "If you don't bring back your two daughters, I will kill you by making you vomit blood. You will find them in such and such a place." The man rose early and told his wife, who exclaimed in great joy that her daughters were still alive. They set off at once, reached the village in the forest where he was told they would be, and found them.[59] In another Bengali folktale, one named Kumara is turned into a goat by the witchcraft of a woman named Hira. This punishment, however, was revealed to his wife in a dream, and she sets about procuring the goat for herself.[60]

A Japanese legend has an old man dreaming of a missing boy in a certain ditch. When he awoke to confirm this dream or to see "if the gods had visited him in his sleep," he found this boy, Umewaka, exactly where the dream had relayed.[61] Osla, from the Scottish fairy tale "Thom and Willie," dreams of a missing person who was on a certain rocky islet on the coast. A boat was manned, and sure enough, just "as she divined," they found the man there.[62] In a collection of Greek fairy tales, we read of a woman whose child goes missing. She soon dreams that a "tall, kingly stranger with long black locks" stood at her bedside, holding her son in his arms, smiling at her before disappearing with the child. She awakens to find the child's bed empty.[63] One Romanian folktale has a man whose sister was stolen from her home by the well-known fairy Sila Samodiva. He leaves in search of her, knowing where she is being kept, having been "directed by a curious dream."[64]

In a myth from among the Modocs, those First People of northeastern California and central southern Oregon, an old woman called Lok had a similar dream that said, simply, "Your brother's body has been stolen." The next morning, she started out to find out if the dream was true. When she returned, she said, "Just as my dream told me, somebody has carried off our brother."[65] An Onondaga Indian from the Northeastern Woodlands told Moss of a dream in which he saw an old man in a snowsuit pushed into a creek. He was badly beaten but still alive. He soon heard that a family friend had been mugged and killed that very night and that, according to the autopsy, he had been alive when he hit the water, as he had been in the dream.[66] The author makes no conclusion as to the timing; however, the coincidence seems clear. Among the myths of the similarly situated Wyandot Indians, we read in "The Woman with Twins and the Wizard" that when a wizard steals both of a woman's children, she receives information in a dream regarding their whereabouts.[67]

According to a story told to Canadian missionary and ethnologist Silas Rand, on one occasion, two Micmac Indians were hunting when, one night, one of them dreamed that there was trouble back home. Immediately upon their return, they found that a war party had been there, that their wives were missing, and that one of their children had been killed.[68]

ILLNESS AND THE DEATHBED

English author and diplomat Dennis Geoffrey, recounting rather matter of factly his childhood experience of attending the coronation of

King Edward VII, wrote that having just cut across the grass to Victoria Avenue, he saw an errand boy appear with a basket on his arm "as though from nowhere." "They've put t' Coronation off," the boy said. "T' King's poorly," he finished, before he "vanished." "Dazed by this apparition," Geoffrey rushed home and discovered that the mysterious message was true in every detail.[69]

Warnings of a Crisis

Just as an interesting number of vardoger accounts relate to illness, so too, unsurprisingly, do the accounts of a general crisis. Canadian biologist and psychologist George Romanes, a Fellow of the Royal Society, described in a letter dated to 1878 that he once saw his bedroom door open and a seemingly shrouded figure walk to the end of his bed. "Then with its two hands it suddenly parted the shroud over the face, revealing between its two hands the face of my sister." Romanes soon discovered that his sister was gravely ill and had only a few days to live.[70]

From the rich folklore of northern Iraq, we can read very similarly of an angel appearing in a dream to a certain abbot and saying, "Yohanan is ill and has not long to live." The abbot soon visited Yohanan and found this to be true. The man also died soon after, just as the dream suggested.[71] Such a typical crisis vision can be found in a folk ballad from northwest India purporting to be a true tale. When, at one point during the ballad, one Dharm Pal is poisoned back at home, his stepmother dreams of him bidding her goodbye. Immediately upon waking, she is told that Dharm Pal is sick and they must visit him fast as he is unconscious and close to death.[72] While the tale is considered part of a genre of similar stories not only in Indian classical literature but worldwide, nothing is said of the dream itself or the extent to which it rather simply mirrors the common kind of crisis visions recorded around that same time by parapsychologists. In a more familiar story too, "Beauty and the Beast," the heroine of the title dreams of her father lying ill back home. She returns and finds it to be so.[73]

A medieval Irish tale, concerned with the crowning of kings by means of divination, has a man, during such a vision, screaming out of his sleep. The man says that he saw "a soft youth, noble, and powerfully made, with two red stripes on his skin around his body, and he standing at the pillow of a man who was lying in a decline at the fort Emain Macha." Messengers were immediately sent, and "the description was found to correspond with that of Lugaidh Reo-derg, the pupil of Cú Chulainn, who was then lying ill."[74]

According to American folklorist Don Yoder, the following memorate was an "extrasensory incident" from a certain family tradition in Pennsylvania. Susanna de Benneville Keim awoke from a vivid dream in which she saw another, "Mountain Mary," in serious distress. This made such an impression on her that she immediately made plans to visit Mary, despite the hard roads and distance between them. "Mary needs me," she told her son, who attempted to persuade her against the venture. According to Yoder, "Upon arriving there, she found her vision confirmed—Mary confined to her bed, and the creatures dependent upon her care in bad need."[75]

In a Portuguese folktale, a young woman hears a voice telling her, "Your father is dying, and does not wish to die without taking leave of you." When she returns home, she finds her father on the verge of death, and he dies soon after they say their last goodbyes.[76] Regarding another auditory account, the highly venerated Arab poet Umar Ibn al-Farid has an account from his own hagiographical account of his grandfather. He tells how Ibn al-Farid met with a greengrocer in Cairo, who told him that he must travel to the Hijaz because he would not become enlightened staying in Egypt. Having spent fifteen years in the Arabian wilderness, Ibn al-Farid heard the greengrocer's voice urging him to return to Cairo, saying that he was dying. He obeyed the voice and returned to Cairo, where he found the greengrocer right at the point of death.[77]

That the individual might take these warning voices seriously remained as apparent in the twentieth century as it had been in the poetry of al-Farid or to the readers of the miracles of Vitalis. One of those cases, told to English author Frank Podmore, had a woman hear a voice telling her to go to a certain town because a friend was in urgent need of her. Here again, we note that these are not simple impressions or offhand thoughts; as Podmore wrote, "The effect produced in this case was so strong that the percipient actually bought a fresh railway ticket and changed her route."[78] Rhine similarly gave the case of a woman from Ontario who, after hearing a voice urgently tell her to return home while she was cutting wood, concluded, "If that voice had not told me [. . .] what would have happened?" As it turned out, there was a large snake poised near her one-year-old son.[79]

The same kind of movement to action is apparent in an account given by Canadian folklorist Helen Creighton. She gave a case from Pictou County in Nova Scotia in which one of two brothers suddenly, while driving, "felt a wall ahead of him," and he said to himself, regarding his brother, "Rod needs me." The feeling was so strong that he turned around and arrived just in time to discover his brother had been in a serious accident after a support came down while he was working on a bridge.[80]

Very commonly, in fact, the information comes in what seems to be an intuitive form; there is no apparition or vision, no sight or sound, merely the conviction that something is wrong. The American doctor of botany Louisa Rhine had a case from Texas in which a woman was expecting her mother and two sons' arrival from Indiana. One morning, sitting relaxed in an easy chair, she suddenly jumped as if she had been struck and called out to her husband that something had happened and that it "must be mother and the boys." When the phone rang twenty minutes later, she exclaimed seemingly knowingly, "That's it," and it was news that they had been in an accident. "I think I jumped and had that terrible feeling at the exact time they were hit," were some of her closing words on the matter.[81]

Irish medium Eileen Garrett once went to bed with a "strange feeling" that something was amiss with her daughter, who lived apart from her. Discounting the experience, she awoke at two in the morning with the impression that her daughter was at her side, speaking to her. "I have not written you, dear, as my chest hurt," she began. "Tonight I am coughing, and have a fever." Garrett, exercising the kind of caution she often would of her intimations, was uncertain as to the validity of the experience; however, she found later in the day that her daughter was "in bed with a heavy chest cold."[82]

Kepelino, a native Hawaiian cultural historian, wrote of these very same intimations as they occurred in his own land, noting that one might weep for their mother and feel a sudden pang of dread. Not long after, he would hear of his mother's death. Our assumption here is that nonfatal crises would elicit a similar response.[83] Such speculations seem to gain merit in the telling of a Hawaiian romance. When a woman of Kohala was "cast out upon the trash," her aunt had a dream through which she was guided to the place where she was and wrapped her in red cloth.[84]

Myths and Monastics

Certain accounts make it clear that these kinds of initial intuitions may later be attributed to a relevant deity. The early modern English Quaker William Edmundson recorded that, "under a great exercise of spirit," the "Word of the Lord" came upon him and revealed that his shop was about to be robbed. It later happened that the thieves had changed their minds; however, they had indeed been spotted that night at his shop.[85]

In an edifying Modoc myth, a certain young girl, around the time of her coming-of-age "maturity dance," dreamed that her five brothers were covered in sores and starving. When she woke, she exclaimed aloud, "I wish I had died long ago, then I shouldn't have brought trouble on my brothers. I have done this by not dancing and by going to sleep." She soon discovered that her brothers had indeed been struck by illness and that they were covered in the very sores she had seen in her dream.[86]

It cannot be overstated the extent to which strikingly similar experiences are to be found among the lives of so many early monastics.

While Columban, an Irish abbot, was once fasting and meditating in the wilderness, something he often did specifically in order to attain such information, something of the same kind was revealed to him. By this particular "revelation," he "learned that the brethren, who were near Luxeuil, were suffering from various diseases, and only enough remained to care for the sick." He soon departed for Luxeuil and soon "saw the afflicted."[87]

DISASTERS AND DECISIONS

In the early 1820s, a Nova Scotian woman named Mary Hichens had a vision of the vessel *Friendship* seemingly sinking off the coast of Seal Island. Having convinced the fishermen to go, they found that the vision had been entirely accurate. The vessel was going down, with sailors scrambling for their lives. The fishermen Mary sent out must have been astonished to see a bad dream come true.[88]

A similar crisis vision, in that multiple people were in danger, was written about in the life of Franciscan preacher Richard of Ingworth. He and some of his brothers lost their way, having set out for Oxford on the eve of All Saints' Day. Knocking on doors for shelter, they were eventually allowed in by some monks, who assumed they were ne'er-do-wells based on their patchy clothes. When they explained they had been devoted to an apostolic life, they were beaten and turned away. A young monk, however, followed them and, fearing they would die in the cold, put them up in a hayloft and brought them food. That same night, having returned home, this young man dreamed of them somewhat elaborately. He saw those who would not allow Richard and his men shelter being hanged on an elm tree for their behavior. When he awoke, he rushed, half-dressed, and found them "struggling with death as if they were being hanged," just as the dream had indicated. Of interest here is that the monk is said to have joined the order at Oxford based on this dream, a vision indistinguishable from those that still occur, however patently edifying this tale might be. That such visions might impact the individual in this way seems to be remembered in the legends and often justifies the reality of the vision itself even before its veridical truth is confirmed.[89]

Rivers and Seas

Something of great antiquity, but alike, is found in one of the legends surrounding the first-century saint, Mark the Evangelist. A young man dreams of a person hurrying quickly along a road who identifies himself as Saint Mark. He tells the man that he is rushing to rescue a ship in danger. "Shortly afterwards," a ship makes port in Venice, and the crew tells the young man they had called on Saint Mark having come to disaster and been in "peril of their lives."[90]

Printed in *The Gentleman's Magazine* in 1787 by a man warning against the "extreme danger of the popular belief in dreams," his anecdote nevertheless extolled their prophetic virtues. While these kinds of incidents are historically often tied to the creation of or generally related to specific significant sites, the same remained true much later. On the island of Alderney, the northernmost of the inhabited Channel Islands, a man of that rock dreamed that a ship had been wrecked near a certain shore and that some of the crew had managed to survive. While his relaying of this information was initially laughed off by his friends, he eventually went with a companion the next morning and found "three poor wretches half started with cold and hunger, and brought them safe on shore." Of great interest in relation to the extent to which dreams and visions have, in all lands, been implicated in the erecting of monuments and structures, this circumstance is the reason the islanders give for erecting three lighthouses there.[91]

From a 1912 issue of *The Illustrated London News* magazine, we read of an Atlanta man who dreamed that a nearby railroad trestle had been washed away. This man, despite being ill at the time, arose from bed and went to the river six miles from his home "to discover that his dream was a reality." The stream had carried away a trestle spanning a sixty-five-foot drop.[92] Another example comes from the folklore of the United Kingdom's northernmost region, the foamy Shetland Islands.

Here, according to Nicholson, an old lady used to tell how once, while putting peat on the fire, she suddenly had a visionary glimpse of a tall-masted sailing ship and a man falling from the rigging. This was "as clear as a photograph," and she realized quickly that this was her brother. Weeks later, she received a letter explaining how he had been severely injured after falling from a height onto the deck of the ship on which he was serving. "It soon became clear," relayed Nicholson, "that the accident had occurred at exactly the same time as the scene had flashed before her eyes."[93]

From Prince Edward Island during the First World War, we read of a Ms. Macmillan who, while sitting looking into her fireplace one evening, suddenly exclaimed, "Look, it's Lord Kitchener and he's in the water." Sure enough, news came the next day with the revelation that Lord Kitchener was lost at sea.[94] Much earlier, and some hundreds of kilometers east on Scotland's mainland, Dalyell gave an account of the same kind. At the very time the husband of a supposed and accused witch, Jonka, was in great peril aboard his fishing boat at Walls, six miles from her residence, she was apparently found, in the manner of Sosipatra, "standing at her own house wall, in a trance," before exclaiming the danger the boat and her husband were in at that very moment.[95]

Earlier still, English writer, trader, and journalist Daniel Defoe, author of *Robinson Crusoe*, relayed an incident from 1729 in which a certain lady of his acquaintance saw her husband walking in the room she was about to enter. Her husband, commander of a ship then at sea on a voyage to or from the Capes of Virginia, as close as they could tell, was seen right around the moment he had an accident.[96] Prolific author and parapsychologist Hans Holzer gave a related anecdote when he wrote about one Mrs. Dorothy T. in California. Although hundreds of miles distant, she dreamed of her son being "brushed by a car in San Francisco." She further saw her mother-in-law being hurt, although not fatally. Two days later, she had a call, finding that the accident had "indeed taken place as she had seen it."[97]

GRAVE MATTERS

Oftentimes, the crisis in question is not directly related to a living person as such. Something of relevance to this point came in 1162 when Nur al-din Zangi, a Turkish prince, heard his prophet calling in a vision for help. Immediately and "without delay," he rode to Medina, where the prophet's tomb was, and arrived in time to foil the Crusaders' plot to desecrate his tomb, which was later sealed with ebony and lead in order to avoid a repeat attempt.[98]

Historically, there are a number of accounts in which a distant tomb's state of repair is supernaturally discovered. According to the ninth-century monk Adrevald, a monk of Fleury named Aigulphus "learned in a dream about the ruined state of the tombs of Benedict and his sister Scholastica."[99] When, in China in 720 CE, men robbed the tomb of imperial consort Hua at Changan, the woman appeared in a dream to her son and informed him that her tomb had been opened and defiled. It should not be surprising that the vandalism of graves could be an issue. Tombs contained valuable grave goods, and ancient China was no exception. A fascinating note here: the robbers cut out the tongue of the corpse in the hope that she would not speak their actions to another in a dream.[100] Comparable was the much later case of a Chinese man who told author Emily Ahern of a dream, which came shortly after a spring grave-cleaning festival. In the dream, he saw rain falling through the roof onto his father. Acting on this intimation, he went to the grave site and found that something had become dislocated, which allowed rain to enter.[101]

Returning to the saints, when a certain bondwoman came to the Irish saint Declan's monastery, she stole from the city a large hide and intended to "wrongly" give it to others. This entire incident, including some further details, however, is something that the late fifth- and early sixth-century Declan apparently "saw" with his "spiritual vision," and he told his story to his brothers.[102] In this vein too, it is written that when Abbot Mummolus of Fleury, Aigulphus—then abbot of Lerins, off the coast of Cannes—and others found and took the relics of the renowned Italian saint Scholastica, the pope was "warned in a dream that the relics were being taken out of his country."[103] Finally here, something of the same kind was recorded in the ancient Icelandic *Book of Settlements* (a medieval Icelandic written work that describes in considerable detail the settlement of Iceland by the Norse in the ninth and tenth centuries CE). When Thorhall Knop pulled down a certain temple on the orders of a dream, a certain woman, Thorhild, "at the same time" had a vision of his deeds. As soon as morning came, she told her men, "Thorhall, my neighbour at Knot-Stead, is gone mad and out of his wits, so that he hath sent his men to break down that worshipful temple that standeth there."[104]

STRANGE CONNECTIONS

One of the simplest and most common kinds of reported extrasensory experience is that in which a distant and nonfatal crisis is variously revealed to the individual. Although very little cross-cultural and historical work has been done in this area, the same dreams, visions, and intimations collected by parapsychologists are found across the depth and breadth of legend and lore. The most renowned saint or medicine man might as much be the subject of such a dream, vision, or other intimation as are the folklorist's informants giving their anecdotes continents apart. While there is much work to be done in collecting, compiling, and finding contextual meaning in this and hopefully other datasets, it seems abundantly clear that the idea itself is a universal one.

THREE

A Date with Destiny

Nearing-Death Awareness in Legend, Lyric, and Lore

> *Prognostication in western medicine has traditionally been based on objective scientific criteria, yet providers often rely on a feeling or "sense" based on experience to provide prognoses. In trauma, some providers believe that patients who express a feeling of death are more likely to die.*
>
> MAURIZIO MIGLIETTA

Anne-Marguerite Petit du Noyer, a renowned early eighteenth-century French journalist, seemingly knowing something those around her did not, arranged her funeral, had her house draped in black, and carried out many other death-related rituals despite appearing entirely physically healthy. After completing the kinds of tasks that would have later taken up a lot of her husband's time at her death, "she died on the day and at the hour that she had indicated."[1]

Austrian psychiatrist and Holocaust survivor Viktor Frankl shared something related in his account of an individual's experience as a captive in a Nazi concentration camp. The prisoner dreams a strange dream in which a voice tells him that his liberation will come on "March thirtieth." On March 29, he suddenly became ill, and the following day he became delusional, lost consciousness, and was dead by the next day. Frankl puts the death down to lowered immunity due to his loss of hope, having initially considered this "liberation" as meaning that of his people; ultimately, however, the voice of his dream, as Frankl observed, "was right after all."[2]

Many mysterious phenomena have long been observed around the coming end of the individual's life. Visions, dreams, lights, and sounds—since the beginning, the dying person, either at or away from their deathbed, has often become privy to secret knowledge. Just as the heroes of legend, romance, and myth had, they often speak of other worlds, of indescribable beings and lands, and of meetings with relatives long past. In the same way that the shaman or other initiate might historically bring himself close to death or participate in similarly stressful rituals to attain his powers or make contact with his deceased forebears, the dying man or woman, in really coming to that same threshold, exhibits those very powers.

MEDICAL MYSTERY

We have already seen in previous chapters that the individual on their deathbed or while ill is often visited by mystery. Although much of this has been approached, perhaps nothing has been so marveled at and so little understood as the strange fact that the dying, and indeed the living, not uncommonly have an uncanny ability to accurately predict the date of their own death, often imparted externally and often at a time when there should be no expectation on the part of the medical practitioner or those otherwise attendant of their imminent demise. "An hour hence I shall depart," were the words of Edward Herbert, 1st Baron Herbert of Cherbury, in 1648, while on his deathbed. The clock that he held while making this prediction later proved him correct.[3]

The physician has wondered aloud as to how their own knowledge might be incomplete in the face of these mysterious yet undeniable occurrences. Medical social worker and author Jeanne Van Bronkhorst wrote that "In every nursing home, hospital, and hospice I've worked at, nurses and social workers tell stories with awe about someone they knew who seemed to know or choose the moment of their passing."[4] A residential caregiver who spoke to neuropsychiatrist Peter Fenwick noted similarly that "this sort of thing happens all the time."[5] These are truly widespread attestations. After calling in to a popular radio show, a paramedic noted this strange knowledge on the part of the dying. "It's very unnerving," he said. "They know, for whatever reason. They have a prescience. It's a definitive feeling that they have that they are gonna die and I would say ninety-five percent of the time they end up dying in front of me. And it's very disturbing to me."[6]

The words of Dr. John Hunter Phillips, formerly a professor of medicine at Tulane University in New Orleans, regarding the elderly patients he cared for, are particularly relevant and profound.

> I became interested in the mechanism of death in the elderly while serving in the nursing home, particularly in those patients who predicted that their death was imminent. They would say, "I'm ready to die," and there was very little the physician could do to prevent it. There was usually no obvious lethal disease process evident at the time, the electrocardiogram might be normal, the chest X-ray normal, the screening blood tests all normal, and yet death would occur, usually within 24–48 hours once the positive statement was made. This made me very uneasy, and continues to make me uneasy when I sign the death certificate under the "cause of death." I don't really know why they died.[7]

Such sentiments might easily be multiplied. "There is no doubt," wrote British physician Arthur Exton-Smith in a 1961 issue of *The Lancet* medical journal in relation to elderly patients accurately foretelling their deaths, "that these patients became aware that they were about to die, but the manner in which this knowledge was imparted to them could not be ascertained."[8] Dr. Joseph Ngeh, in a letter to the editor in the *Journal of the American Geriatrics Society*, noted that such "premonitions of death" are a "curious" and "recognized phenomenon." Ngeh gave the case of a patient of his who died after repeated attempts to revive him. When the patient's family arrived, "they showed no surprise at hearing about the patient's sudden death." The man's daughter soon revealed to Ngeh that six hours before the sudden incident, the man held her hand and told her he would "die tonight." Ngeh concluded that "the occurrence of the phenomenon of POD (phenomenon of premonition of death) may have a psychical, or spiritual basis that is not easily understood."[9]

That something of greatly mysterious proportions is occurring in these cases is clear. These patients, as we'll further explore, really do come into an awareness of just when they will die. By any yardstick, this is no mean feat. Indeed, even the physician's ability to predict death is essentially nonexistent outside of highly acute instances. A *Lancet* study, in fact, found that physicians were extremely inaccurate in making such predictions in the final weeks of patients' lives, guessing even the correct *week* of death only six times with seventy-four patients. That such specificity has manifestly been afforded to the dying patients themselves is, of course, a mystery and a rather plain challenge to current paradigms. Exton-Smith had openly pondered the nature of this information transfer: How did they know? Who told them? As will become clear, the messengers are often mysterious; however, at other times, the dying speak so plainly on the matter that one wonders how often they have even been asked.[10]

NATIVE AMERICAN AND AFRICAN KNOWLEDGE OF DEATH

While such things might seem "disturbing" or may cause "unease" to the modern sensibility, these experiences are and have long been known and widely accepted. With research being relatively sparse in more recent times, the historical, legendary, and folkloric records are, in fact, a far more fruitful avenue for broadening our understanding of these phenomena.

Among the Navaho Indians of the southwestern United States, for example, these capacities on the part of the dying were known, if not collected in numbers. Reichard found that they "tell of persons who, apparently in excellent health, say, 'I'm not going to live long,' give up customary activities and within a few days die." While Reichard was a little skeptical, he noted the cases that came under his purview had been corroborated by other "white men."[11]

American ethnographer George Dorsey tells the same of the Sioux Indians. It is said among those people, spread today throughout South Dakota, North Dakota, Montana, Minnesota, and Nebraska, that the people of the olden times "knew when they were about to die, and they used to dream about their deaths and how they would be when the time drew near."[12]

The Northern Shoshone Indians of southern Idaho and the northeast of the Great Basin believe dreams may impart knowledge of future events. A man called Enga-Gwacu once dreamed that the Sun appeared to him and told him to "build a wikiup all by himself [a hut or tent with a domed or conical roof] that he was going to die, but that he would be allowed to return to life, if he so desired." According to the account, "this was just what actually took place afterwards."[13]

Shifting scenes, according to a diviner among the Temne of northwestern Sierra Leone, it is said that "before people die they dream a lot, and some even dream their death."[14]

We find the same farther south among certain Liberian tribes, where anthropological research associate George Schwab found that "a person may have an unaccountable premonition of his own death. He will tell those about him not to use up any of their substance in having medicine made for him, because it will be no use."[15] As will become apparent, the same idiosyncrasies observed in modern accounts are found consistently throughout these disparate records. Something of striking similarity, for example, was given by one of the previously referenced patients of physician Arthur Exton-Smith, who, before their prediction was accurately fulfilled, "thanked the staff nurse who was doing the medicine rounds for all she had done and said that she would not need tablets any more after tomorrow."[16]

Returning to Schwab's work, though, he was offered several more concrete examples by the Liberians. In one of those, a man named Pepper Cooper told one of his brothers, "I will be dead at about three o'clock this afternoon; I feel it." As is still the common refrain, Cooper was not taken seriously as he was in perfectly good health, though he firmly insisted that "someone told him so." Cooper made a will and disposed of his things before dying at exactly the time stated. Schwab noted that once this story was told, several of the Liberians offered similar others, including from among the northeastern Gio people. There, a man resting at home suddenly felt a pain in the back of his neck and said, "Some people are putting a big rope through my head and body into the background. They want to pull me and the house upward! [...] I shall soon die!" Those present assumed he had been drinking; however, after pleading to be taken outside, he "lingered for a short time and then died!"[17]

Further Afield

We could look much further afield too. Among the Polynesians of the Southern New Hebrides, "men say, sometimes, that they will be dead at a certain hour on a certain day and they are, the end coming at the precise time stated." Just as modern physicians have marveled in such cases, Clarence Humphreys, in his ethnological record of those islands, went on to note that "however we may try to explain this phenomenon we cannot deny the fact of its existence."[18]

These, of course, were not phenomena relegated to the past, those "olden days" or impossibly distant lands, with all their missing time and therefore space for magic and contrivance. American and other folklorists, not even a century later, had collected the same stories. In Adams County, Illinois, a woman was taking care of a man with consumption. "One night," as she tells it, "the lamp went out and the front door opened at the same time. I went and lighted the lamp and closed the door. Just as soon as I sit down by the bed, the same thing happened again. I got up again and my patient said, 'Never mind closing the door, they are coming for me and I will go out that door in a few days.' And he died in three days."[19]

ACCEPTING FATE THEN AND NOW

While not always involving impressively specific dates, some of these *forerunners*, as they are known in parts of Canada and its islands, nevertheless involve strange sightings of one's own form, which are often specifically recognized as portentous, though such omens, often categorized as doppelgangers, have been fairly well covered. For example, a man from Nova Scotia's Saint Margarets Bay met himself at the shore one day, told about it, and was convinced this meant his death was close, which very soon afterward occurred due to diphtheria.[20]

As had many during the Middle Ages, this man of the later twentieth century recognized what seemed to him to be a rather unremarkable and recognizable indication from those natural rather than solely supernatural forces that held sway over his fate. While French medievalist Phillipe Ariès wonderfully speaks to the greater extent to which the medieval mind might more easily accept death and to which the individual may even be spoken ill of if they attempted to resist its call, there are numerous later exceptions.[21] Canadian folklorist Helen Creighton herself puzzled over "why a man will not try to avoid his fate" in reference to a case in which a Caledonian miner who came to his mother and aunt said, "I'll never see you again. I know I'm not coming out of the mine alive." They told him not to be silly, but he was killed that day. "Nobody knew what form his warning had taken."[22]

In fact, despite the idea that such a fate might be accepted more easily by the more (overtly) supernatural-inclined medieval mind, this was not always the case. Weisman and Hackett, for example, noted that patients who became mysteriously aware that they would not survive an upcoming surgery exhibited "little if any anxiety or depression over their conviction of certain death."[23] Conversely, while the medieval mind would have generally found much less of a fundamentally philosophical mystery in the prophetical utterances of the dying as compared to our contemporaries, it is fascinating again to see exceptions so soon after. One Gaspar Lourenco, in 1676, while ill in an infirmary, told his caregiver that the Lord had revealed to him that this very day was to be that of his death and had designated the exact hour the previous night. His infirmarian, visiting Gaspar at daybreak, asked with a "smile expressive of doubt, [. . .] 'Is it not today, brother, that you expect to go and enjoy the vision of God?' [. . .] 'Yes,' he replied, 'as soon as I shall have received the Body of my Saviour for the last time.'" He did, in fact, receive Holy Communion before expiring without struggle or agony.[24]

Something very similar was recorded as having happened over a century earlier, near the end of the life of Stanislaus Kostka, a Polish-born novice of the Society of Jesus who died in 1568. In early August, he had a premonition that he would die on the fifteenth. He became very ill on the tenth, and on the fourteenth he told his infirmarian that he would die the next day. However, the infirmarian shrugged it off, noting that he was not critically ill and therefore would not die. He did, of course, die the following day, his face lighting up as he described how Mary was approaching with her court of angels to take him to heaven.[25]

They Know Something We Don't

In more recent cases, the physician's surprise at the patient's prediction often comes because they had truly assumed them, for the immediate future, not to be at risk of death. This same qualification is made in the historical records. Without doubt, such a qualification in a hagiographic or biographical context serves to ensure the reader's sense that the saint or other person of importance has attained some secret knowledge; the extent to which these things still and actually occur, however, precludes its explanation as a solely literary device. Six years after

Kostka's death, Spanish mystic Catherine of Palma had the time of her death revealed to her and was to similarly surprise her physician with that secret knowledge. She asked for the last sacraments "before her physician thought it necessary they should be administered." She died soon after, passing away on "the very day she had foretold."[26]

While they might constitute their own study, it is interesting again to note that the time of death is often given to the chosen person much further ahead of time. Baronius, a cardinal and ecclesiastical historian who died in the seventeenth century while lying deathly ill, had a related vision. While he thought he was nearing his end, as he lay on his bed awaiting his death, he saw on the wall opposite him the large black numerals LXIX, or 69. As he gazed at this sight, the conviction overcame Baronius that he was not to die of this present illness and that he would die instead at the age of sixty-nine. When that time came and he was in fact dangerously ill, his doctors nevertheless described his condition as by no means dangerous to his life, though due to this experience, he was convinced they were false in their assessments. Baronius, true to his vision, did in the end die at that very age, when "his soul was set free from its worn out tenement."[27]

The sixteenth-century Sicilian friar Benedict the Moor very similarly spoke to his friend as he lay ill. "This time it is our Lord's will that I recover from the malady, but the next time I shall die; this will be before long, because I have finished my career." This happened as he predicted; Benedict recovered, but only for a short time. On the fourth of the following March, he was attacked by a continual and violent fever, which was his end.[28] This was also true of Saint Hedwig, patroness of Silesia, a historical region of eastern Europe. In her last days, she insisted on being anointed before anyone could be persuaded she was actually near death, though her prediction came true despite her seeming and observed health.[29]

More recently, Steve Taylor, senior lecturer in psychology at Leeds Beckett University in the United Kingdom, gave the case of his own father. Despite the fact that his father had Parkinson's and was quite weak, "no one expected him to die at that particular time." He, however, seemed to know something they didn't. "I've found out when I'm going to die," he said. "It will be a week today, next Thursday." He, like those in the previous accounts, was not believed, as he didn't seem seriously ill; however, he took a turn for the worse a couple of days later and died on the very Thursday he had predicted.[30] By unspecified means, too, as it happens, the eighteenth-century Russian Orthodox bishop Tikhon of Zadonsk had it revealed to him that the date of his death was a mere three days away. That day turned out to be August 13, 1783, exactly three days after the intimation.[31]

Perhaps the oldest account in which the seeming good health of the individual is specifically cited as the reason for the knowledge of death being surprising comes from the ancient Jewish *Book of Jubilees*. There, the prophet Rebecca tells her son Jacob, the Hebrew patriarch and grandson of Abraham, of a related dream. "I shall tell thee the truth, my son: I shall die this year, and I shall not survive this year in my life; for I have seen in a dream the day of my death, that I should not live beyond a hundred and fifty-five years; and behold I have completed all the days of my life which I am to live." Expressing the same kind of disbelief as our earlier paramedic, Jacob initially laughed the prediction off due to how healthy and physically able she was at the time; however, she died that very same night.[32]

If any figure could be said to be archetypal in this regard, it would certainly be the Trojan priestess Cassandra of Greek myth. When she prophesied that she and Agamemnon, king of Mycenae, would die, she was very clear regarding the who and the when: "Oh, oh! What fire! It comes over me! Woe, woe! Lycean Apollo! Ah me, ah me! This two-footed lioness, who couches with a wolf in the absence of the noble lion, will slay me, wretched that I amb."

While, in this literary example, she was not at all understood or necessarily believed, she herself was fully resigned to her death, which duly came.[33] Kings, indeed, are often the kinds of important figures around whom such legends collect. Phillip, king of Macedonia, had been warned by an oracle to "beware the violence of a four-horse chariot." Taking the warning seriously, Phillip had all such chariots in the kingdom destroyed; however, he was later killed by Pausanias, who had a chariot engraved on the hilt of his sword.[34]

Clearly, then, not all minds willingly accepted this knowledge as expressed by the dying either in the past or more recently, though again, while this was far less objected to in its metaphysical implications than it is today, the generalization certainly holds. What becomes clear, however, is that whether in the hospices of the twentieth and twenty-first centuries, the medieval infirmary, or upon the Mesopotamian deathbed, the dying and, more broadly related to the theme of this chapter, the living themselves commonly display this secret knowledge. They commonly embodied a mysterious knowing regarding their end, often imparted by another, which rightfully confounds those attending and, at least in our own times, our very sense of things.

AN IDEA AS OLD AS DEATH

Throughout the annals of legend, lyric, and lore, the chosen man or woman seems to move divinely guided through life, either with or eventually coming into a certain knowledge regarding his or her ultimate end. The shaman in the frozen north, the infamous seer of the Scottish Highlands, the hero of romance, and the martyrs and mystics of many lands—his or her fate is often written. He or she is a tool of the divine, bringing the will of fate to bear on the world during their time there. Their beginning and end are known, and their purpose is, to varying degrees, predetermined. Prediction and prophecy abound in the life of the chosen individual. "Thou shalt see me at Philippi," were the famous words of Caesar's ghost to Brutus in Shakespeare's tragedy, *Julius Caesar*, foretelling the fateful moment of that man's death.[35] "I tell you that I shall not live two days" were those of King Arthur's nephew, Gawain, who also knew his end.[36] In Norse myth, Balder, the son of the chief god Odin and his wife Frigg, learns from Hela in a dream, three days before he is actually killed, that he will die three days from then.[37]

While at times the dates are less impressively specific, the idea that one might become aware of the day they will die nevertheless finds us reading from an ancient Chaldean tale. The legendary Ea-Bani, a wartime comrade and friend of Gilgamesh, king of Uruk, is symbolically warned of his own approaching death by way of a "three-fold vision of flames and lightning." A mortal illness comes over him, and he dies in twelve days.[38] The utility and romance of associating these occult intimations with people of importance are again clear. That a very real and indistinguishable phenomenon persists, however, is just as apparent. Perhaps the quintessential seer who foresaw his own end was a hero of Greek mythology, Amphiarus, who famously predicted his own death to his son if he were to, as he did, participate in the war of the Seven against Thebes.[39]

Plutarch tells us that Roman general and statesman Lucius Cornelius Sulla "not only foresaw his own death but may be said to have written about it also." Sulla, in the last days before his death in 78 BCE, seemed acutely aware of its increasing proximity. Two days before his passing, he stopped writing the twenty-second book of his memoirs. He was said to have been told by the Mesopotamian Chaldeans that he would die in his prime, and more tellingly, as we'll later address, he had a visit from his dead son, who was "clad in mean attire and besought his father" to follow him and his mother to the otherworld.[40]

Haterius Rufus, a Roman equestrian, was also warned in a dream of his death, a dream the classicist Henry Walker considered a "very accurate sketch of his future," this being due to the dream having been "proved by its outcome." In his sleep, Rufus saw himself stabbed during a gladiator fight in Syracuse. The next day, he saw the gladiator who killed him in his dream, the final outcome of which soon played out with Haterius's death at his hands.[41] Millennia later, Feather gave the comparable case of a man from North Carolina who dreamed he was standing at a place called Butler's Crossing when a vehicle came toward him at great speed and killed him. Three days later, this exact scenario played out, and the man died.[42]

In 1583, the Jesuit theologian and exegete Juan Maldonado, having been working on compiling a commentary for the Four Evangelists, Matthew, Mark, Luke, and John, also had a mysterious messenger and saw the same vision for several consecutive nights. A certain man came to him and persisted in his encouragement that Maldonado would finish the work shortly and that he would die soon after its completion. The man would then mark a point on Maldonado's stomach. Shortly after finishing the commentary, Maldonado experienced intense pains in this area and died quickly after.[43] Of interest here, the younger Pliny once intriguingly remarked that "the deaths of those who were preparing something immortal seem, in all cases, untimely and immature." In his letters, Pliny gives the case of an acquaintance of his, G. Fannius. That man dreamed that the dead emperor Nero came in, sat on a chair, and took some of Fannius's books from a shelf. After leafing through them, the shade departed, and Fannius interpreted this to mean "that he was destined to come to an end of his writing at the place where Nero made an end of reading" and, according to Pliny, "so it turned out."[44]

The Far East and Others Alike

That the man with knowledge of his own death is in some way elevated above others and that this capacity itself might suggest his status as someone divinely important is brought out clearly in a medieval Japanese tale in which a certain monk, lost in the mountains, takes up residence in a grass hut. Soon, another man, a pilgrim, comes to stay there too, and although our monk initially thought him, based on his appearance, to be "a beggar or worse," it was the fact that this man later stated that he would die "on a certain day of a certain month in a certain year" that called him to reconsider the pilgrim's true nature. This person named each of these variables as opposed to being general about them, and the monk, based "on hearing this," then thought that the man might be a noble sage. On that very day, some years later, the monk returned to the grass hut and found the man who said he would die on this day, which had accordingly unfolded.[45]

According to the fifteenth-century Japanese work, the *Hasadera Reigenki*, a man named Asho had come to the Hasadera temple to ask for its deity's assistance. Three days later, he dreamed that someone had ordered him to try to enter the "Pure Land of the West." The man therefore dedicates his life to a more ascetic path. Of greater interest here, however, is that Asho is said to have displayed "miraculous abilities" toward the end of his life, including having accurately "predicted his death seven days in advance."[46]

During near-death experiences too, particularly those from the Far East, the individual might sometimes become aware, before being sent back to earth, exactly how much time they will be granted to stay. From Vietnam, a judge named Duong Duc Cong died and arrived at a "Black City with the Iron Gate." He was told by two men in purple robes that it had been decided he should have two more eras of life, one of which was twelve years. Duong Duc died exactly twenty-four years later.[47] Of fascinating similarity, the wife of the first-century pope Ananius of Alexandria fell ill apparently because she did "not submit to the truth," in reference to a refusal to renounce her faith. Having been taken on something of an otherworldly dream journey, initially through darker realms, then to those brighter realms where these sojourns so often end, she is told that she will live exactly one more year. She informed her husband about her dream, received communion, and died a year later.[48]

Outside of the mysterious utterances of our own dying contemporaries, who somehow attain knowledge regarding their ends, there has clearly been an ancient and widespread tradition speaking to these things. An old Chinese tale involving Liu Qingsong of Guangling has him visited by a man "clad in court attire," who handed him a tablet summoning him to serve in the other world. When the man came again the next day, telling Qingsong, "You should now report to your post," Qingsong "knew he must die," so he set his domestic affairs in order, took a bath, and that evening suddenly expired.[49]

Secret Knowledge of Death in Celtic Legend

The prophetic dream holds great prominence in Welsh and Irish sources too. Muircheartach Ua Briain, king of Munster and later high king of Ireland, awoke screaming on one occasion as he had a dream of his own death. His next dream was of a shipwreck and a griffin that soon carried him away to her nest, where he was burned alive. Upon awakening, he sent a message to Dub Da Rinn, the son of a druid, asking him to interpret it. The druid told him that the ship stood for his reign, which was about to end, while the griffin was the woman who would cause him to be burned to death. This answer, however, did not get to Muircheartach's hands, as that very night he was trapped in a fire and drowned in a cask of wine.[50]

According to some of Ireland's annals, in the eighth century, Irghalach (d. 702), son or grandson of Conaing and a king of the Uí Néill dynasty, also saw the manner of his death the night before it occurred. The morning after his vision, he stood on a rock and expounded his fate. It is said that among the Britons who were, at that moment, coming to kill him, there was another who dreamed similarly—that a herd of wild boars was all about him and the largest he killed with a javelin—this having been "a presage exactly verified," as the boar represented Sifnigied Irghalach, who was killed by that very warrior.[51] Both early modern Franciscan Bernard Gray and the dean of Armagh were said to have predicted their own deaths in 1549.[52] Later in the same period, Rev. Edmund Hill predicted his own death "a few days before it occurred in 1630," which led some to accuse him of magic.[53] Given much later as a memorate in an 1890 issue of *Folklore* was the case of a young Irish girl from Killeaden, County Kildare, who was standing on Liss Ard when she felt hands take her and pull her forward. Somehow, from this, she knew, and she told that she would die on Lady Day, March 25, of that year. She became ill and died "as she had foretold, on Lady Day."[54]

English historian and cleric Charles Plummer wrote of a man named Fintan from the province of Leinster who, having been unwell for thirty years, saw a vision of a chariot coming from heaven. Two figures he did not recognize rode upon them, though they soon identified themselves as Brigit and Moeog. "Tomorrow is my day," said Moeog, "and the day after tomorrow is Brigit's Day." He went on to note that the man should "be ready for thou shalt die on the third day, and shalt obtain the heavenly kingdom for thy soul." Fintan went to a church of Brigit's in County Kildare, related his vision to all there, and accordingly, "he died on the third day, as Moeog had revealed to him."[55]

Far more obscure, and relayed by Dutch Anabaptist author Thieleman Van Braght, was the case of Hans Hasilbacker, a certain "old and pious" sixteenth-century Swiss monastic who, having been treated poorly in prison, "had a dream in which it was shown him that they would behead him, and it was made known to him in a special manner that he should be punished with the sword." His death came just as it had been shown in the "divine vision."[56]

Symbols and Dreams

As with the Irish accounts and some others we have seen, symbolism and metaphor again play a conspicuous part, as so often do those things of the otherworld. In the Icelandic *Saga of Hromund Greipsson*, one of King Hadding's men, Blind, dreams a number of dreams. In one of those, he sees an iron ring fixed around his neck, and his king, Hadding, one of the earliest legendary Danish kings, later tells him, "The meaning of this dream is that you are going to be hanged; and that will be the end of both of us." Soon after, Blind is bound and hanged in Sweden.[57] Scholar and Arabian biographer Ibn Sa'd likewise records of one Al Hasan that he saw in a dream the words inscribed between his eyes, "Say God is One." When he related this to those in his house, he exclaimed that if this dream spoke truly, then little time remained for him to live, "and he lived but a few days" after that.[58] The dream interpreter with bad news was not relegated to the legendary sagas or other early literature. Greatly removed, and in sixteenth-century Colombia, the then lord of Bogota once dreamed that the waters of his ritual bath were turning into blood. Greatly worried by this vision, the shaman of Ubaque gave his interpretation: the lord, he said, would die imminently. As Reichel-Dolmatoff relayed, "This proved to be true enough."[59]

Reported rather recently in the British Medical Journal was the case of a forty-three-year-old woman in Labrador, Canada. She had been admitted to the hospital for minor surgery, which was completed in an hour. However, shortly after, she complained of pain on her left side and quickly died. She had suffered a rare failure of the adrenal glands but had no underlying illness. Interestingly, doctors at that hospital learned that, as a child, she had been told by a fortune teller she would die at age forty-three. The week before her death, she confided to her sister and a nurse that she was therefore sure her death was near.[60]

As with any phenomenon that, in the end, turns out to be a manifestly real one, these accounts may truly be found among the most seemingly disparate sources. An example from Australian folklore was associated with the horse Nimblefoot's win in the Melbourne Cup of 1870. Some months before the cup, one Walter Craig dreamed that a certain horse carrying his colors would win the cup but that the jockey would wear a crepe armband. Mr. Craig awoke, sure that this meant he himself would not live to see that date. He died that very same night. It had apparently been established that the dream came true in every detail and that it had been relayed before the event occurred.[61]

In something of a twist on the formula, it seems that in some cases, death, despite making itself known, was still a surprise to the individual. In an old tale from Worcestershire, England, in 1779, a certain politician named Tom dreamed that he was in a room into which flew a bird and that the bird turned into a woman clothed in white who told him he would die in three days. Nearing the end of the third day, according to his valet, he was quite cheerful and ordered breakfast rolls for the morning, seemingly happy that he had survived the portent. He sat on the side of his bed, clutched his side, and died in his valet's arms.[62]

MYSTERIES, MARTYRS, LAYMEN, AND SAINTS

It is important to speak to the ubiquity of belief in these experiences as actual phenomena founded upon related anecdotes or memorates, particularly when considering the lives of the saints, where such accounts are found in impressive numbers, as are any number of other seemingly extrasensory phenomena. The learned biographers of the saints, when they weren't recording these events in their actuality, were clearly aware of their reality as events that might literally have occurred around the deathbed. They seemed especially aware of the utility of making it known that those around the person predicting their death would not believe them due to their seeming good health at the time. In fact, in late antiquity at the very least and, in our estimation, certainly far beyond to varying degrees, almost all saints knew the time of their deaths.[63] Likewise, many of the characters in the Persian *Shahnameh*, a large epic poem from between 977 and 1010 CE, foresee their own deaths, often long in advance. One of those characters, Zahhak, dreams of a regal youth, appearing very tall and carrying a mace that looked like the head of a bull, who throws him into a well. This all eventually comes to pass.[64]

As with the vardoger and other related occurrences, while numerous speculations as to why such predictions were so prominent have been put forward, scholars, for the most part, fail to mention the reality of the very much established, if greatly mysterious, nearing-death awareness phenomenon while assessing the related biographical texts, often seeing such episodes as mere functional literary or otherwise edifying devices. Michael Flower, senior research scholar at Princeton University, spoke to this beautifully while contrasting the mythological seer who foretells his death directly against accounts recorded in a historical fashion. "If we had no other evidence," wrote Flower of the related accounts of Cassandra and Amphiarus, whom we shall come to, "that would sound like a purely literary topos—the seer who vainly foretells his or her own demise," before noting, "Yet this sometimes happened in real life."[65] And indeed, despite Flower referencing some ancient lives, this nevertheless continues to be the case. It seems rather, upon closer examination, that hagiographers understood the more common yet mysterious extrasensory phenomena, which historically have been relegated to the holy man, the witch, the wizard, or the shaman, and so on, and the extent to which their ascription to the saint might engage or speak to the reader. These beliefs would have certainly turned up among the legends, ballads, and other lore upon which they so commonly drew.

Saint Maximus, Christian monk, theologian, scholar, and former aid to the Byzantine emperor Heraclius, foresaw the exact day of his death in a vision that occurred in 662 CE.[66] While these accounts are common among those early martyrs, the same capacity was clearly ascribed to many others far distant and was most certainly not relegated to the Abrahamic mystics. Sixth-century Welsh bishop Paul Aurelian is likewise said to have had the very day of his death revealed to him at his bedside by an angel. "Prepare thyself, therefore, to depart from this world on Sunday next," which occurred on that day.[67] Third-century Christian martyr Saint Lawrence was also given the specifics of his death while in prison. In a dream, the Lord asked Lawrence if he would like to live with him now, to which Lawrence replied that he would love nothing more. He is then told that he will be burned alive the next day, but that it won't last very long, and then they will be together. When, on the following morning, Lawrence told the governor in charge of his fate that he knew his plans were to kill him, which soon unfolded, the governor was surprised, asking, "How did you know that?"[68]

We must mention Cyprian, the early Christian theologian and bishop of Carthage, who recorded numerous related accounts and was himself the subject of one of the earlier of these nearing-death awareness kinds of visions. Barely asleep, Cyprian had a vision in which a young man of great stature led him before a proconsul. This magistrate, seeing Cyprian, began to write his sentence, which turned out to be that he should have his head cut off. Cyprian "easily understood" what this meant, and, requesting a day to set his affairs in order, he was granted this grace. His judge writes this on the tablets in a scene rather curiously reminiscent of so many Far Eastern otherworld journeys, especially considering the extent to which they are often cited as unique in this way. These predictions were exactly fulfilled.[69]

The British monk Boisil, living at Melrose Abbey in what is now Scotland, died in 664 CE. Stricken by an outbreak of plague, Boisil, knowing his end was near, called for his disciple, Cuthbert, to read the Gospel of Saint John. He wished it to be divided into seven parts, one to be read on each of the seven days he somehow knew he had remaining, which came exactly to pass.[70]

THE DEAD WHO COME FOR THE DYING

The idea that the dead themselves come to inform the living of their nearing end, some instances of which we have already seen, is an ancient, ubiquitous, and indeed, evergreen one. The martyr or dead saint might come *for* the saint or saint-to-be; a deceased ancestor might come for the native man or woman. This is a reality we find the world over. When we consider the extent to which ordinary people have reported and continue to report being informed of their own oncoming end to folklorists or to physicians in this very manner, we should not be surprised at how well represented the idea is historically, despite the lack of comparative work.

Just three days after her death, the early Christian martyr Potamiana, who died in Alexandria during the persecutions under Septimius Severus, appears to her executioner, Basilides. She places a crown on his head and says, "Know that I have prayed for thee to my God, whom I now enjoy; he will presently call thee to that glory of which I have already been made a participator." The subsequent death of Basilides "proved the vision to be real," as he is said to have embraced the Christian faith after the vision and been beheaded himself.[71]

Another of the older examples was given to us by Plutarch. Spartan Regent and General Pausanias (479–478 BC), "in the heat of his lust," sent for a free-born virgin, Cleonice, from Byzantium, with whom he planned to spend the night; however, for reasons unclear, he became oddly perturbed and stabbed her to death. Having been haunted by her shade that night, he later sailed to the oracle of the dead at Heraclea Pontica and called up her ghost. She told him that, upon his return to Lacedaemon, "he should be free from all his affrights." Pausanias died soon after his return, just as predicted by the dead woman. Plutarch considered the death a punishment from God for Pausanias's actions, as Cleonice had predicted.[72]

Saint Leo, a third-century Christian martyr at Patara in Anatolia, while performing his devotions before the relics of the recently deceased Saint Paregorius, had a vision. Paregorius stood nearby and invited him to pass over, which gave Leo the "hope" that he would soon be honored with martyrdom, which shortly after came to pass.[73] Anselm of Ribemont, a figure of the First Crusade and a lord of that region in the French Valley of Oise, arose one morning and gathered his priests around him. Anselm told them that during the night he had seen the recently deceased Lord Engelrand. He was shown a home in heaven "so beautiful" that he "could conceive of nothing to equal it." Engelrand then told him that a much more beautiful place was in preparation for him, Anslem, and that he would take up residence there the following day. While Anselm knew this meant his death would come the next day, his priests were shocked "since they saw Anselm hale and hearty." Just as we have seen in the modern accounts, however, Anselm's intuition proved correct, as he died that very day.[74]

Bede, perhaps England's premier historian of the early Middle Ages, whose works describe almost all the nonordinary phenomena that early twentieth-century parapsychologists were to become concerned with and later physicians were to write about, has a number of examples. At a monastery located in the West Midlands region of England, a young woman lay ill in the infirmary. Having noted, as still do the dying and those attending them, that the room seemed filled with light, such that she did not mind her candle being put out, this woman told it that a certain "man of God, who had died that same year," appeared to her and gave her the information that at the break of day she would "depart to the heavenly light." The truth of this came to pass as she died the very moment the sun broke at dawn.[75]

An old Palestinian tale has a dead father appearing to his son and telling him, with no indication of ill health, that in an hour or two, he would be "numbered among the dead." While the young man railed against this and attempted to save himself, he eventually died at the given time.[76] French physiologist and immunology pioneer Charles Richet wrote in the 1870s of a man who dreamed he was at an inn, where he met several of his dead friends. In this dream, he promised to visit them again in six weeks. As it happened, exactly six weeks later, he was killed in an auto accident.[77] Among the Maori of Te Ika-a-Māui, the northernmost island of New Zealand, a man dreamed something similar. The night before this man, Manihera, was murdered, he dreamed that several of his dead friends had visited him. The experience made him feel "sure he should be in the Reinga [underworld] himself before the next night." The man was indeed cruelly murdered the same day.[78]

Again and again, worlds apart, the dead come for the living. In a folkloric legend from Munich, immediately after a dream in which he made contact with his dead mother, a man heard seven bells resounding from a small church. He didn't know if this meant he would die in seven days, weeks, months, or years, but he was sure it meant his death. He did, after all, die in exactly seven days.[79] Elizabeth Hastings, an English philanthropist, religious devotee, and supporter of women's education, while ill in bed, mysteriously told those around her that she would soon be able to inform them of the exact time she would be leaving this world. One night, a form came into the room in the shape of the deceased Mr. Nelson, a friend of Elizabeth's. When Elizabeth, asleep at this time, awoke, she had been given the assurance that she would die in six days, and in six days from the vision, she died.[80] The Scottish mathematician, engineer, and indeed, demonologist George Sinclair gave an earlier example in his 1685 work, *Satan's Invisible World Discovered*.

One evening, an Edinburgh man who had recently lost his wife had her appear to him in ordinary clothes, crossing the room and saying, "John will you not come to me?" before vanishing. While no specific date was given to this man either, he died within the month.[81] In an account from the area of northern Italy around Barre, a young girl, Anglica, who apparently had certain psychical abilities, such as the capacity to locate lost items and foretell the future, had a similar experience. Three days before her death, at the age of twenty-two, she had a vision of one of her patron saints, who came to her and told her to prepare herself for this. The day she was sure she would die, she dressed in her best clothes and lay down in bed, awaiting death, which duly came before sunset.[82]

Among the Dakotan people of Tipi Sapa, a woman whose husband was killed in battle suddenly began allowing her hair to grow long and arranging it very neatly, this being against his wishes. When her friends ask her why she has changed her behavior, she tells them, "You suppose I am thinking of some man; but I am not. Things are now to be just as I want them. I dreamed last night that my husband was talking to me, and he said: 'You and the daughter will soon be with me.' That means I shall die soon." Less than two days later, the heavy ridge pole that supported the log house fell where she slept and brought down the roof with it. Both the mother and daughter were instantly killed. "The dream had come true."[83]

That the presence of the dead among the living portends death often comes out even in accounts in which nothing regarding that connection is specified. Thus, when the deceased Persephone appeared to the ancient lyric poet Pindar, she simply complained that he hadn't honored her with his work. Pindar, however, "dies almost immediately" after the encounter.[84] Returning to his less quoted volume, Minot Savage gave just such an account from then-modern New York. A young man from that city told his mother, "I have something very sad to tell you. You must brace yourself and be strong to bear it." Surprised and distressed, she asked him what he was talking about. He said, "Mother, I mean just what I am saying. I am going to die, and very soon. Last night, when I was walking up and down the piazza smoking, a spirit appeared and walked up and down by my side. I have received my call and am going to die." This woman soon sent for the doctor, who gave the boy a clean bill of health. He died, however, just a couple of days later, of appendicitis.[85]

The dead evidently, have been and still are the perennial messengers of death. As recently as in 1944 New York, in fact, a collection of ghost lore found that these spirits "frequently" returned, specifically "to foretell death."[86] These sentiments are found ubiquitously through near-death and related literature. In his excellent 2023 work on terminal lucidity and the paradoxical and sudden awareness of patients with neurodegenerative disease nearing their deaths, Professor Alexander Batthyány gives truth to this idea. The informant's father, who had been in a nursing home for a half year with severe dementia and an inability to recognize his loved ones or converse at all, suddenly began to speak. He told his son that he would not be in that room much longer, much to his son's confusion. "Last night," the man said, "David [his older brother, who had died a month previous] came and said he would take me home." He died that very night.[87] Batthyány gave a number of similar accounts, including that of Monica, who was dying from a progressive brain tumor. In her final stages, she suddenly sat up and said, in a loud voice, "Liz!" This was her best friend, who had been dead for four years. She died just a few hours later, leaving her sister considering the possibility that Liz had actually come to help Monica.[88]

Also more recently, one Judith Wilson, at the age of ninety-seven, in an old folk's home, told her caregiver that her dead sister Alice was going to come for her the next day at 2:30 p.m. Just before that time on the following afternoon, she opened her eyes, whispered her sister's name, and died peacefully. Similarly, in yet another of the many cases given by Fenwick, the husband of one Susan Grant had a visit from his dead mother, and "somehow he knew that her coming meant he was going to die."[89]

Given how widespread is the idea and lived experience that the dead come to warn the living of their nearing end, it should not be surprising that some more general folk beliefs of this kind have developed. The Central African Bakitara, for example, believe that "when a sick man dreamed that his dead parents called him, he would die that day."[90] At the core of these accounts is a fundamental and ancient knowledge: with very little exception, the dead know more than do the living, and the living are sometimes offered this information. Such was the case when in the Bible, King Saul consulted a medium in order to speak with the deceased prophet Samuel in 1 Samuel: 28. Samuel accurately predicted that Saul and his sons would die the very next day. These old ideas regarding the relationship between the living and the dead then, despite our own lack of a broadly accepted explanatory framework, continue.

More recently shared was an account from writer Indubala Kachhawa, in which her father awoke from a dream and told the latter that he should, in his own words, "be prepared I am about to go." Initially brushing this off, the informant's father went on to say that in his dream, his late mother arrived on a train and implored him to hop on with her. The meaning seemed clear to him: that his earthly journey was about to end, and another was about to begin. He died just a couple of hours later.[91]

A FOOT IN BOTH WORLDS

Regarding the Byzantine saint Eupraxia, daughter of Constantinople dignitary Antigonos (380–410), we read that a sister of hers, Theodula, was taken to paradise in a dream where she saw palaces and chambers of "incomparable glory." She saw Eupraxia there, being allowed to pass through to the chamber, though Theodula herself was not. She saw too that this place had been prepared for Eupraxia, and she heard a voice tell that woman that she would die in nine days, which she did after she developed a fever.[92]

While, again, these visions are commonly found among early Christians, the mystics of all faiths often similarly receive their invitation to the next world, finding themselves temporarily there or witnessing their own heavenly abode being prepared for their arrival. Religious scholar and Sufi Arif Jelalu-'d-Din, in 1358, dreamed that he was seated in a chamber overlooking a beautiful heavenly garden. Melodious voices abounded, and he soon met his deceased grandfather, who told him, "The time is come; the end of thy term. Thou must come to me." This invitation caused Jelal great joy and delight, and just days later he fell ill and died.[93]

For something related, we note that Matrona Nikonova of the Russian Orthodox Church, close to her own death, fasted for seven days, in this case specifically to attain for herself a vision of the heavenly home being prepared for her, speaking to the extent to which the possibility itself and such visions were recognized. There she found herself in a beautiful green garden, speaking with divinely attired women.[94] Bracchio of Tours, too, a Thuringian nobleman and avid hunter, once dreamed that he was taken up to heaven, where he saw the prophet Isaiah holding out a book and speaking prophetically in a great voice. When he awoke and examined the dream carefully, he "saw that God thereby announced the end of his life," which soon followed.[95]

Nicetius, a bishop of Trier who died in 566, had a number of seemingly psychical miracles ascribed to him. When the time of his death approached, he too had one foot in this world and one in the next. Before becoming ill, he knew the time of his death was near. He told his brothers, those closest to him, "I have seen the apostle Paul with John the Baptist, inviting me to eternal rest and showing me a crown adorned with celestial pearls, and they said to me, "Here are the things that you are going to enjoy in the kingdom of God." Just days later, having contracted a light fever, he died.[96]

Most of these former accounts are a rather common subtype of vision among mystics and, especially, martyrs. They become conscious of their nearing end, glimpse the location in the otherworld being prepared for them, and draw great comfort from this. While, again, in the martyr's life, such a vision seems a rather helpful and hopeful literary device, marking them as special, we find surprisingly similar reports in our own times. Pioneering hospice nurse Maggie Callanan wrote that those undergoing visions and experiences relating to nearing-death awareness may "attempt to describe being in two places at once, or somewhere in between."[97] The similarities in description are striking, with Callanan also noting that "the experience of dying frequently includes glimpses of another world and those waiting in it."[98]

A Taste of Heaven

Like the mystics and martyrs, dying people still speak with awe and wonder of the peace and beauty they see in this other place. Upon their deathbeds, they can be found speaking of music, lights, and heavenly sights, with one foot already in that other world. Some of them see "beautiful surroundings." Another saw an unearthly garden and heard a voice tell her, "Come to my garden." "If heaven is like that," said another patient after a heavenly vision, "then I'm ready to die." The light is bright, and the colors are unearthly. They hear beautiful music and wonder why others do not.[99] These sentiments are brought out rather beautifully at the end of the life of Madeleine Sophie Barat, a French Catholic saint whose death came in 1865. As she came near her end, she was said to have been "more and more filled with God." The closer she came to that end, she received "more direct intimations of heaven. The veil seemed withdrawn, the union closer. In her prayer she experienced a foretaste of heaven." As the account goes, "In her prayer of mystical union, it would seem as if God had revealed to her the day of her departure from this world." While among those nuns attending her, she said, "My dear daughters, we must really meet today because on Thursday we shall go to heaven."[100]

OTHER MESSENGERS AND PREPARATIONS

With rare exception, in whatever culture we might look to, the dead were common messengers, bringing news of various things, though they were not the only ones. Very often, among those later to be canonized, it was an angel, the holy spirit, or even Mary, Mother of God, who was said to be the bearer of this news in a manner, as we have seen, at least of cursory equivalence to how the shaman's tutelary deity or the Indigenous man's totem might similarly inform.

Ursula, a legendary Romano-British Christian saint, had a visit from an angel while she and her sisters were in Cologne. This angel tells Ursala that she and her sisters will die at the hands of the Huns when they arrive at Basel, which is accordingly fulfilled. While this legend is notoriously disregarded as a historical entity, we are again interested in the value of the literary device and its implications.[101]

Nero Claudius Drusus, a Roman politician and military commander, after multiple successes at war, was preparing to cross the central European Elbe River when an anonymous female of majestic appearance accosted him. "Whither goest thou so fast, oh, Drusus? Art thou never tired of conquest? Know, then, that thy days are at an end." Drusus died the following day.[102] An angel, appearing with "unspeakable splendor," was the messenger said to have come to Kentigern, abbot, early Christian missionary, and traditional first bishop of Glasgow, Scotland. Kentigern is said to have had "some foretastes of the blessedness now at hand." Among other messages, Kentigern was told that "tomorrow ye shall go forth from the body of this death into the unfailing life; and the Lord shall be with you, and ye shall be with Him for ever." The following day, Kentigern indeed fell into a "calm sleep" and died.[103]

Any number of similar visions among Indigenous Indians could be placed among these ranks. Among New Mexico's Zuni Indians, anthropologist Barbara Tedlock was told of a man who was one day cultivating his corn when he, according to her informant, "fell into a dream, or something." A rattlesnake speaks to the man and tells him that he will die on a specific day, this being four days after *Shalako*, the Zuni ceremonies related to the winter solstice. "Four days after Shalako," the speaker concluded, "he died."[104]

The greatly influential English bishop Dunstan, who died in

988 CE, was himself warned by a vision of angels that he had only three days to live. Dunstan took this rather well and announced at his last meal that his death was close. He chose a spot for his tomb and took to his bed. He died exactly when the vision told him he would.[105] Athanasia of Aegina of the Byzantine empire, who died in 860 CE, was warned similarly. While in Timia, she was "forewarned by a vision" that she would be leaving this earthly realm within twelve days. Having been overcome by illness, while in a stupor, she saw men clad in white, angels, this time presenting her with a piece of paper and saying, "Behold your liberation. Take it and rejoice." On that twelfth day on which she did in fact die, her face apparently shone "as a light," something still commonly observed in the dying.[106] The same was true again in coming once more to the incredibly influential Irish abbot and missionary, Columba. He, six days before his own death, had a vision, during which time his face apparently became "radiant with joy." "I beheld a vision," he said, "of an angel of the Lord looking on and blessing us. He is come to demand a certain deposit dear to God." It soon became clear that this deposit referenced the saint's life. It is clear too that Columba was given the specifics of exactly when that would be, telling one of his brothers a "secret" on that day, that he would die that day, that "it is for me the last day of this weary life."[107]

While lacking specifics, Roman politician and writer Gaius Cassius Parmensis experienced something of the same kind. Having fled to Athens after his part in the Battle of Actium (31 BCE), he fell asleep and was twice confronted with a person of "very great stature, with dark complexions, his beard bedraggled, and long hanging hair." This being told him he was a cacodaemon, an evil spirit or genius, and the dream was repeated after Gaius awoke and returned to sleep. First-century Latin writer Valerius Maximus, clearly considering this an indication of his oncoming end, makes note of the very short span of time between this incident and his execution.[108]

An Indian man from Osis and Haraldsson's previously cited study that was published in the 1970s was expected to make a full recovery and was to be discharged on a certain day. Suddenly that morning, he shouted, "Someone is standing here dressed in white clothes. I will not go with you." He was dead within ten minutes.[109] Indeed, while parapsychologist Karlis Osis and former professor emeritus Erlendur Haraldsson had been skeptical regarding certain aspects of these cases, they gave multiple examples, including one reported by an Indian physician in a Muslim hospital. The male patient in question was to be discharged one week after hip surgery. He had no fever and was not receiving any sedation. When the doctor came to him, however, the man told him that he was going to die within a few minutes; this on the authority of a vision in which he felt himself in another word, he saw Christ coming down through the air, beckoning him toward him. The man really died just minutes later, despite his clean bill of health.[110]

Again, according to Bede, a certain bishop attending Sæbbi, the son of Sexred and the joint king of Essex from 664 to about 683, was similarly informed of that man's death date. In a vision "which took from him all anxiety" for the king's well-being, he learned from three men in bright garments that the man was to die three days after the vision. On the third day, the king suddenly fell into a slumber and breathed his last.[111]

As remembered in the medieval *Cantar de mio Cid*, which is the oldest preserved Castilian epic poem and is based on a true story, the Moors, at one point, were on their way to besiege Valencia. El Cid, a real historical figure named Rodrigo or Ruy Díaz, was "favored by a vision of St. Peter," who informed Rodrigo he would die within thirty days. Taking this vision very seriously, Rodrigo "immediately began to prepare for the other world," setting his worldly affairs in order. Accordingly, "the hero died at the appointed time."[112]

While found in such larger-than-life and relatively renowned medieval ballads, messengers carrying their morbid tidings are also to be found in some of the more obscure legends. One of those connected to the Bargello, a former barracks and prison in Florence, Italy, has a "red goblin" haunting its halls. According to the belief, he always foretold every prisoner what his sentence would be before it was promulgated, saying, "Weep, oh weep full many a tear; Make ready; thy hour for death is near."[113] It is recorded of the carer of French saint Austrebertha in the early Middle Ages that, while lying in bed, she had a mysterious indication of her oncoming death from the Virgin, a conspicuously common messenger in accounts of this kind. She was told, "Sister, don't be afraid or troubled. This coming Saturday you will cross over from labor to rest in eternal life." She revealed this prophecy to some of those around her, and it was fulfilled on Saturday when she "migrated from this dirty dwelling to the holy Lord's tabernacle."[114]

Dom Arnold, a Cistercian abbot living at Treves in the thirteenth century, wrote of a monk who, after falling grievously ill, told him that he had come to know when he would die. "Yesterday," he explained, "Our Lady came to me and foretold that in seven days I should go to be with the Lord." The man indeed "fell into his agony on the day and at the hour foretold."[115] Much later in the early modern period, the English Jesuit Edmund Campion had a vision in which he too perceived the Virgin Mary, who apparently "foretold to him his martyrdom." Campion, while returning to London soon after, was killed by a spy in July 1581.[116]

SECRET KNOWLEDGE

These same particulars were said to have been offered to Saint Francis of Assisi, who, armed with this knowledge, used it toward his own ends. He announced to his dearest brother while in the infirmary, "God has revealed to me that I am going to live until a certain day and then die from this sickness." Just as our contemporary dying do, Francis is said to have utilized this knowledge to allow someone in particular to visit him before his end, going on to say, "Lady Jacopa dei Settesoli, who is very devoted to our Order, would be extremely sad if she knew about my death and was not present. So let us notify her that if she wants to see me alive, she should come here at once."[117]

Decisions and Departures

Near-death researchers and others who attend closely to the dying have long noted that the dying often seem to be able to choose when they will leave this world. They seem to be able to, for example, await the arrival of a particular person before passing on, or they may otherwise make specific arrangements. As we have seen to some extent, legend, lyric, and lore tell us the same. Something like this was recorded much earlier about Abercius of Hieropolis, who died in 167 CE. That old bishop, at the time of Roman emperor Marcus Aurelius, was "warned in a dream of his approaching end," so he set about procuring for himself a place of burial and personally oversaw the work on his epitaph.[118] The same utilization of this secret knowledge came later, when an elderly French peasant in 1874 contracted cholera. When the priest came to give her last rites, she told him, "Not yet, M. le cure; I'll let you know when the time comes." Two days later, she said, "Go and tell M. le Cure to bring me Extreme Unction."[119]

More recently, Welsh nurse Penny Sartori noted that during her own career, "it became apparent that patients actually have more control over the time of their death than we realize." Conversely, here, though, Sartori suggested many patients purposely died while their families were, in fact, away, making the transition easier for these particular people. Generalizations in this regard, however, are clearly not justified.[120]

One interesting account attributed to early Mormon leader David Patten Kimball contained an element we have already seen, along with a death prediction. While he is lost in the Arizona desert, his deceased parents appear to him and tell him that a search party is on the way, that he would be fine, and that he would live two more years. In his goodbyes to relatives whom he had paid visits to two years later, the man seemed to have apparently "something about him which seemed to say that he was taking leave of them for all time." His death, as it happened, came two years to the day of the visit from his deceased parents.[121]

English-born Canadian American author Ernest Thompson Seton, in *The Arctic Prairies*, spoke of an old Indian guide at Wayabimika named Omeegi. One day, he suddenly asked those around him, including one Thomas Anderson, for "a new shirt and a pair of pants," the clothes typically reserved for a corpse. He explained that he was to die before Charley, the man in charge there, would return from his ten-day trip and that he would die "when the sun rose at that island" (in seven days). Despite the disbelieving remarks that followed, on that day he said, "Today I die when the sun is over that island!" He died a few minutes after lying next to the fire, exactly as he had predicted.[122]

In the old records of Elias Ashmole, an English antiquary, politician, and student of alchemy, we find that man using his secret knowledge similarly. In 1692, before lying on his deathbed, he sent out a summons to some of the most celebrated occultists of his age. His reasoning was that he had "predicted the day, hour and minute of his demise."[123]

Life Prolonged and Mystics Forewarned

These experiences, still commonly reported, in which the life is extended for a purpose, speak neatly to the archaic Greek concept of *moira*, the idea that one's fate is entirely written and that one has an allotted amount of time; however, it may be not only cut short but prolonged by divine intervention. It would not be surprising if such experiences at the deathbed influenced or bolstered such beliefs. This idea is brought out in a Jewish folktale in which an Arab man dreams of the angel of death standing over him and explaining that his time has come. After this man, however, begs for some extra time in order that he might arrange to leave something for his children, this being takes pity on him and grants him a little extra time.[124]

As we near the chapter's end, we could fill pages with dozens of less detailed references to mystics and saints whose deaths were foretold to them in visions. Truly, in this regard, we have an embarrassment of riches, and a small number here will take us to the chapter's conclusion.

Burgundofara, founder and first abbess of the Abbey of Faremoutiers, is said to have "foretold the day and hour of her going, proclaiming her coming departure from the world."[125] Ceadda, or Saint Chad of Lastingham, formerly bishop of both York and Lichfield, who died in 672, "received warning of his death in a vision."[126] Similarly, Hubert, bishop of Maastrich and first bishop of Liege, was "appraised of his impending death by a vision."[127] Fina, patron saint of Tuscany, was "warned of her approaching release by a vision of St. Gregory" and died in 1253.[128] Finally, here, an inscription from 1151 at the Musée des Augustins in Toulouse likewise tells how the great sacristan of Saint-Paul-de-Narbonne also knew that he was going to die ahead of time.[129]

AN OLD KNOWING

There can be no doubt as to the romance, magic, import, and mystique that such prophecy and vision bring to bear on the lives of the chosen person, the legendary hero, the shaman, the saint. As it happens, though, and as often turns out to be true of the most perennial magic, the old tales often tell true. These accounts, whether they are found at the deathbed of the dying man in the pages of the folklorist, the hagiographer, the historian of the remotest times or in the modern ICU, speak to an old knowledge. Nearing-death awareness and general premonitions of death are long-recognized and recorded phenomena, and while some of the related literature skirts the realms of romance and fancy, the entirety, when taken as a whole, seems to speak firmly to a kind of tradition of secret knowledge on the part of the dying, a secret knowledge they take with them along their way.

To whatever extent certain tales, particularly as they are ascribed to the likes of the holy man or woman, may or may not literally be true, it must be borne in mind that the very same visions and dreams imparting the very same secret knowledge are still recorded, and in the greatest of earnestness. As Ariès wrote: "This miraculous quality, the legacy of times when there was no clear boundary between the natural and the supernatural, has prevented romantic observers from seeing the very positive quality of the premonition of death and the way in which it is deeply rooted in daily life. The fact that death made itself known in advance was an absolutely natural phenomenon, even when it was accompanied by wonders."[130]

FOUR

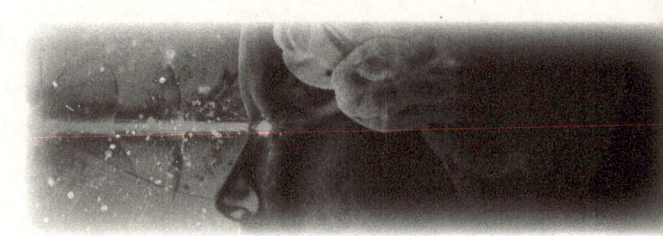

Discoveries at the Deathbed

Veridical Visions and Dreams of the Dying

> *These cases form, perhaps, one of the most cogent arguments for survival after death, as the evidential value and veridical (truth telling) character of these visions of the dying is greatly enhanced when the fact is undeniably established that the dying person was wholly ignorant of the decease of the person he or she so vividly sees.*
>
> PROFESSOR WILLIAM BARRETT

In all ages the dying, and often the ill, man or woman, the closer they come to their end or the deeper they sink into illness, has been imbued with unique and mysterious capacities. That the mortally afflicted person might attain a prophetical or divinatory ability is an idea as old, as we have seen, as are the deathbed visions of Gilgamesh. Former Stanford University consultant Richard Blum made special note of the great age of these notions, writing that such ideas "already existed in Homer's day."[1] Millennia later, Pedro Meseguer, in his book *The Secret of Dreams*, wrote in agreement that "Among all the circumstances in which telepathy is produced, one is outstandingly favourable: the agony and moment of death."[2]

The more recent findings are very much in line with the ancient knowledge. For example, the souls of persons previously killed in war are visible only and specifically to the dying person among the Tlingit, who live across the border between Alaska and British Columbia.[3] Similarly, among the northwest Amazonian Tukano, while the abode of the dead and their spirit houses are spoken of as far away and generally visible only to the dead, Professor Emerita Jean Jackson was told that "some dying people describe the dead-spirit houses they are already seeing."[4] Indeed, those shamans and mystics we have met with so far and others to come, with their extreme fasting, dangerous expeditions, painful rituals, and so on, seem to attempt, in some equatable sense, to approach this final point, this death before dying, in order to attain those very insights, powers, and status for themselves—to attain the clairvoyance of the dead. The closer, therefore, that one comes to death, the more of those powers they take on.

While numerous unusual phenomena occur in and around the deathbed, some of which we have already seen, and others of which we will soon encounter, of most interest here are those mysterious moments in which accurate knowledge of a distant death somehow comes to the gravely ill or dying person. Whatever the ultimate explanations, what is clear is that such discoveries have most certainly been made. These so-called "Peak in Darien" experiences (anomalous discovery of a distant death during or in and around clinical death) and related visionary experiences, in fact, are surprisingly common. As has been established firmly over the previous one hundred and fifty or so years, often, at or around the moment of the distant death of, most usually, someone close to us, the form, voice, or some other indication of the personality makes itself magically known. In my previous work *Apparitions at the Moment of Death*, hundreds of cross-cultural and historical examples of these "crisis apparitions" were collected together for the first time, apparitions that inform the individual of a distant death. The reader, therefore, should not expect as wide a representation here. There is, however, still far more room for expansion, particularly for the reader unfamiliar with that work and the cross-cultural ubiquity of the crisis apparition.

In the present and especially the following shorter chapter, we will primarily present crisis account types that were almost entirely absent in that previous work. The first of these, dealt with here, involves experiences in which the dying man or woman becomes mysteriously aware of a distant death while on their *own* deathbed. Unlike in chapter 3, in which the deathbed was often where the individual became mysteriously aware of their own death date, here, the stricken individual learns of the deaths of others. Likewise, their own death might be revealed to another somewhere distant.

A VIEW FROM THE PEAK

Deathbed visions, which are a range of often numinous sensory experiences reported by the dying or ill, should not be conflated in conversation with the more general visions or utterances of the dying or those otherwise compromised, as they often have been, despite decades of research firmly disputing this notion. As Osis and Haraldsson found, the more drugs the individual had received, the less likely they were to have a deathbed vision.[5] Both authors carried out an extensive questionnaire, still the most impressive work related to this topic this many decades later, of over one thousand nurses and doctors in comparing American and Indian accounts. They showed carefully that the types of deathbed visions experienced "contrast sharply with the hallucinations of those who were mentally ill, where the majority of hallucinated persons were either strangers or bizarre characters." The authors further noted that "the hallucinogenic disease group did not see more dead relatives than the others. On the contrary, their hallucinations were more rambling, disjointed, and concerned with this-world purposes, such as reliving past memories or conversing with imaginary visitors in the hospital." The researchers also observed that "high temperature and sedation such as morphine or Demerol (meperidine) did not increase the frequency of seeing otherworldly apparitions."[6] They found, in fact, a clearer and less medically altered mind more conducive to such experiences.

More recently, Batthyány found in his work on terminal lucidity (the inexplicable return of cognitive functions impaired or destroyed by neurodegenerative disease) that many individuals "experienced, saw, or heard things that those around them did not." "While under normal circumstances," Batthyány continued, "this is precisely what constitutes hallucinations, the primary feature of these episodes still was lucidity rather than confusion."[7] Batthyány, stepping outside of his work's focus a little to address these strange visions, concluded that in this category, he came across nothing related to nonsensical visions of living persons, only cogent and lucid visions of deceased persons. "In view of their somewhat peculiar profile," the author continued, "it might be prudent to just let these reports stand for now, without prematurely writing all of them off as mere hallucinations or delusions."[8]

While a detailed analysis of the deathbed vision is not the focus here, the impact of these unique and often beautiful events on people present at the deathbed should not be taken lightly, particularly by those eager to discredit the words of the dying. Extraordinary and often rather elaborate events have been recorded at the deathbed of those as far apart as Homer, Caesarius of Heisterbach, and Ireland's Lady Gregory, that fundamentally change not only, of course, the dying but those at their side. Perhaps the most mysterious of those is the subject of this chapter, these Peak in Darien experiences.

VISIONS AT THE END

While some work has been done on cross-cultural deathbed visions as they relate to strange knowledge of a death, very little has been drawn from multiple cultures or has been collected in one place. One of those comes from the village of Fu Li in Hualian County, Taiwan. Chi O's father is on his deathbed and approaching the end.⁹ One night, at around 1:00 A.M., Chi O heard a crowd of footsteps outside the front door, where it seemed a large group of men and women of all ages had gathered. This was a party of spirits coming to take her father away. What is interesting about this case is that Chi O was addressed by an elderly man she didn't recognize. The man revealed himself as an "Uncle Ah Ping" who used to live next door to her. He reveals to Chi O that he had in fact died just a year prior and was unknown to her.

This Taiwanese case is strikingly similar to one much better known and reported by Anglo-Irish author, philosopher, and social reformer Frances Power Cobbe. Cobbe's own 1882 work, *The Peak in Darien: An Octave of Essays*, inspired the term "Peak in Darien" experience. Within it she mentioned a number of accounts; one of those follows in her own words.

> Another incident of a very striking character was described as having occurred in a family united very closely by affection. A dying lady, exhibiting the aspect of joyful surprise to which we have so often referred, spoke of seeing, one after another, three of her brothers who had long been dead, and then, apparently, recognized last of all a fourth brother, who was believed by the bystanders to be still living in India. The coupling of his name with that of his dead brothers excited such awe and horror in the mind of one of the persons present that she rushed from the room. In due course of time, letters were received announcing the death of the brother in India, which had occurred some time before his dying sister seemed to recognize him.¹⁰

Cases such as those given by Cobbe have been recycled many times in an area still greatly lacking in historical anecdotal volume. Something similar, in any case, had been recorded around the time of the death in 587 CE of the Thuringian princess and Frankish queen, Radegund, who founded the Abbey of the Holy Cross at Poitiers. On the day of her death, another man, Domnolenus, was himself wasting away with a serious disease in a farther town. He dreamed that Radegund was approaching his town, and he soon met her and asked what her business was. She revealed multiple auspicious things to this man, as the dead are wont to do, including the location of some relics. Most importantly, though, when the man came to, he recounted what he had seen to his wife, saying, "Indeed, I believe that at this hour the saint has gone from this earth." He then sent someone to the city to confirm the truth of this. The messenger returned and reported that Radegund had left the world at that very hour.[11]

Far more obscurely, English Benedictine monk and martyrologist Bede Camm relayed the 1628 case of one Father Edmund Arrowsmith, a priest of the Society of Jesus, who died in Lancaster, England. That very night, he appeared "in glory" at the bedside of another dying man, Father Barlow. Barlow soon wrote a letter to one Dom Rudesind, noting the following: "I believe I shall suffer, for Mr. Bradshaw [this was one of the names used by Father Arrowsmith], the last that suffered martyrdom, the night after he suffered, whereas I knew nothing of his death, spoke thus to me, standing by my bedside." The words Arrowsmith spoke to him were, "I have suffered, and now you will be to suffer; say little, for they will endeavour to take hold of your words."[12]

From entirely another world, though not far distant in time, just a few decades earlier, something comparable was reported in a Chinese tabloid. A soldier who lived near the informant's house was killed in battle. This man's uncle, who himself was dying at that time, called the informant to his bedside, saying that he was about to die. He also told them that the aforementioned soldier had appeared to him and told him he should soon join him.[13]

The next deathbed vision, from 1894, finds us in Fiji. A South Sea Islander named Ganna, while working in the cotton industry, knew a man sick with dysentery. She and others would look out for him however they could, although one day he was found insensible, speaking, but apparently not with his normal voice. Ganna herself knew "very well" that he did not speak her language, and yet he told her all about her own country and "what people were dead there." According to Ganna, "he told true, because I find it out after, from them other boy that come from my place after. So we must believe it, you know."[14]

Remaining on that side of the globe, we read more recently of a family visiting their great-grandmother in New Zealand. She was apparently "kind of senile" and "not usually lucid enough to have a conversation," although she nevertheless told them, "Jimmy [her adopted son] and we had a conversation and he was sort of crying." This was apparently two weeks previous, which was exactly when Jimmy had died. The informants looked at each other and thought it was all a little eerie. "We're not like a religious family," one of them remarked. "It really made me think. Could he really have come and visited her?" No one, as it turned out, had told her that her son had died. No one had called her, as they were sure her condition would preclude her from a full understanding of the situation.[15]

An Irish milkman in his seventies died on a Tuesday in Connecticut—the day after his sister's death in Ohio. According to Osis and Haraldsson, "he mentioned seeing his sister Mary in the hospital, but he did not know that she was dead. He and Mary were very close."[16] According to a hospice worker in North Carolina, an elderly man, Mr. Sykes, entering the final stages of Alzheimer's, in which he could not recognize anyone or even know where he was, suddenly sat up and spoke "clear as a bell." He was looking upward and carrying on a conversation with "Hugh," whom the worker assumed was a deceased relative. However, they later found that Hugh was her own husband's brother and had died suddenly of a heart attack "right about the time that Mr. Sykes miraculously came back to life."[17]

While parapsychologists have collected many, these deathbed vision types are also found widely among the memorates of the folklorists and in volumes far greater than can be represented here. These are avenues that should be much further explored. Margaret Coffin, for example, recorded indistinguishable experiences among her own American collections. Charles Baldwin, a stonecutter, gave the account of his daughter's death from diphtheria and the death of his wife, which tragically occurred right at "about the same time." According to Baldwin, Lizzie "must have had a premonition about the little girl," because although folks at the time claimed it to have been impossible, Lizzie claimed she knew of Etta's death because she "saw the shadow of her coffin pass the chamber door."[18] Similarly too, and speaking to the historical precedents and diversity found among these accounts, at the moment that one Father Corbinelli died in 1591, Italian aristocrat Aloysius de Gonzaga, himself very ill at the time and just three days away from his own death, announced aloud that the soul of Father Corbinelli had, at that moment, "entered into glory."[19]

Some centuries earlier, a brother named Augustine, who was then minister of the brethren in Terra di Lavoro (historical region of southern Italy), having come to his final hour in 1226, suddenly cried out, "Tarry for me, father, tarry for me, lo, even now I am coming with thee!" When the brethren asked who he was speaking to, he gave the answer, "Did ye not see our Father, Francis, who goeth unto heaven?" This was the very same day that Francis had died far off.[20] The same was true when General Serrano, one of the chief military politicians of nineteenth-century Spain, was lying exhausted and paralyzed by a long illness. One morning, to the astonishment of those present, he jumped up of his own accord and shouted, "Ready! An adjutant, on horseback, to the Prado! The king is dead!" Those gathered around the deathbed that day thought he was delirious and tried to calm him; he fell back into the chair in a faint, but a few moments later, he again got up and said in a weak voice, "My uniform, my sword! The king is dead." Those were his last words, and he died a few seconds later. That morning, it was learned that the king had in fact just died; his illness had been kept secret.[21]

Much earlier in 1569, another such experience related to the killing of Louis I, Prince of Condé, the military leader of the Huguenots in the first decade of France's Wars of Religion. His wife, being at that time perilously ill at Metz and having a half-dozen loved ones around her bed, including King Charles IX, cried out that she had seen the battle of Jarnac as it was then happening. "See how they fly! My son has the victory! Do you see the Prince of Condé dead in that hedge?" All those who were present thought she was dreaming, but the night after, M. de Losse brought her the news. "I knew it well," said she, "did I not behold it the day before yesterday?"[22]

Pioneering French chemical engineer and parapsychologist René Warcollier recorded a relevant case in his own family. Warcollier's uncle contracted yellow fever in Venezuela while separated from his family. During his death throes, he called out names of people he was apparently seeing in his delirium. Later, when Warcollier's family returned to France from an American trip, they discovered those names represented recently deceased friends of whose passing they had been unaware and Warcollier's uncle could not have known about.[23]

While in some cases, then, people around the deathbed are unaware of the death in question and discover it from the insights of the dying person, at other times, they *do* know and note that they had specifically kept that information from them so as not to further burden them. This, however, does not always go to plan. In a nineteenth-century example, psychologist Edmund Gurney and classical scholar Frederic Myers originally reported the case of two brothers, ages three and four, who died of scarlet fever on successive days. Harry, the younger brother, died on November 2, and David, the older brother, died fourteen miles away on the following day. David's family took care to keep him from knowing about Harry's death, and they felt sure that he did not know. Nevertheless, about an hour before he died, David sat up in bed and, pointing, said distinctly, "There is little Harry calling to me."[24]

More famously, philosopher William Barrett reported the case of a woman who, while on her deathbed, saw her deceased father beckoning to her and said, to the puzzlement of those around her, "He has Vida with him." The woman was referring to her sister, of whose illness and death, which occurred three weeks earlier, she had not been told.[25] While this account has been very widely reproduced, something of impressive similarity was recorded by Bede the Venerable many centuries before Barrett's account of Vida. In a certain monastery, there was a boy of around three years named Aesica. He had been struck by the plague and at the point of death called out three times for a certain maiden, "Edith, Edith, Edith!" as though she were in the room. As it happened, the maiden whose name he called was, on that very day, stricken by the same sickness in the place where she was.[26] Relatively more recently too, Technicolor pioneer Natalie Kalmus wrote an account in a popular magazine, subsequently reprinted in several books, of her sister Eleanor's last moments, in which she began calling out the names of deceased loved ones whom she was seeing. Just before she died, she also saw a cousin named Ruth and asked, "What's she doing here?" Ruth had died unexpectedly the week before, and Eleanor, because of her condition, had not been told.[27]

In *Dialogus Miraculorum* by the Cistercian prior Caesarius of Heisterbach, a collection of 746 miracle stories, there seems to be a reference to just such a vision. "Meantime there was a pleasing sight," were the words of a thirteenth-century man, Meyner, priest of Hammenrode.

> I saw a beautiful street stretching above me, making a road from earth to heaven. One of our order suddenly appeared in the midst, who, entering this road, sought the realms above. Full of joy and uttering praises, fenced in by troops of angels, having suffered no agony at all, he was taken into heaven. Yet that brother was not named to me.[28]

I SAW YOU DIE

At other times, the moment of the death of the person upon their deathbed becomes mysteriously known to another far off. Minot Savage gave a case from among his notes that occurred in nineteenth-century Maine.

One of two sisters, living many miles apart, was gravely ill and had promised that if she were to pass away, she would somehow announce this to her sister. One evening, the sister in good health went to her daughters and told them, "Your aunt is dead. She has just appeared to me and announced the fact." The family, according to Savage, "lived several miles from the post-office, and the snow was deep, so that it was a day or two before any news was received. When it did come, however, it announced the fact that the sister in question had died at the time when the apparition had been seen."[29]

These variants also have an impressive historical pedigree. When Italian widow and Dominican reformer Clare Gambacorta (1362–1419) was about to leave this world, her fate was revealed to one of her sisters in a symbolic dream. She saw a group of nuns wearing black veils over their faces, which shone oddly. One was especially glowing; a voice soon explained to her, "This is our prioress" (meaning Clare).[30]

In ancient Ireland, at the time Brito of Columcille was dying, Columba, while in the courtyard, was seen by another brother "looking upward." Upon questioning, Columba told him, "I have seen just at this moment the holy angels fighting in the air against the power of the enemy, and I gave thanks to Christ, the Judge, because the winning angels have carried to heaven the soul of this stranger that is the first to have died among us in this island."[31]

One example from the eleventh century has a monk dreaming that he had been transported to a monastery where another was dying alone on a straw mattress. The dreamer heard the song of angels coming to collect the monk's soul, which came out of his mouth and departed seemingly with Saint Michael.[32] The same was true in a thirteenth-century account in which a monk foretold his imminent death in seven days. While that man was dying, another monk had a vision while sleeping of a crowd of white-robed people entering the dying man's cell and telling him that they had come to take him away.[33]

The French monastic Hugh of Lincoln, after administering the last sacraments to a brother of his, Morinus, who had fallen gravely ill, had to take leave for Sleaford, a place around twenty miles distant. A number of days later, at the time of the man's death, Hugh dreamed that he was in the cell of his dying friend, who, as was confirmed by a messenger, was passing at that very moment. He saw a dove fly from one end to the other, seeking a place of rest. When he awoke, and recalling our "interceptions" from the first chapter, he gave the order that horses should be prepared so that they could meet the coffin of Morinus, which he knew would be coming from Stowe to Brüer. The funeral took place in the very place where the coffin was seen.[34]

The Italian Conventual Franciscan and Christian mystic Joseph of Cupertino, who lived in the village of Assisi, Italy, had a related experience when his mother was distantly suffering on her own deathbed. She bemoaned the absence of her son, crying aloud, "Oh, my son, my son! Shall I never again meet you on earth?" As she was dying, the room "blazed with exceptional illumination," and the mother, beholding her son coming through the flaming light to her bed, extended her arms and exclaimed, "Joseph my son!" At this very hour, Joseph, her son, was praying in church and told those present that his mother had just died. According to the sources, this apparition of the living man by his mother's side was confirmed by letters that, soon after the death of the mother, were received in Assisi, and the fact was further proved by the sworn testimony of those who saw the saintly man at the bedside of his mother.[35]

Some centuries later, an anonymous author offered the similar case of a woman who lived in Rhode Island. While on her deathbed, she expressed a great desire to see her son, who was then in the west Indian Ocean. At the very moment of her death, she appeared to him during the night and delivered her message before disappearing into the ocean.[36] Conversely, Portuguese Jesuit John Cardim, "at the moment of his death" in 1615, appeared to his mother, who was miles away, and said, "Rejoice, mother, for I am now on my way to enjoy the vision of God; I owe a great part of my present happiness to you for the holy lessons you taught me."[37]

A physician and British professor of physiology, Ivor Lloyd Tuckett, relayed a related incident from an early twentieth-century newspaper. A boy of twelve in Capua, Italy, was found crying. When his mother asked why he was distressed, he said that he had just seen Mr. Smith at the point of death in America. The next morning, a letter came from America announcing the father's death. The boy's mother tried to keep this experience secret for fear that the boy might be considered to have been possessed in some way.[38]

According to a vision at the death of Mary of Saint Peter in 1848, a Carmelite nun who lived in Tours, France, was said to have converted a skeptical nun to her sanctity. At the moment of Mary's death, this sister had a dream in which "it seemed to her as if she were with the other nuns, round the bed of the dying sister, who expired before her eyes." According to the sources, the day following, "she felt entirely changed."[39]

Whatever the truth of each particular vision in a more legendary context, that the individual might be fundamentally moved and changed in light of these mysterious events is a truth clear not just in those texts but in more modern accounts, and the old knowledge reflects the recent realities in this way. A Jewish example from Eastern Europe has an elderly woman cut off from her family and finally dying alone. Her great-grandson, far west in Germany, lived alone and had no contact with the family either; he was a recluse who lived in the woods. The first night after his grandmother's death, he dreamed of her approaching his bed dressed in white. "I am your great-grandmother and I have just died yesterday," she told him. This experience, occurring so close to a death he was unaware of, "changed his way of thinking," and he found his way back to his family after.[40]

DEATHBED DRIFTERS

In so many accounts of this kind, the dying person is seen out and about at a time when they are, in reality, physically on their deathbeds.

These are common and impressively widespread tales in the collections of folklorists, though they are rarely compiled or related to works of parapsychologists, and while only a few will be presented here in the final section, these tales, in their thematic similarity, will also lead us nicely into the next chapter.

From the shores of the remote Shetland Islands, respected scholar Andrew Cluness was told by an informant that he and two others saw a woman they knew called Betty Clarke coming out of her house. The informant, who had some days earlier made a straw basket for her, told her as much as they crossed paths, but she completely ignored him. The second time, she turned around and looked at him, but didn't answer and moved on. When he was later told that Betty was not expected to live through the night and was mortally ill four miles distant over the hills, this man replied that he was amazed, exclaiming, "But I've just spoken to her or tried to speak to her less than half an hour ago." Next morning, the postman brought news that she had died just a short while after the vision, the kind of thing that in the Shetland Islands has often been called a *feyness*.[41] Farther south, indeed, to the north of England, where such apparitions were often referred to as *wafts*, William Elliott, of the same place, saw his neighbor Mary Brown cross the yard and disappear into a straw house. Knowing her to be very ill, he made instant inquiries and discovered that she had died at the moment of his seeing her.[42]

In 1952, a Hispanic New Mexico informant told an author and former professor of Spanish at UCLA that one night, his uncle goes outside and sees a woman he knows standing by a woodpile. He knows it can't be her because she is very sick. He leaves for the woman's house with his sister, but when they arrive, they find the woman whose apparition he had apparently seen died "about thirty seconds before they arrived."[43] Far from there, among the northwestern California Yurok Indians, a certain man went to the coast to find a doctor for his sweetheart, who lay ill. While he was returning, across a little lagoon, he noticed the form of a woman approaching. He thought to himself, "It seems as if

I knew her." And he soon realized it was his wife out and about, so he tried to intercept her. He only felt wind against himself when he came to her, however. When he came home to Turip, he discovered that she had died while he was away.[44]

Virginia Sutter, author, elder, and enrolled member of the Northern Arapaho Indian Nation, was once working in a hospital when they brought in a seriously ill Arapaho medicine man. They became rather close over the period of his stay, and, very early one morning, Sutter dreamed that an Arapaho elder came to her and told her that the medicine man back at the hospital was dying. Arriving to the hospital soon after the dream, she found him dead, and she believes the dream was "his way of telling me he was leaving the world."[45]

In a similarly fascinating case relayed by journalist and author Patricia Pearson and colleagues, the informant was walking to a main street after dropping her daughter off at school. "I saw my uncle walk past me and head to Chester Subway," she said. "I thought, 'that's my uncle.' I stopped in my tracks. I nearly followed him, but then thought, 'No, that's crazy.' My uncle has had Lewy Body's dementia for the past ten years and is confined to a bed. When I got home, there was an email from Dad. My uncle had died that afternoon."[46]

Also in this vein is the account of one Marshal De Moltke recorded in the much lesser-known work of French occultist Jules Bois. While dying in his bedroom in 1904, Moltke's apparition appeared to the sentries of his palace, who knew nothing of his then-critical circumstances; the form was seen simply leaning on a bridge over a river. These soldiers related the event in their guard book, and Jules Bois tells us that the hour of the sighting coincided with the marshal's last breath.[47]

It is clear in these cases that knowledge of the individual's illness is not a requirement to receive such a vision as to their predicament. This comes out in the legend and lore as much as it does in the accounts of our contemporaries. Likewise, in a fairly obscure volume, American Lutheran minister Isaac Funk was told by an informant that when an aunt of theirs died suddenly at midnight in the house where they were then residents, her son-in-law, living two miles away, around the time of the death, was going for water at a spring some distance from the house. He saw a very clear apparition of his aunt standing by the well, though he "knew nothing of her illness."[48]

However disparately these accounts are found, the similarities persist. In the thirteenth century, at the monastery of San Pantaleo at Cologne, there was a young man named Godfrey who was attending another in his agonies. Godfrey told the man he feared even going to dinner in case he should leave this world in his absence. "Go," the brother replied, and assured Godfrey that he would see him before then. Godfrey left, and while sitting down at a table in another part of the monastery, he saw the sick man open the door of the refectory, look at him, and give his blessing. The sick man turned and disappeared as if to go to the oratory. The brother thought his patient had been cured by some miracle, but just then he discovered that man had just died.[49]

A certain Newfoundland navy man once separated from his Scottish wife, who needed to move back to her homeland. Much time passed until his memory of her began to fade. Once, however, he had an encounter with her apparition, who told him she was sick. He went to the airport to fly to her, having confirmed her illness by telegram. As he stepped out of the ticket office, he saw her again standing there to greet him. This time she told him she had died that very morning and had come to say goodbye. He learned later of the truth of his vision.[50]

Finally, returning to the work of Canadian folklorist Helen Creighton, who recorded so many related experiences, we read, in fact, of one of her own. One morning, Creighton awoke from a dream in which she saw the archdeacon of her town walking along a street, though he seemed very intently focused and ignored her. Helen knew the man was ill, even in the dream, and surmised he could not be out and about, so this must be his spirit. It turned out he had died during her sleep, "probably at the time" when she saw him.[51]

EXTRAORDINARY ENCOUNTERS

Visions and apparitions of a distant death, which later turn out to be accurate, have been a long-known phenomenon. Crisis apparitions, Peak in Darien experiences—these omens fall under many categories, but fundamentally, they are veridical messages of a distant death, and they are ubiquitous. Even in this short analysis of their deathbed variants, the age and cultural spread of these extraordinary visionary events are plain to see. In this historical and cross-cultural context, however, much work still remains to be done. As far as those messages and indeed messengers are concerned, though, we move now to apparitions, and not just of the seemingly nonphysical variety.

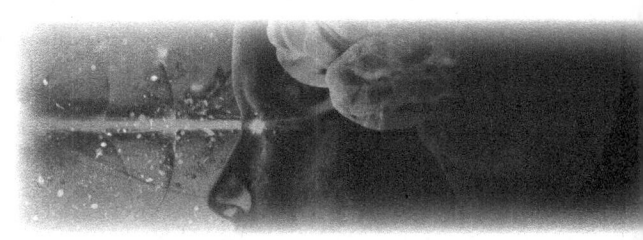

FIVE

Revenants, Wraiths, and Disinterested Shades

Vampires, Zombies, and Mysterious Knowledge of a Distant Death

> *What we do know is that a large minority of people all over the world commonly experience contact with their dead—sometimes regularly, sometimes as one-offs—and that there is both an academic and a personal need to know why.*
>
> ALLAN KELLEHEAR

From the rich folklore of a ghost-haunted Guatemala, we read in a Chuj Mayan memorate of a man who had not come home for a little longer than usual. His wife was not particularly worried, as he was often away for days at a time. While she sleeps, however, he begins to arrive at night to work on the wool, as is his usual habit. Some time later, after finding his finger, she concludes he might have come into some trouble. The authorities are alerted, and the man's remains are soon found.[1]

Following on very much as an elaboration upon our "Deathbed Drifters" section, encounters such as these, in which the apparitional figure of the deceased, unknown to have been dead, is seen simply going about some prosaic or unremarkable daily activity, often ignoring the subject of the vision entirely, are incredibly common. Such tales speak to an interesting point of intersection between account types, one that warrants further exploration. From cultures as far apart as the old tribes of Mexico to the rural inhabitants of the Shetland and Orkney Islands, the seemingly apparitional figure may sometimes present in a way that suggests physicality, such as practicing some worldly activity or interacting (by some seemingly "physical" means) with the world. At other times, the figure behaves in a more typically ghostly manner (passing through walls, floating, etc.). Distinctions, however, can be hard to draw, and at times, the figure might display both behaviors. In this way, they might qualify historically as either a *wraith* or a *revenant*. This is to say, either a typical apparition with news of its death or something more akin to a more literal, walking-dead "zombie" or vampire. While the timing between the death and the encounter is often much longer where the revenant is involved, of sole importance here is that, according to the tales, both may qualify as supernatural death messengers; both may inform of a death not previously known and later confirmed. It is fitting, then, that the two have been interchangeably used so widely.

Revenants in the Writings

Perhaps the most well-known account of a revenant in antiquity is the timeless tale of Philinnion from the second century CE. This has been called "one of the most detailed and one of the most significant ghost stories in all of ancient literature." Philinnion emerges from her grave to meet a certain man at her father's house. During this time, and just as with the Chuj Mayan man from our opening account, Philinnion goes about her normal domestic activities, much to the shock of a certain member of her family.[2] The man in question, as Lacy Collison-Morley importantly noted, had no idea until he was notified that he was speaking to a woman who had died.[3]

While this tale is generally considered to be of the revenant variety—that is, again, an account of a physically reanimated corpse as opposed to an apparition or ghost as such—it is clear that these needn't be mutually exclusive types. The ancient Greeks, in fact, had no separate word to describe *revenants* and used the term interchangeably with "apparition."[4] The revenant, indeed, often later becomes the wraith or shares the traits of both at different times. In Apuleius's *Metamorphoses*, for example, the ghost who kills the miller could be touched, which suggests a solid form, and yet she soon disappears from a locked room.[5] Much later, the Danish king in *Hamlet* appears substantial at times yet similarly fades away at others.[6] We read in a Korean tale that similarly stresses this simultaneously corporeal and incorporeal nature of a man named Chon, a magician living around 1550, who seemingly visits his father and asks for a book entitled the Tu-si, which his father duly hands over. "I had no idea," said the father later, "that he was dead and that it was his ghost. I gave him the book, though I did not learn till afterward that he had been dead for a long time."[7]

In this case, despite the physical interaction, the informant later refers to the being as a "ghost." As noted in a previous paragraph, even Summers himself referred to the Philinnion tale as a "ghost story." The dual nature of these encountered forms is nicely illustrated in a Polynesian example. While fishing one night in his canoe, a Papuan Mawata man was joined by a mysterious stranger. It was apparently a significant amount of time later before he found out that his companion was a ghost. On their way back, the spirit disappeared underneath the burial ground, and its very physical footsteps were visible there.[8] This simple encounter, which entirely echoes the Western accounts, speaks directly to this apparent dichotomy. Clearly, while these "undead" are commonly associated with certain European regions and writings, they have, as it happens, walked the world from end to end.

WORLD OF REVENANTS

Revenants in the Family

In a memorate collected on the outskirts of Arequipa, Peru, a woman saw someone off in the distance, his head covered with a big hat. When she asked him how he was, he insisted that he would be going to bed in her house. While they slept, the woman dreamed that a lady, seemingly the Virgin herself, came and told her that her husband was dead and that he was, in fact, a *condenando*, a malicious kind of vampire with which Peruvian folklore abounds.[9]

Whether by way of the revenant or wraith, such supernatural announcements of a distant death are found widely in Peru. In another of its tales, it is the male who takes on the role of revenant, something that seems to be rarer in the lore. A boy returns home to tell his father he has been married, but his father accidentally kills him later. This man, now also a condenando, returns to his wife, who thinks nothing unusual is happening. Muleteers passing by, however, inform her that her husband is dead.[10]

Much farther north, and from a New Mexico anecdote told in Spanish, a certain woman living in Socorro, Mrs. Chavez, while walking home one evening, saw brightness in her house in a room that had no light. When the woman looked in, she saw her aunt sitting next to the fireplace, but she would not respond. News soon came from the town that she had died that very night.[11] Similar, although featuring a more talkative figure apparently carrying on their daily routine, was a tale from a Zapotec-speaking community in southern Mexico. A traveler returning to Mitla met a woman named Paula bathing herself. "Where have you been?" the traveler asked. "Looking after goats in the mountain," came the nonchalant reply. When the traveler reached Mitla, he learned that Paula had been dead for two weeks.[12]

Taken from among a community of Quakers in southern Indiana, one Susanna Satterthwait was sleeping in a room with a fireplace when suddenly she saw two women sitting together by the fire. She looked at the clock on the mantel and noted the time. They vanished. When she described them to her father later, he recognized his great-aunt and her grandmother. A few days later, a letter came saying the man's great-aunt had died at the same time as the vision. They received a letter in a few days saying that his great-aunt had died at the time Susanna had noted on the clock.[13]

Death Messengers

The fact that the figure appears so lifelike and their otherworldly nature was not even suspected is a refrain still commonly recorded regarding the appearance of the apparition. At other times, however, their nature seems immediately apparent. From the Yaquit ethnic group, those being Native American people of Arizona and Indigenous people of Sonora, Mexico, a man named Benjamin Red Owl awoke one night to the feeling of someone touching his neck. He soon saw the image of a small Indian girl. This man "immediately knew she was a spirit" as she looked "vaporlike" and "luminous." He got the earthy scent of wet grass, and she soon disappeared, but not before he perceived mud around the base of his neck. After he found that someone had been shot in that area two months prior at the same spot on the neck, his friend Jerry told him a spirit messenger had come to acquaint him with this news.[14]*

These kinds of accounts recall more typical and ongoing "haunter"-type apparitions, which can of course qualify as a death messenger when the death is later revealed to the person involved. In 2024, Elsaesser relayed the story of her informant, who, at thirteen years old, would often greet an old neighbor of his. One afternoon, after greeting him as usual and receiving a reply, the informant was surprised to learn later that the man had died some months before.[15]

The interesting account of Theobald III, Count of Champagne, in France (1179–1201) is worth mentioning for its fundamental similarity.

---

*Apparitions displaying the manner of their death are recorded widely among parapsychologists, and have a long history. The reader can find further examples in chapter nine of my previous book *Apparitions at the Moment of Death*.

Not far from one of his castles, there was a cottage where a leper lived, a man whose feet he would often wash before giving alms and departing. One time, during Theobald's absence, this leper died. The count, unaware of his death, was passing the cottage some days later and went to visit with him as usual. He did his work and came out "with a full heart" and exclaimed, "I am so glad I have been to my leper today." But they told him this was impossible, for the leper was both dead and buried. Having been assured of this truth, the count rejoiced, for he considered himself to have been considered worthy to receive such a holy experience.[16]

One of the oldest encounters of this kind relates to Aristeas of Proconnesus, the supposed author of the epic poem of antiquity, the *Arimaspeia*, whose chief evidence comes down to us from Herodotus and was well known in his day. He was a semilegendary Greek poet to whom a number of miracles have been attributed. Aristeas died suddenly in a fulling establishment in his hometown. When the owner of the business locked up the fullery and departed to tell his relatives of the unfortunate news, a certain man from the ancient Greek town of Cyzicus disputed that Aristeas had died, saying that he couldn't be dead as he'd just met him on the way there and spoken to him.[17]

We can pivot to the less-mentioned 1980s work of psychologists Celia Green and Charles McCreery, *Apparitions*, for a strikingly similar account. One of their informants saw a man named Bill Smith standing in his garden wearing a summer shirt. He looked ill and ignored questions. Three days later, the informant was with Bill's wife when he was mentioned in conversation. There was a "ghastly silence," after which someone noted that Bill had suddenly died six weeks ago. Just as that man of antiquity noted of his meeting with Aristeas, the informant here said that this was impossible as she had spoken to him only three days ago, the form, in both cases, seemingly presenting realistically enough to fool the observer.[18]

In what was a rare mainstream approach to the topic of crisis apparitions, CNN reported on a number of similar accounts in 2011, including that of Nina De Santo, who was about to close up her New

Jersey hair salon when she saw someone standing outside the shop's glass front door. It was Michael. He was a customer of her salon whom she had previously comforted in a time of need. When De Santo opened the door that Saturday night, Michael was smiling. "Nina, I can't stay long," he said, pausing in the doorway. "I just wanted to stop by and say thank you for everything." That Sunday, she received a call from a salon employee. Michael's body had been found the previous morning—at least nine hours before she talked to him at her shop. He had committed suicide.[19]

Removing ourselves distantly to Japan, which is brimming with such tales, we read that a samurai, having been awakened by a din, opened his bedroom door and was greeted by a beautiful woman. She told him, "I am O Kei San, Ko's younger sister. Though you have not seen me, I have several times seen you, and I have fallen so madly in love with you that I can think of nothing else but you." Having initially refused her advances, he eventually agreed to visit with her for a month, which led to their disappearance for a year. As it turned out, the spirit was actually another woman, O Ko, who the samurai hadn't realized was dead, as they had apparently been going about their usual days together.[20]

Remaining in Japan, a samurai leaves his wife in order to find better fortunes. Years later, he eventually comes to miss her so much that he returns. He met with her, as it seemed to him, and they spent the night together talking, laughing, and crying. The samurai soon drifted off to sleep, and come morning, he realized this had all been some sort of fantasy or dream as he found the skeleton of his wife, who, as it turned out, had died of grief in his absence.[21]

In another example, coming to us from the *Nihon Ryōiki*, a collection of old Buddhist tales recorded at a time when a great plague was raging, we read of Kinume, a girl who falls ill and dies. Eventually, another, also named Kinume, from a distant village who, likewise, had lost her life, takes the body of the former and returns to her *own* parents. In this way, the parents, who eventually believe her story, learn of the distant death of the other Kinume.[22] Also involving possession is an old Chinese tale that has two friends, Gao and Liu, making a pact that whoever died first would return to tell the other what the afterlife is like. Some months after Liu died, Gao heard a knock at his door one night and the voice of his friend requesting that he douse his lamps and let him in so they could speak in the dark. As they were talking, Gao was disturbed by the smell of a rotting corpse and found that Liu's had possessed the body of a barbarian. Gao later found that he had, in fact, been dead for seven days.[23]

In another Chinese account that writer and educator Anthony Masters noted shared multiple features with its European and Near-Eastern counterparts, we read of a courier called Chang Kuei who, in 1761, was caught in a storm and his lantern was blown out. He soon made his way to a rest stop and was ushered into a cottage by a young girl. The next day, at dawn, he found that he was lying on a tomb in dense undergrowth, with his horse tied up close by. When he delivered his cache hours later, he was questioned and related what had happened. The authorities made inquiries and learned that a girl named Chang had hanged herself at that spot.[24]

In early eighteenth-century Hungary, a soldier, as he was one day sitting at a table near his host, saw a person he didn't know come in and sit at the table with them. The soldier had no idea who this man was. But with the master of the house dying the very next day, the soldier made inquiries. They told him it was the body of a certain man who had been dead and buried for ten years.[25] As an interesting aside, English scholar and clergyman Montague Summers considered that if this tale were to be true, it would be evidenced by the fact that the strange man's death was unknown to the soldier until after the encounter.[26] Amid the work of prolific French Benedictine monk Antoine Augustin Calmet, he gives an old account in which a Parisian maidservant who went into a cellar was horrified to find herself staring into the immobile face of a stranger, silently standing between two casks. This revenant was later identified as the body of a dead man who had slipped from a cart and fallen to his death through the cellar window.[27]

Jean Gobi, a fourteenth-century French Dominican author, tells us a story regarding the interrogation of a revenant, in which the messenger was an unwilling one and gave information pertaining to the death of another. At the twenty-second question asked by the prior, the dead man "spoke of purgatory and answered by using as an example a brother who had just died then in Bologna." The tale strongly speaks to the extent to which confirming this kind of information would give credence to such a tale.[28]

From Russia now comes a tale in which a young girl named Marusia was celebrating the feast of Saint Andrew in her village cottage. She soon met a handsome man, and they both took to each other quickly. Later, Marusia told her mother about him, and she suggested her daughter should find out where the boy lives by following him. The next time he came and left, she trailed him across roads, hedges, and ditches, eventually making it to a church. She looked in one of the windows and saw him standing beside a grave, devouring a corpse. She didn't realize it till then, but he was a *Nechistoi*, a dead man.[29] Similarly, in a Portuguese folktale, a woman followed a handsome prince she had met to a palace. Having seen everything it contained, she came to a house, and after entering, she suddenly uttered a scream and ran out. She said to the maid with her that she had seen a dead man; the handsome prince was a dead man.[30]

The same was true in Philostratus's third-century *Life of Apollonius* regarding the tale of Menippus, a man hailing from what is now Turkey. While walking alone toward Cenchrae, he met the apparition of a woman who nevertheless "took him by the hand" and told her she was a Phoenician woman who lived in a suburb of Corinth. She urged him to meet her. He visited her that evening and many times after. Apollonius eventually tells Menippus that this woman is a *lamia*, a vampire of sorts, a woman previously dead.[31] This is exactly the kind of tale that had been adapted and was included in the complete *One Thousand and One Nights* regarding the story of Adul Ahassan, the son of a Baghdad merchant who fell in love with and married a woman named Nadilla. When he noticed she didn't eat food and left bed every night, he decided to follow her and found that she was visiting a graveyard; she was a living corpse.[32]

From East Africa too, revenants with word of death and, indeed, a curiously similar aversion to food are found. In the Mboni district of Ulu "a long time ago," a certain young man went for a walk one night and met a very beautiful woman on the path. Eventually ending up at his mother's house with him, the woman surprised everyone by saying, "I do not eat food." In the morning, the man's parents woke up and noticed their son and this woman had disappeared. The mother called out and said, "This woman must have been an evil spirit in human form for she would not eat and now my son is lost to me for ever."[33]

While in these tales, then, and in line with extrasensory experiences generally, there is most commonly a strong bond between the parties involved, this is by no means always the case. Brunvand relayed the much more modern example of a Korean taxi driver who once picked up a young woman. When the cab arrived at her destination, the girl told the driver she did not have the fare and asked him to wait until she could go into the house to get it. Despite offering her grace, she did not return. The driver became impatient and knocked at the closed door. After repeated attempts, a certain Mrs. Shimo showed up and asked the driver what he wanted. She seemed to know nothing about the girl or the fare; however, after the driver described the young lady, Mrs. Shimo showed him a picture of her daughter on the wall.[34]

In an Icelandic folktale that inspired dozens of pieces of artwork, the deacon of Myrká, who lived in times of old, falls into a river while riding to meet Gudrun, a woman he loved. A special mention was made of the fact that, due to the thaw and floods at that time, no news traveled between Myrká and the town in which Gudrun lived. His form, along with his horse, knocked at her door, and they rode together, though she had not yet heard of his death. She saw him go into his own grave before she returned home and heard the news that he had died.[35]

Worlds apart, the object of the vision expresses the message similarly. An old story from Lehigh Valley in eastern Pennsylvania claims that a young woman, whose husband had left her to fight, dreamed continuously of her wayward lover. One night, she dreamed she was swept away by a ghostly form atop a white horse. It was her husband! In the darkness, the soldier cried out, "Brightly shines the moon. Swiftly ride the dead!" The phantom steed carried the couple to a cemetery, where it deposited them at a freshly dug grave. She awoke the next morning and soon was given the bad news: her soldier husband had died in a battle.[36]

To reiterate, however long has passed between the death and its discovery, these supernatural messengers first and foremost inform of a death, just as might a typical revenant or wraith. Some of the originally contrived and arbitrary time periods within which one must have died in order for their appearance to another to be called a crisis apparition are irrelevant here.* The fact that a distant death, either in space or time, has been discovered to the surprise of the informant is the important element. In a sense, then, a crisis apparition has no need to be strictly concurrent *with* said crisis.

DISINTERESTED SHADES

As with our opening Mayan account and some others, it is again notable how often the form of the dead or dying person simply acts out a normal ritual of theirs or ignores the percipient entirely. As opposed to the often rather dramatic and literary kind of revenant or wraith, these stand out in their relative "mundanity" and perhaps read more believably for that reason. Lillian Li gave a then-recent instance, told to her and published in *California Folklore Quarterly*, that took place in Peking, China. When Yu Mei, the roommate of her informant, An Chen, left for home for certain domestic duties, they decided to exchange letters in the interval. At the end of a semester, after a long period of no communication, An Chen, at the time amid friends on

---

*As noted by the authors on page xix of *The Phantasms of the Living Vol. 1*, "As regards the interval of time which may separate the two events or experiences on the agent's and the percipient's side respectively, an arbitrary limit of 12 hours has been adopted."

the grass on a sunny spring day, felt her attention drawn away from the group. She was "amazed to see Yu Mei coming down a narrow path toward the party." As An Chen approached her, however, she vanished. The next day, she found a telegram from Yu Mei's parents telling of her death on the preceding afternoon.[37]

Relayed in 1859, celebrated poet and novelist Miss Anna Maria Porter was once living at Esher, in Surrey, when an aged gentleman she knew who was often in the habit of visiting entered one evening as usual and sat down without speaking. She addressed him, but he made no reply, arose, and left soon after. Astonished, she sent her servant to his house to make inquiries, and the news was that he had just died within that same hour.[38]

In Texas in 1956, a student told Grover Allred that once he went to bed and suddenly felt the springs pushed down as if someone had sat there. He turned and saw his grandmother on the bed, looking away from him and combing her long black hair. The next day, he received a telegram telling him of her death. He learned later, too, from relatives that she had called for him just before she died.[39]

In Irish folklore, such forms or apparitions were often referred to as a *fetch*, a superstition that, according to an 1834 volume of the *Dublin Penny Journal*, was "so prevalent among our peasantry, and which, from its wild singularity, deserves a more lengthened notice than I have seen bestowed upon it."[40] That notice, unfortunately, has not been forthcoming. The following account, however, was given by Patricia Lysaght, an Irish folklorist and Professor Emerita of European Ethnology.

> Well, my mother was washing one day at the back window of the cottage at home," her informant began, "and a distant cousin of hers used to stop [i.e., stay] with her and she saw him coming up the garden and she was waiting for him to come in and he didn't come. So she went out to see where he was and there was no sign of him anywhere. And, she thought, maybe then she was only imagining it and that night when she went to get his bed ready for him word

came that he had been found dead where he'd gone off for a walk across the roads. He was found dead: he died, and he came back to her to let her know that he was going. She believes that.[41]

From Scotland, in 1745, a Mr. Adam Bell was murdered on his way from Dumfriesshire to Edinburgh. At the same time, back in his house, his housekeeper saw him enter, though he made no reply to her. After asking if he needed a fire or drink, he still remained silent, soon leaving and disappearing into the woods.[42] More recently, from the work of Elsaesser, the day after feeling the strange presence of what was apparently a tall male on her stairs, the author's informant said that her husband's cousin was missing. Later, making the connection between the events, she dreamed of him. He showed her a certain location in town. Later, it was found that he had killed himself at that very place.[43]

From Adams County, Illinois, and once more tapping the vast folklore collection of Harry Hyatt, one of a number of similar accounts has the informant noticing something strange in the early hours. "One morning just at four o'clock," the account begins, "I looked out the window and there was my uncle looking in at the window with a white shirt on and no head." Later, it was found that "he died at four o'clock that morning, just when I was seeing him looking in at the window."[44] From France too, highly influential chemist Michel Eugène Chevreul saw a phantom between two windows in his study. Frightened, he turned away, but when he looked back, it was still there. Soon afterward, he heard that, at the time, a close friend who was to bequeath his library to Chevreul had died.[45]

A Maori example from New Zealand has a young boy awakened from his sleep and seeing the form of his uncle, who was supposed to be farther north at the Bay of Islands, leaning over his bed. The boy spoke to the apparition; however, it suddenly vanished. "The next mail," according to the informant, "brought me news of his death." The same boy, as a man, once saw another Maori standing between him and his window. It was his uncle, Ihaka, who was also unresponsive to his calls. "I had not expected to hear of my uncle's death," the man explained, "for I had seen him hale and strong a few hours before." He soon discovered, however, that he had gone into the house of a missionary, and he was poisoned by eating a pie made from spoiled tinned meat.[46]

In a Canadian folktale relayed by author Maria Leach, a man named Joe saw a fisherman on the road ahead of him in high rubber boots and a billed cap. He recognized the figure as his brother Wilfred, whose name he then called. The figure turned and returned his gaze but made no answer before vanishing. When he returned home, his wife, Luella, cried out, asking him what was wrong. Joe replied that something was going to happen to his brother, as he had "just seen his forerunner," before weeping. The next morning, Joe waited for the news he knew would come, and later, it was confirmed by messenger that his brother had died at sea at the very time he'd seen the vision.[47]

Once more, in the following memorate given by Professor Daryl Dance in her compilation of African American folklore, the apparition ignores the percipient, despite being the bearer of important news. An elderly woman was said to have seen her boyfriend, who was gravely ill in the hospital at the time. That evening, around dusk, she was in her kitchen when the doorbell rang. And there was Frank. She addressed him. "Frank, I thought you was in the hospital. Where—?" He didn't reply; he just stood and stared blankly at her. "Say, Frank, don't act like that; you scare me." She then turned around to run, and she slammed the door behind her. Soon after, word came that he had died right at the time of the encounter—a fact that the woman stated she would "tell on her dying day."[48]

VISIONS AND WRAITHS

To end this chapter and the subject of discoveries of death at a distance, a small and varied collection of more typical cross-cultural and historical crisis apparitions and visions follow. Again, drawing from the ancient Icelandic *Book of Settlements*, we read of a bishop who had a vision one night in which a man he "did not know" stood in the middle of his hall. "Thorkel sainted" were his only words. The bishop awoke and told his archpriest, "Rise up, brother, and let us go to church and praise Almighty God, for priest Thorkel our brother is now departed out of this life," as indeed, it turned out, he was.[49]

According to an old Icelandic legend, a certain Asmundr dreamed one night that his uncle visited him and said, "Now is the time for you to come to me; bring good and active people with you, and horses enough for the journey." Asmundr awoke, quickly gathered his horses and his men, and rode for the valley where his uncle had lived. When he arrived, he found that his uncle had died, and he brought the coffin home to Fjall and buried the man.[50]

From the Edda's legends to the hamlets and hovels of the Scandinavian countryside, the idea and the reported experience of discovering a death by means of a supernatural vision or apparitions are extremely common in those lands. According to one account, in the autumn of 1780, two men were lost with all their guides and sheep while attempting to cross some mountains. Nothing was heard from them for the winter. The folks living back at Reynistad first began to suspect how things had gone when the sister of one of the dead men dreamed that he, a man named Bjarni, came to her in a dream and related the circumstances in a manner that is rather common in Scandinavian folklore, a verse:

> *No one now can find us here,*
> *Neath the snow in frosty tomb;*
> *Three days o'er his brother's bier*
> *Bjarni sat in grief and gloom.*[51]

Much older even than the sagas, four years after Greek mythology's Heracles left the company of the similarly legendary twins Castor and Pollux, they visited the great seer Iamos at his sanctuary as they wished for tidings of the man. "This very day," said the seer, "that great spirit has departed from among men. Yes, for it was shown me in a vision how he met the doom of fire, and entered by that flaming gate into everlasting bliss."[52]

Such capacities were clearly expected of the mythological seer, and like so many of those skills we have seen, they were also taken for granted much later by many North American Indians. Among the Pueblo Indians (primarily of New Mexico), for instance, when a young man failed to return from the hunt, his parents consulted a medicine man to see if he might locate the missing man using his "searching stones." We will see such magicians locate bodies after the death is known; in this example, however, the death itself is also discovered. He soon said simply, "This young man has been killed," before letting them know where his body could be located. They found him exactly where he indicated.[53]

In another case from among the Puebloans, this time regarding a young medicine man in the making, Chips, his skills were sought out by a certain family. They had come two hundred miles for his help in locating their lost young boy. After a ceremony in which Chips consulted the spirits, he told them, "I see your son, and you'll see him too, in seven days, but I don't know whether you'll be happy to see him," before also telling them exactly where. Later, however, he revealed to another, his uncle, that he had later seen this young boy drown in the Missouri River in real time, watched in his vision, and avoided telling them the entire truth. They found the boy seven days later, as Chips had indicated.[54]

The fact that the information was known and somewhat manipulated in this way brings us to the Pima Indians of Arizona and New Mexico. These people have "speeches," portions of their cosmology recited, among which there is one that tells of the Pima's approaching battle with the Apache. Of interest here, the Pima medicine man casts a spell on an Apache, forcing him to dream, so that when he awoke, "he thought it was true that his younger brother and his uncles had been killed."[55] Tedlock recorded something very similar among the Zuni Indians. When a man named Hapiya fell ill, another dreamed that he was discussing the text of a creation story with him and that two lines were missing, before suddenly awaking, "thinking he'd been with a man who was already dead." Consulting his teacher, the man "divined" the meaning of his dream, noting of Hapiya, "Already he is dead."[56] If we may make the comparison, Benedict the Moor, a sixteenth-century Sicilian Franciscan friar, was likewise said to have announced aloud the deaths of Bianca, a sister of a Sicilian princess, "which was fully verified."[57]

Returning to these skills as they are given in the lives of the saints, when Duke Henry II was killed during the 1241 battle between the Mongol Tartars and the Poles, "his death was known to Saint Hedwig three days before the news was brought to her." She told her companion, Dermudis, "I have lost my son [. . .] He has gone from me like a bird in flight, and I shall never see him again in this life."[58] The sixth-century Irish saint Berach sent a monk, Sillen, on an errand to Rathonn. Nine robbers killed the monk. This, however, "was revealed to Berach," and he set out quickly and found the body.[59] Brad Steiger, who had a similar intimation, wrote that when his mother died in the early fifties, he "happened to be in California. I needed no message from home. I knew the day and the hour when she left her earthly surroundings."[60]

In an old oral poem with multiple variants from among the Tatars, those Turkic people living from west-central Russia and east to the Ural Mountains, we read of a raid in which a man named Manas, while attacking a neighboring village, is wounded and must return home. After his return, he is poisoned by the Kalmuck prince Kokshogos and dies as a result. In another variant, he dies from the initial wound. Importantly here, though, in both cases, one who loves him, Kanykai, learns of his death supernaturally—by means of a dream and by means of "second sight," respectively—before finding his body.[61]

Told to Louis Jones in 1940s New York was the story of a woman whose husband, a man of the navy, had drowned at sea. That same night, he appeared in their child's bedroom, looked down at the child, and left without opening the door, simply passing through; the telegram later confirmed his death.[62] As explored in detail in *Apparitions at the Moment of Death* and as we have seen in numerous accounts so far, these visions of a distant death often present symbolically to the percipient. It is written in this vein that, in 1202, a certain unnamed noblewoman had a vision of a French-born Benedictine and Carthusian monk, Hugh of Lincoln, pushing away a candidate of King John's, a bishop who was to be Hugh's successor after his death, with his staff. The next morning, just as she was relating this dream to her friends, "startling news" was brought to her that this candidate had died.[63]

In 1958, a certain Colonel Pritchard saw Douglas Jardine, a British cricketer who played twenty-two test matches for England, in a bar and raised a glass to him, receiving the same gesture in response. Just before the game started, news that Jardine had died the previous day in Switzerland was announced over the loudspeaker.[64] Priest and hagiographer Sabine Baring-Gould recalls in his book, *Early Reminiscences*, that in 1840, his mother had been reading the Bible in her dining room at Bratton Clovelly, an English village, when she saw on the other side of the table an apparition of her brother, Henry. A month later, news came that he had died on that very date.[65]

Finally here, an old account from Canada, more specifically Nova Scotia, about 1774, one of the earlier examples of their "forerunners." At that time, a considerable number of families went out of Yorkshire to settle in Nova Scotia. Among them was one man, whose name was Brian Kay. The eldest of his daughters was great friends with a neighbor back home, Polly Smith. When these two girls parted, they shared much mutual distress. Some weeks after they left for Nova Scotia, this same Polly Smith had a most afflictive dream or vision concerning her absent friend. The room lit up, and she saw her friend standing by the bed all in white. "O Betty," said she, "what is the matter, thou lookest so ill? What, is not Nova Scotia as good as old England?" Betty answered, "No, no; but it has been a good while since I left Nova Scotia." Betty then said, "Your father will receive such a letter as this from my father, which will tell you all." Polly then became quite awake. In tears to her mother and father, she could not be convinced this was but a dream, and sure enough, Polly's father received a letter from the said Brian Kay, exactly of the size and shape of that which Polly had seen in her sleep, bringing news of her friend's death at that very time.[66]

THE MESSAGE OF THE MESSENGERS

Here, as with the previous chapter, an indication can be given to the reader as to just how widespread these tales and experiences are—these revenants, wraiths, and disinterested shades. While they have been collected in large numbers by parapsychologists, from a complimentarily cross-cultural and historic perspective, they have been greatly underrepresented. Regarding the wraith that announces the death of someone at a distance, this is a fundamental aspect of the human experience, occurring with surprising frequency at all ages and times, despite being little spoken of. It is not rare that these apparitions do not interact with the informants and yet still inform of a death. Conversely, these apparitions and visions commonly perform a consolatory function, preparing the mind of the individual for the news of a death and often changing how they think about the universe itself, often suggesting to them a far more connected and meaningful cosmos.

Regarding the revenant, without doubt, many of the instances of apparitions that still occur would, at a different time, qualify as revenants with their surprising physical or "psychokinetic" interactions with the world. Lecouteux noted that "the belief in revenants and ghosts possesses two roots: the fear of the departed and the stupefaction caused by any abnormal death."[67] It seems, however, that experiences from as long ago as the Philinnion tale of antiquity and the romances of Japan to those of our opening Chuj Mayan account would qualify as a third root, a very clear avenue by which such beliefs might be formed. "My mother convinced me that the dead come back," wrote playwright David Belasco, after all, following his own encounter with the form of his mother at the moment she exited this world and left him with her mysterious and hopeful message of survival.[68]

SIX

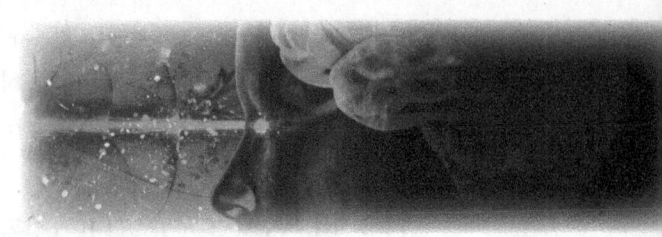

Treasure, Tombs, and Visionary Boons

Cross-Cultural ESP Involving Mysterious Knowledge of an Item's Location

It is readily acknowledged that our time has surpassed all epochs in history for the accumulation of technical knowledge, physical power over our environment, and economic might. It is less often pointed out, however, that our age has generated, and continues to generate, mythical material almost unparalleled in quantity and quality in the rich records of human imagination.

JACQUES VALLEE

While the things of crisis, death, and dying are most commonly the subjects of the kinds of worldwide extrasensory visions and dreams we have explored so far, the things of vanity and fortune, as it happens, are very much at the center of many others. The finding of something hidden or lost, such as treasure, tombs, bodies, relics, and important ritual items, by way of visions, dreams, or other means, has been a persistent tale through the ages. Just as we have seen with the vardogers and missing person cases from the most ancient times, while the specialist was often enlisted to locate missing things, from bodies and bones to treasure and coins, the layman might dream the same dreams, see the same spoils, and find the same treasures.

While such things have been wonderfully and carefully written about previously, rarely are they (a) compiled from such varied sources, (b) compared to much more recent anecdotes, and (c) considered specifically in the context of broader extrasensory phenomena—this strange magic in the mind with which we have been dealing. In this way, it is hoped that a contribution can be made, especially for the new reader in these areas.

TREASURE AND TROVES IN THE WALLS AND THE COVES

Truly, there are riches in the hills and in the caves. For a number of reasons, through time, there has been cause to hide valuable things. Helen Creighton noted that the sheltered coves, bays, and beaches of Nova Scotia, where tales of treasure are a "favorite topic," made excellent hiding places for pirates of the earlier days to hide their booty.[1] Creighton makes it clear that whatever the source of the treasure, which features so heavily in Nova Scotian lore, there is no doubt that, in actuality, "money and other wealth have been extricated from the ground" and that "people known to be poor have suddenly grown rich."[2] The author then gives the example, among numerous others, of a woman at Clam Harbor who dreamed of a hidden treasure before subsequently finding it with a mineral rod. She and her husband unearthed a copper pan containing a "sizeable amount" of English sovereigns, with which they could then buy horses and send their sons to college.[3] Author Sterling Ramsay noted, in a somewhat disparaging tone, of the nearby Prince Edward Islanders that, in fact, they "love to dream of finding the wealth which some one else has accumulated and buried."[4] "The wealth of the

Astors," wrote American author Charles Skinner, referencing a powerful family, "hardly exceeds the treasure that is supposed to be secreted here and there about the country" before going on to mention "caves and cellars" as prime locations.[5]

The dreams that locate such treasures and other things of importance to the unsuspecting individual may be found in every quarter. As apparently elaborated upon by the then prime minister of Korea, the mountains there, too, were said to "have their pot of silver or pot of gold concealed."[6] Accordingly, the mountain god is said to have sometimes made known in a dream the place where the pot is buried. The former prime minister goes on to note that some of the treasure had been left behind by Japanese invaders. Similarly, and conversely in New Mexico, Applegate notes that the Mexicans of the hinterlands believed that the old Indians buried "great amounts of treasure" to keep it from the hands of the Spaniards.[7]

Eighth-century Chinese emperor Hsuan-tsung once dreamed that an old man appeared to him and told him that a huge white boulder had fallen to earth in the Chungnan Mountains. First thing in the morning, Hsuan-tsung sent his official to look for the rock, and they "found it and brought it back." He had it carved into a statue and placed next to his villa.[8] British civil servant and journalist Nicholas Dennys, writing much later in the mid-nineteenth century, spoke of the faith in dreams as an "every-day belief" among the Chinese and those relating to treasure being an "old, old subject." He relays multiple instances, including from a journal out of Shangai and the case of Chang. This man dreamed he was at a particular spot behind a certain temple in Shangai City, where he found a trove of gold. Being so impressed with the vivid nature of the dream, Chang immediately made for the "enchanted spot" with a pickaxe and, sure enough, found a box weighing heavily with gold.[9]

Greek travel writer and mythographer Pausanias gave an ancient dream in which prominent Athenian Epiteles was guided to the location of a bronze urn enclosing mysterious texts.[10] Something similar can be found in Claire Rougemont's early twentieth-century collection of "well-authenticated" dreams. A poor peasant living near Rheims in Champagne, France, was taken in his dream by a mysterious young man to the base of an old wall. The youth pointed to a large stone and recommended that he raise it up the following day, which the peasant did and revealed a vase filled with golden coins, enriching him and his family.[11]

In Ireland, too, such dreams were especially commonplace. In County Clare, for example, Irish antiquarian, folklorist, and archaeologist Thomas Johnson Westropp noted that "treasure-hunting is, so far as I have learned, in nearly every case in consequence of a dream,"[12] while O'Reilly, in 1986, found ninety such tales in a survey of the National Folklore Collections material.[13] Just as in Korea, it was advancing armies that in the seventeenth century forced the concealment of valuable treasures in churchyards and other places. Farther east, according to old Bohemian belief, if the finder of a fern seed bloom climbs a mountain that night with it in his hand, he might either find gold or have it revealed to him in a vision.[14]

Secrets in the Walls

Coming again to the work of folklorist Charles Leland, he found the same in Italy. Despite mostly disbelieving in the ghosts of the stories he had carefully collected, Leland noted that much treasure is to be found in the walls and floors of Florence and that during the Middle Ages, so great were the risks to men and women that they must surely have hidden things away from prying eyes. The author gives a concrete example recorded in the newspaper *L'Italie* from 1891 in which an "immense treasure of very ancient gold coins" had just been unearthed in Bologna, which conformed to rumors of a centuries-old treasure buried exactly there. Leland gives stories of the more traditional form as well, in which the dead once more offer information, in this case a legend related to the Palazzo Strozzi in Florence. There, it is said, a spirit came in a vision to a man and recited, "Remove the wall which here we see, and thou wilt read the mystery, and learn where 'twas thy father fled, And find a fortune with the dead." The wall was thus removed, with both the body and "bags of gold" being found.[15]

According to a wide variety of legends, in fact, the walls or floors of the house, either owned by the individual or temporarily resided in, are a prime location where one might find hidden things. One of the earliest and best-known of this kind relates to an ancient Athenian haunted house and to a ghost said to have scared away all previous tenants. Finally, a Pythagorean mystic enters, fortified with esoteric books, and withstands all attempts by the ghost to dislodge him. At last, the man corners the phantom and drives him down into the earth. Our victorious exorcist marks the spot; the next day, a moldering body is found six feet away, and after exhumation and reburial, the hauntings stop.[16]

Many ages apart, at Fjälkinge, a locality situated in Kristianstad Municipality, Skåne County, Sweden, a late seventeenth-century tale is told in which one Madam Margaretta, coming to an inn during her travels, was insistent on sleeping in the "ghost's room," where apparently another traveler had been murdered some years previously. At midnight, she was awakened by the lifting of two floorboards, from which a bloody form appeared. The following morning, she insisted the bailiff assemble the people at the post office, where she demanded the boards be taken up. The body was discovered exactly where she had dreamed of it.[17]

A famous Spanish scholar, physician, and "master of magic" of the sixteenth century, Dr. Eugenio Torralva (who, incidentally, is mentioned by Cervantes in *Don Quixote*), was once consulted by the cardinal of Santa Cruz for something of the same kind. A certain woman, Donna Rosales, claimed to have seen by her bed the figure of a man covered in wounds, pale, and in apparent pain. Torralva, being "acquainted with the spiritual world," later asks the spirit its motive. "I seek a treasure" was the reply. Soon after, the cellars of the house were dug up, and the corpse of Aman, stabbed to death with a long knife, was discovered.[18]

A folktale from Baghdad, Iraq, has a woman who, along with her husband, is in dire financial straits. One night, the prophet Elijah comes to her and tells her of a small aperture in her bedroom wall behind a cupboard where money is stored. The woman awoke, frightened, but found the money exactly where the entity had suggested.[19] We can read a comparable case relayed by prolific English cleric, theologian, and evangelist Rev. John Wesley. He gave a "remarkable relation" from 1745 in which, the evening before a man was to be tried and killed during the seventeenth-century Siege of Carlisle, his wife dreamed someone came to her and said, "Go to such a part of the wall, and among the loose stones you will find a key, which you must carry to your husband." After initially ignoring the dream but dreaming it again, she donned her cloak and hat against the weather and found the key exactly where the stranger in her dream had said it would be.[20] From a similar Armenian account told by one Mariam Serabian, we read that "many generations back," some gold was buried in a certain house, which for generations no one could find. One day, however, the informant's great-grandmother dreamed three nights in a row that she was told its exact location. She soon found an extraordinarily beautiful Turkish coffee cup made with gold, though cracked in half.[21]

PERENNIAL LORE

Before further and unapologetically dipping in and out of such seemingly disparate sources, it should be made very clear that these strange happenings are very much ongoing, still reported, and in significant alignment with the older legends and lore. "My files," wrote Diana Arcangel, just eighteen years ago, "contain many reports whereby apparitions directed their surviving loved ones to large amounts of hidden cash."[22] In that same year, Sally Rhine Feather, in an analysis of 2,878 ESP experiences, found almost one hundred cases dealing with locating missing articles.[23] In a fascinating analysis of then-current New York ghost lore, Louis Jones found that, according to the memorates collected over four years by his students, ghosts very much still "tell or try to tell where money is buried,"[24] even noting that the buried treasure lore required "special notice" for their ubiquity among native New Yorkers, Sicilians, and Italians.[25] Regarding Sicilians and their old beliefs in this regard, we can reference in passing the words of folklorist Gustav Henningsen. He noted that historically, "the assistance given by the fairies to poor Sicilians in their untiring search for hidden treasure is a whole chapter in itself."[26]

Much more soberly, yet of striking basic similarity to the events that unfolded in that ancient Athenian house, Arcangel was told by an informant that they dreamed of a recently dead friend who had a message for another. "Tell Lorraine to look in the hall, at the dead end, just south of the bedroom, to the right of the light socket. I've left something inside that wall." Sure enough, according to Lorraine, "I just dug into the wall where Murphy told Charles to look and I found a whole lot of cash—thousands and thousands of dollars."[27]

Returning to the Manchester sample of the previously quoted Gillian Bennett, one of her informants, Maura, while looking for a document relating to the recently deceased wife of her friend, suddenly, seemingly automatically, exclaimed, "I expect it's hidden under the paper in the bottom of the wardrobe." And they found it exactly there. Maura expressed her belief that her sudden inspiration was a message from that dead woman herself.[28]

The Guggenheims, in their seminal study of after-death communications, give the case of a Floridian named Ruth. While searching for $5,000 worth of savings, which she knew her dead mother had left but was unaware of the location of, she was about to give up. Suddenly, however, she heard her mother's voice: "Oh, you dummies. They're in the bottom of the garment bag." According to Ruth, the voice was "so distinct," and she soon found the bonds exactly where indicated.[29] In another case from this study, one of the Guggenheims' informants had their dead father appear to them while they were lying on the couch. He revealed the location of some money, which the informant wasn't aware existed.

These accounts, particularly when the item is found, are often enough to strongly convince people of the reality of the soul's survival.[30]

Eighty years earlier, something related was given by the longtime president of the American Theosophical Society, Louis Rogers. A certain Mrs. Reeves from Ohio, after the death of her mother, had trouble locating important bonds needed so that she could adjust the relevant financial accounts. After "every conceivable nook and cranny" of the house was searched, they could not be found. This woman's deceased mother later came to her during a dream and told her:

> "Don't worry any more about those bonds, you'll find them in the morning. I had them at the house just before I was taken ill, and had them in my hand when I went up to the garret floor, and laid them aside while busy there. I forgot them when leaving—and then came the illness and confusion that followed. But they are there, and you will find them in an old tomato can, covered with a board, near the end of the large black trunk."[31]

While her husband remained incredulous, the bonds were found exactly where indicated.

A gentleman from Texas told Horace Hutchinson that, around 1896, he bought his daughters a lady's knife each, their first knife, which greatly delighted them. During the excitement of their games during the day, one of them lost theirs, which apparently "nearly broke her heart." During that night, this young girl of around eight or nine years dreamed that her dead brother came to her, took her by the hand, and said, "Come, my darling, I will show you where your little knife is," before revealing to her the exact place. Both girls hastily searched and found the knife exactly where the dream specified.[32]

It seems no corner of the earth can be excluded in the collecting of these surprisingly similar stories. In an old Filipino folktale, a ghost appears to a young prince in a dream and tells him, "Your father left a hidden treasure of gold and diamonds, which he forgot to mention in his will. Should you care to have that treasure, go to the city of Black," before mentioning that it will be in a cellar behind the palace. The man eventually finds the loot exactly where it was indicated.[33] The idea itself is even expressed satirically by Italian scholar and early Renaissance humanist Poggio Bracciolini in his book of jokes, first published in 1470, in his short piece, *A Man Who Found Gold during His Sleep*. This tells of a man who claimed to have found gold in a dream. In another account, someone else says something similar, although with a less agreeable ending. In this case, the devil is said to have been the messenger of the gold's location in the man's dream, and he led him to the gold, which eventually turned to turd.[34] Very commonly, in fact, such tales do not have a happy ending; the individual, in their greed and haste, often fails to carry out the necessary steps to rightfully attain the bounty. The extent to which such narratives agree in their specifics with the folkloric tales could reasonably be posited as being related to their genesis.

Regarding a memorate fairly well removed from Bracciolini's humorous tales, Skinner recorded that a farmer near Oneida Lake, New York, dreamed several times of a buried treasure at a certain point and was told that if he were to dig there at midnight, he could make it his. He made an attempt and hit something that seemed like gold. The dream, however, had instructed him to turn around three times beforehand, which, in his hurry, he forgot. He was struck dead on the spot by lightning.[35] The same was true in a tale from the Scottish Highlands. Craigie gives the example of a "navvy," or laborer, who was working on a road around the year 1840. He dreamed that if he were to rise early on Monday morning, two days from then, he would see a crow sitting on a stone, under which he would find the gold that was apparently hidden there after the murder of a Norwegian prince. The man was in such a hurry that he went the evening before and thus failed to retrieve the gold.[36]

FINANCES, TRANCES, SAINTS, AND SHAMANS

American anthropologist Rosalie Hankey collected a story in California in which the informant lived on a farm previously owned by a man who died without divulging the location of his fortune. One of the men on the ranch who "frequently went into trances" apparently had the dead owner himself appear to him and had him follow on a horse to a bare spot where he was buried. The treasure was pointed out by a crooked branch.[37]

Such "trances," under the influence of which certain secret knowledge is revealed, should by now be familiar to the reader. They would be entirely familiar, of course, among innumerable Indian tribes, who would make use of them for the very same reasons. Among the Paiute of Nevada, certain of their shamans were commonly called upon specifically to locate lost or stolen property. "People would come to my father," an informant told Willard Park, "and say that he had lost something."[38] The man would always have to go to sleep first and would wake up with clairvoyant knowledge of the item's location. More pertinently, among the Paiute, one "Doctor Dick" was consulted by a man who buried money but could not remember where. That night, "Doctor Dick" apparently "went into a trance," and the following morning, he revealed where the money was located.[39]

The parallels, when laid out in number, seem to speak to something perennial that manifests either at the whim of the specialist or in the mind of the unassuming individual. In 1682, the Franciscans in New Mexico heard from a man named Juan Anton, whose belongings had once been stolen. Juan therefore took a "big dose" of the psychedelic cactus peyote to induce a helpful vision. An old man and woman appeared to him and told him not to worry, "for if he went to a certain place, he would find his belongings." Juan awoke, "went to the place indicated and found the things that had been stolen."[40]

Canadian anthropologist Diamond Jenness, living among the Copper Eskimos, once lost a tin full of matches, after which a shaman "discovered in a dream" who had stolen them.[41] These are common stories sharing basic similarities and found oceans apart. Dr. Barend Laubscher, studying divining among the people of the eastern Cape Province of South Africa, gradually became convinced that, apart from some obvious cases of fraud, genuine clairvoyants were to be found among them, giving the example of a diviner who located stolen cattle sixty miles away and named the thief. Laubscher noted that "the native territories abound" with these stories regarding the discovery of lost items.[42] Similar skills, of course, were attributed to far less renowned "professional clairvoyants." A man living in seventeenth-century County Mayo, Ireland, named Brian Rua, was said to be able to "disclose where gold was hidden in the earth."[43] Similar stories and concerns are nothing new. The procurement of "professional clairvoyants" to discover things lost is referred to in a fragment of an ancient short play by Roman dramatist Pomponius.[44]

Another of the oldest accounts in which the location of something hidden is revealed comes from Pliny the Elder and a near-death experience in 77 CE involving two noble brothers by the surname Corfidius. When the older of the two brothers stopped breathing and appeared to die, his will being opened and his funeral being arranged, he later revived in the present of a greatly surprised undertaker and told that he has just been at the house of his younger brother, who himself had just died. This was later confirmed to have occurred while the older brother lay "dead." Of interest here is that the man, while seemingly having met his maker, reveals that he had discovered that his brother had buried some gold underground. Accordingly, this gold, "of which no one else knew," was found in the place indicated.[45]

One can imagine, when considered against the evidence of history, if Pliny were not so openly inclined against the truthfulness of the majority of these visions, how many more he might have recorded. Indeed, when Plutarch wrote of the decline of the oracles and why they ceased to give answers, he noted that they might be asked "about treasures buried in the ground."[46]

In a twelfth-century Jewish tale from Germany, a man whose widowed mother died without leaving a will knew she had been wealthy but could not find where her fortune was hidden despite looking seemingly everywhere. Finally giving up, and in the same manner a shaman or ancient seer might be called upon, he enlists the help of a famous witch, who, after an elaborate sequence, finally locates the box.[47] The similarity of the skills so disparately employed are often striking. Estonian historian Juhan Kahk noted that, at least in the seventeenth century, "Across many different parts of Europe one can find [. . .] the use of witches and wizards to recover stolen property."[48]

Such specialists, in fact, still have their place. Psychoanalyst Elizabeth Lloyd Mayer tells us that in 1991, when her daughter's rare hand-carved harp was stolen, her familiar world of science and rational thinking was soon after "turned on its head," when, having failed to turn up any leads, a friend suggested she call a dowser, a man who apparently specialized in finding lost objects. Mayer agreed, almost as a joke. Within two days and without leaving his Arkansas home, the douser located the exact California street coordinates where the harp was found. Elizabeth noted that this changed everything and caused her to embark on a fourteen-year journey collecting similar accounts.[49]

With this said, it follows that even in communities where such capacities were known and accepted, these visions and dreams also came spontaneously to the nonspecialist. A tale from among the North American Lenape Indians has a young girl dreaming of a doll her parents had thrown away. She dreamed that the doll appeared to her and said, "Find me and keep me always, and you and your family will ever enjoy good health," before instructing her "exactly what to do" in order to find her. The girl told her parents, who "immediately looked for the doll and found it."[50]

An ostensibly true folktale told among the Indigenous Yurok, Hupa, and Karok of California has a young woman digging for bulbs before her carrying basket is blown away. The woman and her grandmother searched but could not find it. That night, the girl dreamed of "someone" who told her exactly the location of one of the bulbs. "He is lying close to the river," were the last of the stranger's words. Awakening, she thought, "I dreamed strangely. I was dreaming about that boy [the bulb]. I had better go see," and she found it exactly there.[51]

The very same slew of messengers we have seen turn up in these accounts too. In a story given by Rumi meant to illustrate that the dead can be greater benefactors to the poor than the living, we read of a man from Tabriz, Iran. He was trying to raise funds for a poor man but had no help from the citizens. Having visited a prefect's tomb, that man appeared to him in a dream the same night and gave him directions on where to find a great treasure to offer the poor man. "Thus," wrote Rumi, "the dead prefect proved a more liberal benefactor than the citizens of Tabriz." Such edifying tales with a basis in real folkloric notions and generally accepted ideas are extremely common in Sufi compilations.[52]

Something with a similarly moralizing bent comes from the Antilles, an archipelago bordered by the Caribbean Sea, the Gulf of Mexico, and the Atlantic Ocean. After a woman sends her sons out to earn a living, they sleep in the house of an old woman and dream that in a certain place there is a jar of money. They are told not to bring anyone else, but they bring their mother and find the money. When she puts her hands on it, the jar disappears.[53]

Messenger Saints and Laypeople

The little-known saint Lupus, or Leu, archbishop of Sens, France, from 609–623, nevertheless had a number of legends ascribed to him. One of those has the saint digging the ground at a certain spot in search of a treasure that had been "revealed to him in a dream."[54] In 775, Liudger, a missionary among the Frisians and Saxons and founder of Werden Abbey in Germany, was dispatched to find the grave and relics of Saint Lebuin, patron saint of Deventer, in the Netherlands. Greatly frustrated that he could find nothing, he turned to the construction of the new church when, as the story goes, a vision came to him. He saw Lebuin himself and heard his voice exclaim, "Dear brother Liudger, good is your work in the Lord. Those relics of mine for which you are searching you will find buried under the wall which you are raising on the south." Liudger found exactly what he was looking for at that spot.[55]

Once again, we see the saint take on the geographically widespread and historically typical role of the messenger, and more particularly, of the duties performed by the deceased in other cultures. A sixteenth-century Scottish "cunning woman," a medical practitioner, Bessie Dunlop, was said to have delivered babies, healed the sick, consoled the bereaved, identified criminals, and, pertinently, recovered lost and stolen goods. In one case, she told a Lady Thridpairt precisely where the lost contents of her purse would be found.[56] As we had seen with some South American cultures, old Scottish seers' reputations often hinged on the success of their visionary insights and other intimations, and they, too, often attributed their capacity to find lost things to an external familiar. In 1669, one Harry Wilson claimed that "when anybody came to him to inquire about things lost or stolen, that he gave no perfect answer, but appointed them to come to him some other days and in the meantime, the said woman appeared to him in the night and informed him how to answer."[57]

We may again draw an interesting parallel from among the mystics of the church. At times, certain people came to Saint Theodore Phanariot to locate lost items, including a man who wished to know the location of his escaped servants.[58] Just as we have seen the shaman or other clairvoyant consulted, other saints were similarly capable of discovering the location of lost or missing items. In the ancient Broccan's Hymn to Saint Brigit, from no later than the ninth century, a slave woman is given a brooch by the king of Leinster. Her husband threw it into the sea out of spite. Brigit happened to have come to the poet's house around that time and "prayed to God that the brooch might be revealed to her." An angel came and told her where to find it and how to get it, which, according to her, "was done."[59]

There are multiple references in old records describing different kinds of divination similarly used among the laity of early medieval Ireland to find "something stolen" or recover what had been lost.[60] The Irish Rev. John Ashton was accused of using "invocations and conjuring," specifically to obtain aid from spirits to find a lost cup and locate gold.[61] The dead, then, not only come spontaneously to the living in these cases to point out something lost, they are specifically invoked, their capacities being known. In France, too, in the year 708, Saint Michael appears to Aubert, bishop of Avranches, in a dream vision and tells him that a certain stolen bull would be found at the top of Mont Saint-Michel, where later it was found.[62]

Treasure and the Power of Dreams

The extent to which a dream was believed to have been a legitimate means of learning the location of something lost, something valuable, even allowed these traditions to be taken advantage of for one's own gain—and this being an ancient reality. Virgil tells of three men who came to Rome and buried a pot of gold in a certain spot. Afterward, they declared themselves to be soothsayers and dream readers, went to the Senate of Rome, and told them if they were to dig at a certain spot, they would find the gold, whose location they had dreamed of.[63] So ingrained, in fact, was the geographically ubiquitous idea that treasure is often protected by such a guardian, and often a ghost, that a group of Sicilian robbers once murdered a young boy and buried him with their treasure specifically in the hope that his spirit would watch over their booty.[64]

Like the Polynesians and so many others, among the Muria tribe from the regions of Chhattisgarh and the neighboring areas of Madhya Pradesh in India, dreams are generally considered to be the experiences of the soul leaving the body. It therefore follows, as it does from many similar beliefs worldwide, that such exploits might provide real truth, to be veridical. "Long ago," a Muria man fell asleep in a blacksmith's shop. Another person near him saw his soul leave his body in the form of a lizard. The soul went to a certain anthill and apparently saw a pot full of rupees. When the man awoke, he told the other what he had seen: "And they went to the anthill and around the rupees." This was apparently a "true tale."[65]

From the capital and largest city of the northern Indian state of

Himachal Pradesh in the Himalayas, a young woman dreams that she hears the cry of jackals. She heard them say, "Near the river lies a dead man; go and look on his finger and you will find a ring worth nine lakhs of rupees." Accordingly, the woman rose, went to the river, and found the dead man.[66] As recently as 2010, Rodney Davies gave the similar example of the widowed Monica, who could not find an important ring. "I kept saying," Monica explained, "I wish I could find that ring. Then William [her dead husband] directed me to the place where it was."[67]

Given Jones's surprising discovery that such things, in line with the old tales, were still going on in 1940s New York, our interest should at least be piqued to discover that, and to reiterate, nothing much has changed. In the following account, again from Elsaesser's 2018–20 sample, one of her participants lost a ring that was very important to them after lending it out. However, as the participant describes, "my grandmother in a dream told me the exact location where it was," which proved accurate.[68] Elsaesser places such experiences and others under the category of "practical ADCs," or after-death communications. Worlds away, Bayar Odun, a Mongolian woman, also dreamed of her dead grandmother, who was holding four mirrors. Some weeks later, she noticed a reindeer circling a spot on the snow. When she dug it up, she "found the four mirrors from her dream."[69]

BODIES, GHOSTS, AND TOMBS

With certain exceptions, particularly among more sea-bound or seafaring cultures, proper burial of the body has historically been of great importance. One can imagine then, as is borne out from the ancient seers of the Near East and Greece to the tribes of the deepest Amazon, the premium placed upon those claiming the ability to find lost bodies, persons, or indeed, tombs. Each of these categories, in their historical ubiquity, could take up chapters, and we will primarily avoid the more commonly repeated tales and references, the following paragraph notwithstanding. It is often not clarified in these tales, in which the body's owner appears in spirit form, whether or not their death was known. Here, then, the focus is on the veridical information pertaining to the location of their body. At the end of the fourth century, Augustine of Hippo wrote, in reference to the challenge of denying the reality of such encounters, as they so commonly appeared in the lives of early Christians, that "it is said that either in dream or in some other manner, some dead men have shown themselves to the living who did not know where the bodies of these dead people lay buried. The dead people directed them to it and requested that the sepulcher that was lacking be provided."[70]

While such tales exist in number in the well-trodden literature of the classical world, here we begin in Japan and the long-lost grave of Gyōki (668–749), a Japanese Buddhist priest of the Nara period. His body is said to have been rediscovered in a dream. According to the sources, his own spirit appeared in a vision to a monk called Keion and told him the exact location where his bones could be found. A group of monks went and confirmed the reality of the vision.[71] Farther west, a Chinese king, Wen (1152–1050 BCE), while taking a daytime nap, dreamed that someone climbed his city walls and exclaimed, "I am the dry bones of the north-eastern corner. Bury me without delay, with the ceremonial appertaining to a king." Upon waking, the king ordered his officials to find the spot indicated, and they actually found the bones, which he quickly ordered to be buried. The tale tells that this act greatly endeared the king to his people, with respect for the dead being greatly valued.[72]

Fridolin of Säckingen, a legendary Irish missionary, when arriving at the church of Saint Hilarius in Switzerland, was shocked to find it vandalized by the Goths. After spending some nights in prayer, the location where its holy patron was buried is mysteriously revealed to him. The lost tomb is soon found, and, like the Chinese king Wen, the vision is credited with bolstering his reputation and assuring his installation as the abbot of an adjoining priory.[73]

These tales are so widespread that any compilation will seem somewhat scattered; here, however, they are united under the general concept of finding something hidden by nonordinary and seeming extrasensory means. This ranges from the hidden treasures in the mountains of our earlier paragraphs to the lost doll in the case of the Lenape Indian girl. Thus, in 1238, a Knight Hospitaller of Saint John of Jerusalem at Cologne, Ingebrand von Rurke, dreamed that he was visited by a beautiful girl. She requested that he dig her up. "You will find me," she specified, having appeared in a second vision, "in the orchard of the priory, under the filbert tree." After learning her name, Cordula, he tells his prior, "We must unearth her tomorrow." Accordingly, on the following day, they dug under the filbert and found bones, which were later venerated as sacred relics. Of interest too, on account of these visions, Cordula "forced her way" into the German and Roman martyrologies and is celebrated with a certain feast.[74]

In a Russo-Jewish legend, certain "sires" were inspired by a vision in which the location of the sepulcher of Moses is said to have been revealed to them. After searching the caverns of Mount Pisgah, lying directly east of the Jordan River and just northeast of the Dead Sea, they discovered the structure where indicated.[75]

Peter the Fuller (471–488 CE), patriarch of Antioch, is said to have been visited in a dream by Barnabas, later to be the patron saint of Cyprus. Barnabas revealed to him the location of his tomb, "which had not previously been known," and he found it where the vision suggested.[76]

As repeatedly noted, the specialist was not the only one capable of such things. Indeed, among certain First Peoples of the North American continent, it was such visions of the spontaneous kind that might be their making and might call them to the mystical path in the first place. As collected among the Canada-based Salishan and Sahaptin tribes, we read of a man who falls in love with his younger sister and is killed for it. His murderers deposited the man's remains in a distant lake over many mountains, assuming that "the girl can never find us here, and she will never find her lover's remains." She discovered later that he had been killed, but she had no idea where his body was. According to the tale, at last, "in a dream, she saw the body of her brother on the islet in the lake." This experience, in fact, was her own shamanizing, and she later used these abilities to help others.[77]

The very same kind of thing might have marked another from the recent sample of Elsaesser had they undergone their own experience in a different time or place. The day after feeling the strange presence of what was apparently a tall male on her stairs, Elsaesser's informant said that her husband's cousin was missing. Later, making the connection between the events, she dreamed of him. He showed her a certain location in town. Later, it was found that he killed himself at that very spot.[78]

Printed in *The Gentleman's Magazine* in 1761 was the case of a Gloucestershire farmer who went missing. His father, having searched the country for him in vain, discovered that a relative of his had dreamed that his son was drowned in the well of the public house. His body was found exactly there.[79] Somewhere around 1865 in Maitland, Australia, a farmer named Shaun Cott went missing. Months later, a man named John Anthony moved there, and one week after his arrival, he called Sergeant McLean of the police force; he had dreamed a "vivid dream" in which Cott appeared to him, told him who had been his killer, and "revealed the exact spot on the farm where his body lay buried." Just over an hour later, the body was found at that spot.[80]

People and Things

Something of a passing similarity among the Yucatan Maya can be noted, in that they use certain supernaturally infused crystals in order to help locate lost children.[81] Although less spoken of, even still, these specialists are enlisted in missing persons cases. During the 1990s, Polish clairvoyant Krzysztof Jackowski, to whom hundreds of cases had been attributed, including corroborating police testimony, came to prominence after the families of three missing men asked him for help. Using a photograph that was provided of the men, he sensed that they were dead, their throats cut, and their eyes, sadly, removed. He then saw three headless bodies "at a specific location." A few days later, Russian police "revealed the bodies had been found as Jackowski had described."[82] Something similar was reported in the *New York American* on October 18, 1915. A mother dreamed accurately, as was later shown, of her son's body being lowered into a pauper's grave, which led to the discovery of the body. This was apparently "one of the strangest incidents in local police history."[83] The folklorist has sometimes observed that these visions are now less dramatic than they had been in older accounts; this is a simplification, however, as many of the old accounts, mostly those that have been ignored in this context, are equally trite and commonly lack embellishing details.

Once more, among those Canadians hailing from Finland, a man was involved in an accident while working on a railroad bridge. No one could find him; however, one woman stated that she could tell exactly where the man was because she had a dream showing what happened. She reported that she watched from a vantage point and saw the man say, "Tell them that I am here in this spot." Accordingly, "the man was found on that spot."[84]

Such beliefs and capacities have been long-held in those regions. In sixteenth- and seventeenth-century Finland, in fact, people who had been robbed "often turned to a sorcerer in order to find the stolen goods."[85] These are truly old ideas then. Speaking to this, an incident recorded in the Old Testament (I Sam. 9:6–8, 20; 10:2) has Samuel very much expecting to locate his father's missing animals through the help of a "seer" or a "man of god," and his services would be paid for. Likewise, on Ambae, an island 1,800 kilometers east of Australia, in case of theft or any hidden crime, some wizard who understands how to do it drinks kava and so throws himself into a magic sleep. When he wakes, he declares that he has seen the culprit and gives his name.[86]

Somewhat likewise, and according to Sally Rhine Feather, a woman from Ohio managed to locate her mother's stolen car "with the help of accurate information received during a clairvoyant dream, surprising the police."[87] English anthropologist Edward Evans-Pritchard found that the Central African Azande ethnic group employs "magicians" in order to "retain stolen property."[88] These skills, in fact, are commonly recorded on that continent. The Bantu diviner, too, the *inyanga*, is instructed in dreams in the art of "finding hidden things."[89] Far removed, an Icelandic tale from 1780 speaks of a "wizard" who would specifically be employed to locate the bodies of brothers who had perished, and according to the tale, he was successful.[90]

Returning to the work of South African journalist Lawrence George Green, he gave a related case that came to him from that country, the evidence of which was "absolutely reliable." Magistrate Frank Brownlee, a friend of the author's, was "convinced that certain natives were clairvoyant." He came across a case in which a man's money had been stolen, and, after police failed to find the thief, a diviner was enlisted, according to whom the money had been "buried near a large rock at the source of a [specific] local stream." The information proved correct. Brownlee was apparently "certain" the diviner had no knowledge of the theft before the consultation.[91]

There is an ancient dream in Cicero's *De Divinatione* in which a god reveals to the poet Sophocles the identity of a thief who had stolen a golden bowl from his temple. Of great interest here, Oppenheim made the connection between this account and how often they turn up among traditional cultures, noting that the letter on which it is found "furnishes us with a unique example of a very primitive type of dream."[92] Much removed, a certain Sufi sultan once dreamed of the recently killed Shemsu-'d-Din. He was told where to find the body, which he and some others soon recovered from the bottom of a well.[93]

FACT, FANTASY, AND MAGICAL MESSENGERS

Like some we have seen, these tales also commonly feature a third-party seemingly intent on either helping or hindering the suspecting or unsuspecting mortal. While the dwarf, fairy, martyr, or other divine being commonly takes on that role, at other times, as we have seen in some of the previous accounts, the messenger is entirely anonymous.

Returning to the Pawnee Indians of the Central Plains, among whom innumerable similar tales exist, Handsome Boy once dreamed of a man standing near him wearing fine leggings fringed with human scalps and trimmed with eagle feathers. "I want you to go towards the southwest until you come to a high hill," the man said. "I have placed something for you upon that hill." The next morning, the boy mounted his pony, found the hill, and discovered a flint knife in the ground. He took it as his own, and "he knew that it was what the man had promised him in his dream."[94]

Once, among the Menominee Indians of Wisconsin, a young boy fasted for eight days until he was very weak. On that eighth day, he "dreamed" that one of the sacred monsters who lived in the falls appeared and told him, "Look yonder and you will see something laced there as your reward for fasting," pointing to a rock in the center of the falls. When the boy got to the spot, he discovered a "sacred kettle," before later being directed exactly where to find and kill a bear.[95] At the age of fourteen, while very ill, a Shoshone Indian boy dreamed that a supernatural being, Nunumbi, appeared to him and told him to go west of Washakie, Utah, where he should sleep in a cave and where he would find a feather. He did so and located the feather.[96]

Among the Melanesian Tanna people, it is more generally and relevantly believed that dead ancestors can remind their living namesakes of the location of lost incantations or forgotten ritual procedures. In one more specific example, a man named Mak dreamed that his ancestor came to him in a dream and pointed out a spot where he should dig. Mak grabbed a spade, began digging, and found an important power stone.[97] Despite the cultural and geographical disparities, the similarities continue to impress. A Muslim diviner, Pa Abdul, in an initiatory experience was called into a sacred forest by his deceased father. He was sent off to sleep when he met a "fine white lady" offering a choice of multiple gifts. "Whenever something is hidden," Pa Abdul told her, "I was to know how to find it." This gift was duly granted.[98]

While the messenger varies, the fact that a third party is claimed to reveal the location of something hidden, often through a dream, is a worldwide and ongoing phenomenon. From another time and place, and in another Jewish tale, this time from Eastern Europe, a young man dreams of a "little man" who "told him that he would find a wrapped coin" under a certain mayor's window. He soon went and found it exactly there.[99] In an old folk prose from Athens, the then vizier told a man named Moda that he must dig the ground, plant certain seeds, and bring the vizier the fruits of his labors in a year. The man had no money or tools, however, and, having been traveling, eventually grew weary and fell asleep. He dreamed of an old man who claimed to be his "mother's blessing" and who told him to go ten paces in a certain direction until he saw a white slab at the foot of a mountain. "Raise this slab," the spirit says, "and under it thou wilt find tools, take them, and go about thy business." Moda awakens, finds the tools exactly where indicated, and sets to work.[100]

While such anonymous messengers turn up in these accounts, it seems that, more commonly, some traditionally known beings reveal the secret knowledge to the individual. Recalling traditions such as those of the Yucatan, for example, "Both dwarfs and fairies are also reported to have revealed to their favorites the places where the finest rock crystals could be found," wrote Guerber regarding Swiss traditions.[101] In a fairy tale from Nicea, *The Story of Little Mouk*, a dog tells Mouk in a dream that, using a certain stick, he could locate buried things. Using the stick, he later unearthed a hefty pot of gold.[102] Finally, the devil himself was once again the treasure seeker's guide in the ninth-century Irish romance *Scéla Cano meic Gartnáin*, in which he helped Aodhán mac Gahbráin locate a "hidden vat of treasure."[103]

TRINKETS AND BAUBLES AROUND THE GLOBE

As the Native American tales of the lost doll or the sacred kettles have shown us, by no means are the only "treasures" revealed in this manner of the monetary kind. In *Panther and Deer Woman*, an Upper Coquille Indian oral tale retrieved from Canada's boreal northern climes, one named Wildcat "dreams of the whereabouts of another named Panther's stolen pancreas, confirms the truth of his dream, and is sent to retrieve it."[104]

In a thousand-year-old Chinese tale, *The Widow and Her Son*, one Yao-Moi dreams of an old man in flowing white garments and gold embroidery. This man calls Yao-Moi by name and tells him how well he has lived his life, how he has looked after those he loves, and how he has never asked for too much. "Tomorrow morning," the spirit continued, "you must arise early and go to the East Mountain by the wilderness. There you will find many meats and nuts and seeds." That same morning, Yao-Moi went and found exactly what he had dreamed and precisely where indicated.[105]

From the previously referenced *Nihongi, The Chronicles of Japan*, we read of a man named Kumano no Takakuraji who dreamed that the deity Amaterasu no Oho-kami told him, "My sword, which is called Futsu no Mitama, I will now place in thy storehouse." The following morning, just as instructed, he went to his storehouse and found that there was indeed a sword on the plank floor.[106] In one of her visions, the famed folk hero and more familiar Catholic saint Joan of Arc was similarly told of a sword that lay in a certain tomb near the high altar of Saint Catherine's Church. The tomb was later opened, and the sword was duly found.[107]

Among the Papuan Gulf's Elema people is a story tells that of one Maikere, who loses an arrow while patrolling the beach with his brother Maikree. That night, Maikere dreams, "and is thereby enabled to find the spot next morning." They discover the arrow where the dream had told them.[108] Far more anciently, it is said that the Egyptian deity Horus, while at Hermopolis, dreamed that Thoth appeared to him and revealed the location of a magic book that was hidden in a chest inside a certain sealed chamber of the temple library, which Horus soon found exactly there.[109]

That dreams and visions that accurately describe the location of things might give rise to real-world effects are clear and speaks both to their impact upon the individual and to the extent to which the hagiographer or other author might therefore implement this similarly. The ancient convent named *Chrysobalanton*, meaning "golden purse," has an interesting and relevant origin. Irene of Chrysovalantou, a tenth-century abbess who died in Constantinople, once dreamed that she would find what she needed in a place near the Church of the Holy Apostles. There, she discovered the purse and named the monastery after it.[110]

Likewise, according to a history of the Middle Eastern Sharvan and Al-Bab regions in the tenth to eleventh centuries, a man named Muhammad built the town of Janza after dreaming for three consecutive nights "that a treasure was buried in the middle of one of the hills." He heard a voice say, "Ascend it and stop thy horse there; and where the horse has struck its foot, order to dig, then remove what is there and with the find, build a town and call it Janza [treasure]." He did so and found three kettles, one filled with dinars and the other with dirhams (currency), with which he founded the town.[111]

Regarding a then-modern Greek festival at Koroni, two related *ikons*, a Hellenistic terra-cotta figure and a bronze Greek weight from the third or fourth century, were said to have been found in an old cistern "as the result of the dream of an old woman in 1896."[112] It was similarly recorded that, in 1209, the relics of Mary Salome, a follower of Jesus who briefly turns up in canonical and noncanonical writings, were discovered "through a vision" seen by an unidentified man of the city of Veroli, Italy.[113]

While many a vision is attached to the life of the saint and his or her relics, the concerns of the messengers and the subjects of these dreams and visions, especially in more recent times, are often rather prosaic. An Irish woman told pioneering polymath Andrew Lang that, after walking in a wood near her house, she lost an important key of hers. Later, she dreamed that it was lying at the root of a very particular tree, where she found it the next day.[114]

THE END OF THE RAINBOW

Very clearly, tales of treasure, with all their room for lessons in vanity and greed, offer fertile soil for the magical or edifying tale. By no means, however, should this be confused with being the sole origin of such tales or of the belief that such things are possible. If anything, the extent to which the dream, visions, or other intimation in varying cultures was considered to have the capacity to reveal such things would have often been the reason they were implemented into the tales in the first place.

The riches that a person craves being revealed to him in a dream might seem like a most obvious literary device; indeed, the suggestion has been that in certain cases, the tale is very much of the allegorical kind, symbolizing one's search for oneself, one's own inner treasure, etc., and without doubt, diffusion has played a role in the dissemination of some of these tales. Those, however, are only a number of what are commonly rather forward, sober anecdotes, which, as it happens, are still being recorded entirely unconnected from those traditions. This would be well to remember.

SEVEN

I Knew the Cure

Sacred Healing, Other Worlds, and the Origins of Botanical Knowledge

> *During recent decades, academics developed a culture of disbelief regarding the supernatural. Psychologists and sociologists have insulated themselves from folk accounts and beliefs and therefore have failed to recognize the prevalence and universality of common forms of anomalous experience. They ignore the experiences that earlier scholars found significant.*
>
> JAMES MCCLENON

Numerous further areas could be explored in which the veridical dream or vision has borne fruit in the waking world—experiences that impart great value and give rise to tales, traditions, connections, creations, and beliefs. Many of those tales have featured the dead; we have heard some intimations of another world; here, however, our focus shifts to the attainment of a different kind of treasure and a more direct confrontation with that great beyond.

If health is wealth, then none of the bountiful boons from the previous chapter can compare to the tonics, healing, and aid that have been attained, as we'll see, by similar means. Such an experience might reveal the actual location of certain plants, roots, or herbs, the medicinal properties of which will cure the ailments of either the visionary themselves or another in need. At other times, one might be brought into the role of shaman or healer by means of such an event. Our contemporary visionaries and otherworld travelers too, during their near-death experiences or otherwise, might display strange healing of ills and ails. While anomalous experiences of this kind are myriad and each warrant their own more nuanced studies, here we are concerned with uniting a number of reports and tales from both relatively and, at times, particularly disparate sources under a certain umbrella, accounts that share a specific theme, that of veridical and seemingly invigorating contact with other worlds. This is what most strongly unites the accounts that follow.

ANCIENT HEALING AND THE GRACE OF THE GODS

It would be hard to overstate how seriously the general idea that healing might come from contact with other worlds and their inhabitants was taken in the ancient world, various places and times to follow, and presumably since dreams have been dreamed. Dream incubation, the specific attempt to dream toward certain purposes, can be found in relation to such healing among greatly unconnected cultures. Most famous in this regard are certainly the hundreds of Asclepian healing temples of the ancient Hellenistic and Roman worlds. Asclepius, the man after whom these temples were named, was said to have been a skilled doctor whose powers included the capacity to raise the dead. According to the tales, a snake licked his ears clean and taught him secret knowledge, later even pointing out a very specific herb Asclepius could make use of.[1] As will become apparent, the events surrounding the life of Asclepius are, in important ways, indistinguishable from traditions found across the globe regarding the attainment of such medicinal knowledge. These ideas were later to permeate the legends and folklore that would follow. Furthermore, the extent to which similar experiences are still reported might speak to a mysterious idea, a tradition involving the exchange of experience and knowledge between the individual and the beyond.

Returning for now, though, to those old temples where men and women, often for a price, would attempt to gain the favor of the gods to treat their ills of body and mind, we can read the inscription of one Marcus Iulius Apellas. He was advised by a god on a number of specific steps he should take to recover from his illness, including taking lemon rind and soaking it in water to rub on himself against a wall near the "place where supernatural voices are heard." The advice to use honey as a laxative was also offered. The man was soon restored to health.[2] The ancient Roman and Greek physician Galen, suffering from a potentially fatal abscess, dreamed at an Asclepian temple of opening an artery between his thumb and forefinger and letting it bleed out fully. He awakened, "knowing" this was the cure, and successfully performed the procedure.[3]

We could reference a dozen similar and often reproduced accounts related to the uniquely popular Asclepian cults: the blind man dreaming that Asclepius opened his eyes, another with crippled fingers having his hands restored, and so on.[4] Such dream incubations, however, specifically those attempted in order to attain healing, have been a long-standing practice as culturally distant from the Mediterranean as is Japan. Indeed, in those ancient times in Japan, it was the emperor alone who exercised this link with the supernatural world. He was the principal "dreamer," and incubation was an important part of his religious duties.[5] His palace, therefore, always comprised a special hall where such dreams could be solicited, equipped with an incubatory bed known as a *kamudoko*. More specifically, chapter 65 of the *Kojiki*, an early Japanese chronicle of myths, legends, oral traditions, and semi historical accounts written in 712 CE, states that the emperor Sujin, grieving that so many of his subjects had died in a terrible epidemic, lay down upon the kamudoko in the hope of learning through a dream the cause of the sickness. Sure enough, the god Ōmononushi, a Shinto deity associated with Mount Miwa in Sakura, appeared to him, speaking oracular words advising how the calamity might be averted.[6]

We could point to dozens of examples of similar incubations on the North American continent too. The Ojibway, for example, would use specific bathhouses to bring about healing dreams and to attain knowledge of healing from various deities.[7] Jackson Steward Lincoln, in fact, suggests that among North American Indians, the process of producing certain important kinds of dreams "is often similar to the ancient temple incubation" practiced in antiquity.[8] Similarly, in certain parts of the Indian state of Punjab, people suffering from snake bites are brought to the shrine of Guga, the snake god, where they will sleep, attain a vision, and hopefully receive a cure. The author here, too, makes a comparative reference in the footnotes to the Greek Asclepian shrines.[9]

In medieval Europe, cures were sought by the hundreds through fundamentally comparable kinds of invocation. A French woman was unable to move and prayed at the tomb of Benedict for his saintly intercession until he "appeared in a dream and cured her."[10] Despite the risks of generalizing, Kittredge noted how strongly one is "reminded of the ancient practice of incubation" in such cases. The author gives multiple examples, such as a maddened girl whose parents brought her to the tomb of Saint Oswin. After staying the night, she returned home cured.[11] The Church of Michael at Constantinople likewise became famous as a healing site after a ninth-century dream vision in which a candlemaker, Marcianus, met with the deceased Michael. This otherworldly man dipped his finger in oil and made the sign of the cross on Marcianus's forehead. Marcianus replicated this technique on an ill doctor who was "miraculously healed."[12]

People would attempt to attain healing from within and around the relics of these saints, where miracles were considered more likely to occur. An eleventh-century text tells of a German man named Henry who was told in a dream that he would be cured through the merits of Maximinus of Micy, a French saint associated with the bishopric of Orléans. Having followed later instructions from an "angelic vision," the saint himself appeared to the man and struck him on the legs, and he was no longer lame.[13]

Although less known outside the Islamic world, here, too, *Istikhāra* is commonly practiced, in which similar guidance during the day but often through dreams is sought and solicited, a practice that, according to several hadiths, was taught by Prophet Muhammad to his companions. Anthropologist Vincent Crapanzano, in fact, found that certain Moroccan Muslims will similarly attempt the "very important practice of visiting a saint's tomb, or some other sacred place, in order to have a dream."[14] Farther south, among the Temne of Sierra Leone, their healers also use divination in the name of their clients, constructing an amulet or writing a passage from the Qur'an with the client's name on paper and praying for the solution to the problem before the client sleeps with his head on the written sheet, the answer being revealed in his dreams.[15]

Such beliefs and practices persist. In a more recent Mexican account given by Shockey, a woman was given six months to live after cancer was discovered. No signs of remission occurred over the next few months of treatment, so, in desperation, she traveled to a certain church and wished, "Please heal me—or do your will with me." Soon after hearing buzzing and feeling heat, she was convinced she had been healed. This was apparently confirmed by a disbelieving doctor the following day.[16]

In its most basic sense, then, the idea that contact with or from the otherworld promotes healing is widespread and ongoing. This is a belief very clearly related to the anomalous experiences of the individual in which, often, there is contact with some higher power. It is to those individual experiences in their broader sense that we now turn.

GIFTS FROM THE GODS

The most ancient and renowned cults of Asclepius, in their tales of that figure and others, share similarities with distinct shamanic and other healing traditions. Like the experiences of Asclepius, spontaneous visions and dreams were our first and truly archaic technique of ecstasy. The vision or dream, of course, came before the incubated or otherwise visionary trials and adventures of the specialist. Worldwide, in fact, it is the spontaneous vision that commonly offers the call to shamanism or doctoring in the first place. In some cases, such as among certain Mayan doctors, this was the *only* path. None of them, as it happens, sought out a vision but were instead "chosen to learn by supernatural beings."[17]

Doctors in Disguise

Here we remember that Asclepius was given his secret knowledge of healing by a snake and even observed specific herbs that were to be used. The fact that such specialist and specific knowledge was imparted by a nonhuman or seemingly supernatural entity has been claimed far and wide and is plainly apparent in both the creation myths of numerous groups and the folktales of ordinary women and men. As far as one might imagine from Asclepius, we can read of a Northern Paiute woman who had dreams of her dead father urging her to become a shaman. A rattlesnake soon followed and "gave her the songs she sings when she is curing." Later, as a shaman, she "is told how to cure sick people in this way."[18]

Speaking broadly, the comparisons to Asclepius are no singular or flippant allusions: these are persistent stories; that the recipient then becomes a healer is similarly widespread. Deep in the past, the Ojibway Indians claim that the sacred Midewiwin bear appeared to their early ancestors and gave them knowledge of "several hundred kinds of medicine through a horned serpent."[19] "My grandmother," wrote Barbara Tedlock much later of her Mayan elder, "followed the bear path; she received many of her best remedies during dreams and waking visions in which she encountered a female bear who became her teacher."[20] More specifically, in this way, a Native American man from an unspecified Western tribe was severely wounded in battle, when he dreamed of a great white bear, who became his "guide and adviser" from that day on. The bear told him that if his friends were to kill a buffalo, extract its heart, and feed it to the man, he would be able to rise and walk. The next day, the man was able to go with them.[21]

Especially among South and many North American tribes, these beings are often understood as humans in animal form. An anecdote from Lady Gregory's collection in the west of Ireland has a surprisingly similar feel. A girl, out tending to cattle, has her dead mother appear to her "in the form of a sheep" and tell her exactly what herbs to find to cure her sick stepbrother.[22]

As with the prescriptions given by the gods in those ancient Asclepian temples, the instructions can also be rather strict and elaborate in the legends and lore. Returning to the Menominee, they have many similar tales. In one of those, a boy dreamed he had received a powerful medicine from an underground panther. He soon went to the shore, where the panther had promised to meet him. Apart from a white stone, one of the gifts he was offered was *pewisitcupa*, a black root. "Scrape a little from the stone and pulverize it with the root," the panther said, before continuing, "add some *manik* (Colorado root), and the three will make a powerful medicine." The medicine has since been known as one of the most powerful among those people.[23]

Boas gave us the tale of Nau'Kalakume, the Kwakiutl Indian, whose soul shrank to the size of a fly until he left his body. After his soul was returned, the beings responsible for this, apparently certain wolves, taught him to cure illness and rid others of disease.[24] A Chilean Mapuche candidate, Machi Tomasa, during her own shamanic training, dreamed that two mermaids, and in her own words now, "told me what herbs to use with my patients. [. . .] They named the herbs and they showed them to me."[25] The people of the Peruvian Quechua religion speak of the *auki*, a mountain spirit that their specialist diviners consult during their trances if someone falls ill, during which time "the cause and treatment of the malady are revealed."[26]

The Tukano medicine man of the Colombian Amazon, while imbibing his own sacred intoxicant, *yajé,* for sometimes months at a time, will see the radiant shapes of plants, vessels filled with medicinal potions, cups filled with draughts, and other things "all demonstrating how this or that disease might be cured." All the while, the voices of the deity Viho-mahse show them exactly which herbs to use for which poisons.[27]

Ancient Egyptian sorcerers, too, would attempt to learn in a dream which plant was best for which disease. A deity was then thought to appear in their sleep and was "supposed to indicate the plant specially attributed to him, as the one divinely destined to subdue the disease."[28] The very same was true as far away from the Amazon and Egypt as the Himalayas. There, as Tedlock wrote, in fact, "wherever healing is highly developed, shamans consult psychoactive plants—what are called 'traveling herbs' [. . .] to learn which ones are to be used as herbal remedies and which are to be taken to travel into alternate realities."[29]

Fairies and Dwarves

In a Turkish folktale, a farmer lowers a rope into a well and pulls out the "Padishah [Persian sovereign title] of Fairies." "In return for your kindness," the farmer was told, "I shall teach you something very useful. I shall tell you how to cure those who are sick and at the point of death."[30] An Irish folktale has some especially benevolent fairies too. A man whose back had been injured since childhood got lost or "stupefied" on his way home from a fair, when he had to sit down and fall asleep. When he awoke, a passage between two pillars had opened nearby, inside which was a large, vaulted room with hundreds of lamps and many strange small men and women with green and red coats. After he sings with them to their satisfaction, they cure his back, and he wakes up feeling "as if he had wings."[31]

Fairy beliefs and cults flourished in seventeenth-century Italy. The interactions of the fairies with the would-be healers may be notably similar to those of the traditional shamanic healer or medicine with his own deceased ancestors or gods. The 1630s in southern Italy had a wise woman who, tending to a patient, claimed that her "ladies," seemingly fairies, "had shown her how the sick woman was to be cured."[32]

An old Icelandic story about a man with an illness speaks of a dwarf, one of the last two in the country, who "had an ointment that could cure him of his infirmity."[33] He sets out, finds the dwarf, and is healed by the supernatural entity. Similarly, in another Irish legend, a young girl nursing a long-injured leg is cured after her mother has an encounter with a fairy. "Take this ointment," the tiny being said, "and rub it where you will see the purple mark, and I hope that your thoughts of me may be pleasant." The leg was quickly returned to health.[34]

Divine Assistance

From China, we hear how Chin Tsung, the third emperor of the T'ang dynasty, was afflicted with a grievous boil, which the imperial physicians could not cure. There was a Taoist priest at Tai San called Yen He, who declared that the goddess of the mountain had appeared to him in a dream and directed him to go to the capital and cure this boil, revealing to him exactly how to proceed. The priest soon prescribed the treatment, and the boil was cured.[35]

According to a 1531 Latin American folktale, a man named Juan Diego set out for Tlatelolco to fetch a priest for his ailing uncle. On his way, he came upon the "Lady of Guadalupe," the Virgin herself, who told him not to be troubled and that Juan should "know that he is already cured." According to the tale, "his uncle became well at that moment, as was later learned."[36] Similarly, according to the fifteenth-century *Hasadera Reigenki*, one of Emperor Montoku's sons, Seiwa, fell ill. In one of his dreams at the Hasadera Temple in the city of Kamakura, one Fujiwara no Iemune dreams of seven beings calling themselves the "tutelary deities" of the mountain upon which the temple was built. They handed Iemune some medicine wrapped in paper, within which the man found a mysterious white powder. They instructed him to heal Seiwa with it. Iemune later found the time of the dream corresponded with the very moment Seiwa was observed to have become strangely fragrant at the mouth, as if he had drunk sweet dew and "completely recovered."[37]

In antiquity, Plutarch wrote of Pericles, who was of the tribe Acamantis and was a Greek politician and general during the Golden Age of Athens (480–404 BCE). Amid the construction of an acropolis, one of its chief architects, the best among them, fell from a great height and lay in a "miserable condition, the physicians having no hope of his recovery." Pericles, while much aggrieved, dreams that the Roman goddess Minerva appears to him and orders a very particular course of treatment, which he quickly applies. In just a short time, the man was cured. This vision was the reason for the subsequent construction of a brass statue in Minerva's honor.[38]

Servilius Damocrates, a Greek physician in Rome in the middle to late first century CE is said to have discovered the flowering plant, candytuft. According to Servilius himself, however, he ascribed the discovery "to an imaginary person."[39] Of great age, too, was an incident in Homer's *Odyssey* in which Hermes bestowed a drug called *moly* upon Odysseus, the legendary Greek king of Ithaca. While he is on his way to free comrades who had been turned to swine by the goddess Circe, Hermes appears to him and offers the moly as an antidote to Circe's own magic drug.[40]

Like the Pajé of the vast Amazon or the shaman of the snow-capped Himalayas, in fact, the ancient Greeks and Romans ascribed the discovery of a number of botanical cures to the gods. Among numerous other examples, the discovery of the herb *Heracleum* was attributed to Hercules; the discovery of the herb *Opopanax chironium* was likewise attributed to Chiron; and the discovery of the shrub *Parthenium* was said to have been made by Hermes.[41] The pagan Zosimus, a Greek historian who lived in Constantinople, describes something similar related to the discovery of *seculum*, an "excellent remedy for the plague, consumption and other diseases." He tells us of Valesius, who, after his children fell ill, consulted both physicians and soothsayers to no avail. Begging for the help of the virgin goddess Vesta, he heard a voice that gave the instructions, "To carry the children to Tarentum, and there to warm some Tiber water over the fire of Pluto and Proserpine, and to give it to the children to drink." This, however, caused him despondence, as Tiber was so far off, although, hearing the voice again, he obeyed the command. After carrying out the task, his children drank the concoction, fell asleep, and were "perfectly cured."[42]

Healing Dreams

That some benevolent messenger from another world instructs the visionary regarding otherwise occult medicinal knowledge is truly, then, an old idea and an idea by no means particular to shamanic and related traditions. Whether induced amid the sleepers of the old temples or by the doctor in the depths of the jungle using some psychoactive brew, whether attained spontaneously after a fall such as that of Pericles or during an otherwise dangerous episode that might call a tribesman to the medicinal or mystical path, something patently perennial seems to lie at the core. While neither Odysseus nor especially Servilius or Pericles were medicine men and neither were they soothsayers nor shamans, such experiences, as we have seen in many cultures, would most certainly have qualified them at least as being such a candidate. Furthermore, the encounters themselves are, in some archetypal ways, either indistinguishable from or share a majority of similarities with certain episodes among the widely separated folktales that were later to follow. In those tales, too, some of which will be presently described, we can detect the basic thematic similarities.

Things of this kind are still recorded and range from examples in which the visionary actively helps the supplicant to those in which they simply become aware of the healing of another. Guiley gave the case of psychotherapist Carol Warner, who dreamed of a patient named Tina, whom she knew to have been given three months to live with ovarian cancer. A religious woman and setting intention for prayer, Warner dreamed of being alongside the Virgin Mary and sending luminous globes into what she somehow "knew" were Tina's ovaries. Warner awoke and simply "knew with the most inexplicable and profound certainty that she had just witnessed Tina's complete healing." Tina's doctor was later "astonished to find no trace of the cancerous lesions." Carol ascribed the healing to her Virgin Mary.[43]

Relayed in 1901 was the case of a Chicago journalist who was affected by an aneurysm of the popliteal artery, for which he was under the care of two eminent surgeons. About two days before the appointed surgery, the wife of the patient dreamed that a change had taken place in the disease, in consequence of which the operation would not be required. On examining the tumor in the morning, the practitioner was astonished to find that the pulsation had entirely ceased, and, in short, this turned out to be a spontaneous cure.[44]

A Scottish woman, having come down with a mysterious skin disease that went on for some time, dreamed that an "angel" came to see her and told her that the problem was coming from inside her. The angel encourages us to think of certain happy memories while she "peeled away all the itching skin." The woman attributes the sudden and protracted improvement of her skin condition to this encounter. "It needed intervention," the woman concluded, "from somewhere completely different to show me the way towards recovery."[45] Noted American sculptor Richard Hunt had an aunt who was cured of a "blockage" when "she saw something like an angel come down and take something away from her."[46]

Speculatively speaking, if at least some of these experiences qualify as actual contact from other worlds toward the benefit of mankind, then we might reasonably assume less need for such contact over time as it pertains to the more specific cures and remedies and therefore a lesser volume of accounts. This, one would imagine, would be particularly apparent regarding traditional groups among whom Western drugs had been introduced. With that said, certain of the like are seemingly still reported. Margot Grey, for example, gave the case of a leukemia patient who, during his near-death experience, reported communication with a being who told him to "heat the body up to kill the germ, then cool the body off to get rid of it" and that they were to disseminate this information in the world.[47]

Continuing this line of thought, it would seem to follow that the majority of modern examples would involve the individual being informed they were ill rather than being given more particular instructions regarding the cure or its location. The author of *Healing Dreams*, Marc Barasch, dreamed so consistently and so vividly of the likes of iron pots being held under his neck, being chased by an axe murderer who wanted to behead him, tribesmen sticking needles into his "neck-brain," a bullet lodged in his neck, and so on, that he visited the doctor. A malignant tumor was soon found in his thyroid. Barasch noted a "twinge of vindication" regarding the seeming truth of his dream in light of his doctor's initial skepticism.[48]

Of great similarity and much better known, actor Mark Ruffalo said that while working on the set in 2000, "I had a dream that I had a brain tumor, and it was like no other dream that I'd ever had." Having told his set doctor and receiving a disbelieving reply, a tumor the size of a golf ball was nonetheless discovered behind his left ear, with Ruffalo himself later saying, "I knew it."[49]

THE DEAD, HEALING, AND SONG

Healing Wisdom from the Dead

Returning to the lore, Kamanga, a Central African Azande man, told Evans-Pritchard that when on an expedition to learn the medicines of witchdoctors, he himself being in training, "ghosts would come and show them the plants for which they were looking."[50] Farther distant, among the Tikopia of Melanesia, a medium there described how, regarding the curing of his patients, "My ancestor entered from the realm of spirits, flew into me to deal with the sick person."[51] Much removed, in an old Palestinian tale, a father who had taught his son the ways of medicine was speaking with him on his deathbed and told him that in the future, after he died, he would be beside his son, aiding in his work, but that only the son would be able to see him.[52]

Once more, then, it is not only more general otherworldly or supernatural entities imparting healing and related knowledge, but the dead themselves. Just as we have seen the dead relay news of who is coming or information regarding the location of missing items, here, too, they offer similar aid. The *pajé*, or shaman, of the Brazilian Parintintin would, during healing ceremonies, specifically summon various such spirits to "blow on the sick person and sing over him or her."[53] Likewise, a fasting Ojibway will dream of a dead person who tells him, "I will give you power to make this bone of mine into medicine."[54]

More pointedly, among the Santal ethnic group of the Indian subcontinent, a Norwegian missionary, linguist, and folklorist, Paul Olaf Bodding, rather incidentally recorded a relevant account. A man dreamed that a dead relative told him how to cure *puni*, atrophy in babies, through the consumption of hummingbird eggs. "This is just mentioned," wrote Bodding, "because it may be of some psychological interest."[55]

The extent to which the dead are involved varies between groups and individuals alike. Among various Thai groups, however, it is almost always a "benevolent spirit" who offers secret remedies and medicines. This is so ingrained that they have a term, *yaa phu book*, which means "medicine revealed by a spirit."[56] From among the Chilean Araucanians, too, Hilger notes that "Health restorative knowledge has its origin in dreams." One informant told her, "I had hiccoughed for 40 years. Then, one night in a dream my dead aunt told me to find the plant chanchan. I found it. I squeezed the juice of it through a cloth into water as cool as it came from the spring, and I drank it. That ended my hiccoughs."[57]

Returning to the work of anthropologist and ethnologist Craighill Handy, an authority on Pacific religions, he noted how commonly the native people he worked with received messages from both departed ancestors and unrecognized others. Handy wrote of a friend of his, a native of Hawaii, who, after taking a remedy advised to him in a dream by an "unknown man arrayed in a native dress" was "cured of an illness."[58]

A Korean folktale has the dead performing the same duties. Set around five hundred years ago, the father of a girl called Sim Chung was going blind. In a dream, her dead mother tells her the means by which she could restore his sight.[59]

Saints Bring Healing

The reader by now may not be surprised to find that those very particular otherworldly prescriptions we have seen both in antiquity and from the Americas also turn up in the lives of the saints. Theodore, a seventh-century Cypriot suffering from paralysis, had a visit from Saints Cyrus and John. They prescribed him an ointment made of roasted pig lungs mixed with wine before revealing the cause of his illness.[60]

While tales of such miracles involving the interaction of the common person with long-dead saints are easy enough to find and are variously explained, in our broader context we can see what seems to be another guise under which these far more ancient and widespread ideas regarding the nature of contact between the living and the dead seem to manifest and persist. In a legend attached to Saint Francis and immortalized in a piece of artwork by Italian painter and architect Giotto di Bondone, Francis appears to a man who had been gravely wounded by robbers, attended by two angels, and heals him.[61] According to the Christian writer Sophronius of Jerusalem (c560–638), an Alexandrian paraplegic named Theophilos is visited by two saints in a dream and told to go to the harbor, offer coins to some fishermen, and make sure to buy their next catch, sight unseen. Doing as he is bid, the man sees them haul up a small box, and he finds a bronze statuette with nails driven into its hand. This, as it happens, was a voodoo doll from which a nail was removed in order to cure Theophilos's limb.[62]

In certain examples, the old folk traditions and the later or otherwise dominant religious traditions are clearly intertwined. Like a medicine man, a woman from Sarajevo called Sadeta, who was an Islamic Bosnian healer, was "called" to the practice of healing in her dreams. She is visited by a dead *shadid*, or martyr, who tells her that she is to become a healer and use her skills to help people.[63] This cross-pollination is strongly apparent in certain groups, such as, and returning to, the Yucatan Maya. Kunow noted of their curers that "whether deities are Maya, Catholic, or some combination thereof [. . .] they intercede with the supernaturals on behalf of patients and seek their guidance in the selection and location of suitable medicines."[64] These chosen healers, then, were in touch with other realms and accessed those realms, often to attain otherworldly assistance in healing others. Commonly, he or she might be given special music, tools, or even songs toward this end.

Such tales are more common than could reasonably be, or indeed, need to be represented here, although some indications are offered. Among the California Yuroks, for example, their doctors might use an *U-pahsoi*, a form of "curing by recital."[65] These are old ideas. Just as, for example, among the Navajo Indians, a medicine man might similarly sing over an injured patient and the patient might proclaim, "I got well again,"[66] it was said of Greek philosopher and polymath Pythagoras, a man who, according to the philosopher Empedocles, "knew countless things," that when his friends were unwell, he comforted some "with incantations and magic spells, others with music." He was said by the Greek philosopher Diogenes to have "had songs that were remedial even for bodily illnesses."[67]

Once more, the dead themselves *continue* to bring these messages. Lynn Geosits had a visit from her dead uncle in which he told her to eat fish. When she later developed a tremor that arose from a lack of protein and iodine, having ignored the advice, she switched to fish and the tremor cleared up.[68] A link between these disparate traditions and this reality seems a reasonable one, which may be relevant in certain cases.

FOLKLORE, AILMENTS, AND THE TRUTH OF THE TALES

Locations Revealed

Recalling the previous chapter, and as we have seen to some extent, the actual location of certain remedies and cures is often described in these similarly veridical experiences.

The companion of Wolf-Man, a Pawnee Indian man, once asked him how he had so much endurance. Wolf-Man responded that he used a certain powder from a root, which he then offered him to try. The companion, having taken up the offer, felt "as though it were morning and he had not been traveling all day." Amazed, he wondered who or what gave him this root. Wolf-Man told him of a dream in which a horse brought him and showed him the location of the root, which he dug up and tasted. The next day, he went out and found the root there, and it tasted the same.[69]

Now from the Philippines, in Visayas, a woman dreams that her husband is dangerously ill and that only a certain plant can cure him. She collected said plants, went and found him, just as in the dream, and cured him.[70] The same was true in Indonesia during an experience in which an unspecified elderly man appeared to one Rohanna Ler in a dream and told her to apply a certain stone to her son's eyes. She woke up with the stone and used it to successfully treat him.[71]

During soul travel induced by the consumption of *Datura*, the Quechua man of the Ecuadorian jungle, while a woman guards his body, is similarly shown "secret plants with curing properties, and also where soul stones containing ancient Runa souls are hidden in the forest floor or in the bases of trees."[72] Among many Maya doctors of the Yucatan, beings called *balam* (fairy-esque supernatural beings) would point out in dreams the locations of crystals that could be used to heal others—the doctors' personal crystals, which would from then onward be a link between themselves and the other world. Recalling the fairies of Switzerland, who would point out the location of rock crystals, when Marianna Kunow asked a Mayan doctor where he got his crystals, some glassy and others "like onyx," he replied simply, "where they told me to look, that's where I found them."[73] Likewise, among the Chorote of Argentina and Paraguay, the botanical utility of their own bitter manioc root was revealed to the Indians by Thlamé, a denizen of the underworld. He instructed a shaman to fetch it from certain people living to the east, and thus it was that the Chorote learned how to make use of this plant.[74]

According to the entirely unconnected *Acts of Sylvester*, a series of legendary tales related to that fourth-century bishop of Rome,

Constantine the Great, while afflicted with leprosy, dreamed of Peter and Paul. They advised him as to the exact location of Sylvester and that he could further reveal the location of a pond where he could be cured, all of which came to pass after the dreamer took action.[75]

According to Gallo-Roman historian and bishop Gregory of Tours (538–594 CE), an unnamed man appeared to another blind man in a dream. "If you want to be cured," the stranger said, "go and prostrate yourself in prayer in front of the altar of the basilica of St. Nicetius, and there you will receive your sight." The man is said to have been restored.[76]

A thirteenth-century Cistercian legend has a priest, Adam, of the monastery of Lucka in Germany, breaking out in "dreadful sores" for which he could find no remedy. One night, during prayer, he noticed a bright light in the church and saw before him seven beautiful ladies, one of whom identified herself as "the mother of Christ." "Gather some fruit of the sloe tree," she tells Adam, "and get your head washed with the juice of it three times before the Mass in the name of the Father, of the Son, and of the Holy Ghost." Adam tells another woman of the experience who gathers some of the fruit marked out, and his head, being washed with it, "was immediately cured."[77] Similarly, when the husband of the Iroquois Sky God, Aataentsic, became sick, he dreamed it necessary to cut down a certain tree from which "those who abode in Heaven obtained their food; and that as soon as he ate of the fruit, he would be immediately healed."[78]

This idea, so common in the legends and lore, that the location of a particular remedy might be magically revealed crops up in Apuleius's great Greco-Roman literary work, the *Metamorphoses*. Here, the goddess Isis reveals in a dream to a certain priest that a particular rose would cure a young man who had been transformed into a beast, further telling where it might be found. The man regains his human form upon its later discovery and consumption.[79]

After defeating the Indian Brahmins in the fourth century BCE, the Macedonians were horrified to find that the Indians' arrows were tipped with poison. One of Alexander the Great's closest friends,

Ptolemy, was himself afflicted. According to Curtius, Alexander, who refused to leave his friend's side, "saw" in a dream that "the plant would cure the poison."[80] His soldiers located the referenced plant, administered it, and cured Ptolemy in this way.

While it could be argued that perhaps the cure was already known among the Indians, whose doctors would have specialized in snake-bite wounds, and the dream later added, here we are just as interested in why this would be the manner in which the discovery was said to have been made. While the goal of linking Alexander to the god Asclepius seems as forthcoming a reason as any other, such tales take on new meaning in the wider context of these worldwide tales.

In Persia, the medicinal use of roses is common and stretches back as far as anything that is known about that flowering plant itself. It is said that in distant times, Milto, a maid, had a tumor on her chin which threatened her beauty. The goddess Venus appeared to her and "bade her apply roses from her altar to the swelling," the cure being entirely effective.[81]

According to an old Austrian folktale, the eldest of a certain king's three sons, Ludvig, went to check on his ailing father. "A white figure appeared to me in a dream," were the king's words, "and told me that I should not get better until I had eaten a fruit out of the accursed garden."[82] Another truly archaic example of this kind is recorded from the ancient Near East, in which an unspecified "apparition" appears to the wife of Khamuas, son of Ramesses II, and offers such information, telling her that she should recover a certain plant from a particular spot and make medicine from it. The remedy proved entirely effective.[83]

In "Three Brothers and the Hand of Fate," another Turkish tale, it is once again a supernatural entity who provides the information, in this case, a magical jinn. In this tale, the jinn tells one Keloglan, in reference to the incurable blindness of a certain prince, that only he knows the cure and that on the edge of a certain village "there is a stunted poplar tree whose leaves hold a powerful medicine. If the prince's eyes were rubbed with leaves from that polar tree, he would see as clearly as a mirror." The man Keloglan finds this poplar tree, and as the jinn had told him, the prince's sight gradually returned following its application.[84]

TALKING PLANTS AND THE MYSTERIOUS ORIGINS OF BOTANICAL KNOWLEDGE

Even upon a relatively cursory examination, it seems, just as with our accounts of strangely revealed trinkets and treasures, the idea that the location of a remedy, or the means by which such a cure might be concocted or applied, can be variously and "supernaturally" made known to the receptive individual is a ubiquitous one. However ideas surrounding such phenomena might evolve, this fundamental notion is represented from the most ancient Near Eastern and Greco-Roman literary works to the shamans of the rainforests and tundra, and furthermore, widely among the lives of the saints and the folktales and fairy tales of all parts. Even in light of their variety, the means, messages, and messengers, too, share surprising similarities.

Plants Impart Wisdom
One of the more interesting and widespread claims we have seen is that the individual's skills were taught to them by the gods, the dead, animals, the dead masquerading as animals, and certain other supernatural beings. Of great interest, too, is that the plants themselves are said to have imparted this knowledge to the individual who finds themselves in a suitably altered state. This refrain is either expressed generally or is plainly apparent in some legendary tale and seems to make perfect sense, even conceptually, when one considers how commonly psychedelic brews are used to attain clairvoyant information. This is to say, the flora themselves. However, even before such attempts and experiments were made at some distant point in the past, the tales also tell that the plant might, in fact, "make the first move."

Among the Algonquian-speaking Maliseet Indians living on the Saint John River, at a time when great disease came, one man dreamed of a stranger who told him his name was Ke-whis-a-wask. This was no ordinary man, but a human figure representing a particular root, and his features even "looked like what this root is." The location of the root was revealed in this way, and after drinking with it, "they grew better and were soon all healed."[85] Coming to the Eastern Cree too, who are "expert botanists and even recognize many obscure plants" and the curative properties with which they are "well conversant," we find something alike. A Cree man dreams of a woman in a black dress trimmed with downy feathers. She held in her left hand a clamshell and in her right a powdered root. Singing a song, she said, "When you are doctoring a sick person sing this song, hold the shell and the dust of the root; drop it into the shell; when you have finished singing give it to the patient and he will become well." Interestingly, it is said that the woman from whom he learned these songs "was none other than the root itself" and that this man became a great medicine man.[86]

The Pawnee, also, whose mythology could be excavated for many similar stories, speak of a great flood, after which the "Big-Black-Meteoric-Star" god comes to a man in a vision and "told him where to find the roots" to be used medicinally. The roots are explained as literally being the remains of the giant people who lived on the earth before the flood. Later, while singing, the man speaks directly to the plants as he removes them from the earth, saying, "I thank you. I am to remove you, so that you may remain in the medicine-man's bundle, and I am to use you for the sick."[87]

The Cherokee of Oklahoma say that when a doctor is unsure about how to proceed with their patient, "the spirit of the appropriate plant will suggest the proper remedy in a dream."[88] In Oregon, some of the doctors of the Coos Indians dreamed of a tree that, appearing as a person, "brought knowledge of medicines."[89] Something of this kind among the Ojibway is related to the origins of corn. In this case, however, the knowledge was very specifically sought out. An Ojibway boy had reached the age when he would attempt to attain a guardian spirit. Retreating to a special lodge, this young man had something very particular in mind: he wished to know how plants grew and learn about their properties in order to help his family and others. On the third day, becoming weak and almost fainting from fasting, he encounters a being claiming to have been sent by the "Great Spirit." This being seems eventually to identify themselves as the actual corn, stating, "You will strip off my garments and throw me down, clean the earth of roots and weeds, make it soft, and bury me in the earth" and some further skills regarding its upkeep. The young man carefully carried out the instructions over the course of the spring until green plumes came through the ground. The appearance of the corn was idiosyncratically akin to the spirit he encountered, and henceforth came the knowledge of corn.[90]

As distant as Thailand, there are similar legends relating to the origin of the mango fruit. A Thai boy from the "early days" fell ill and dreamed of a "god's voice" telling him that in the mountains of northeastern India, there grew a tree that bore the fruit that would cure him. The tree was later found, and its fruit was used in this manner.[91]

Just twenty-three years ago, social anthropologist and ethnographer Henry Sharp wrote of Phil, a troubled Athabaskan-speaking man of the boreal and arctic Canadian Dene people. Sharp notes that most of their men must first dream of plants before they could heal with them; Phil was different. "As Phil walks through the world," Sharp explained, "the plants sing out to him even through the snows of winter, telling him their locations and their uses."[92] Such things were known as far from there as Turkey, where a folktale tells that, upon ingestion of a certain brew, one may "understand the language of plants," stipulating, however, that it is the plants themselves who "know" the illnesses they can respectively cure.[93] A folktale from among the Aimol of Manipur, in northeast India, has God coming to the king, Selek, and telling him to look at a certain spot on the ground, where in the morning he himself, God, would be growing there in the form of a magical plant. Selek found the plants where described and used them to cure disease.[94]

Ethnomusicologist and anthropologist Marina Roseman made an observation among the Malayan Temiar people that is highly relevant here. For them, plants had souls that could appear visible to mediums "during trance in the shape of humanoid mannikins." During these visionary experiences, the plant entities themselves, according to the Temiar, "indicate their 'homes' [e.g., a particular plant or animal species], thereby making their origins known to the dreamer despite their generalized form."[95] It follows, of course, that such trances could also be of the spontaneous kind. Of the fifty related dream narratives Marina Roseman collected among the Malaysian Temiar "30 percent came from plants." In this case, they were those the dreamer had previously tended.[96]

For our own contribution, an informant told us that while staying among the Melanesian Fijians, she was taken on a walk by certain "healing women" who showed her plants and described their healing properties. When the informant asked the women how they had such wide knowledge, "they looked at her like something was wrong with her." "The plants tells us," was the simple and seemingly disbelieving reply.

One can see the dramatic, compelling, and utilitarian nature of such narratives, memorates, and myths. The plants themselves, of *course*, one might argue, are not literal spirits but are later represented in this way in the tales in deference to their contribution. This, however, ignores how commonly the visionaries themselves suggest that literal communication with plants is possible in altered states. Schultes and Raffauf found, for example, that certain medicine men of the Colombian Sibundoy Valley had an "unusually extensive knowledge of medicinal and toxic plants." Salvador Chindoy, one of their most renowned doctors, insisted that his knowledge of the medicinal value of plants "has been taught to him by the plants themselves through the hallucinations he has experienced in his long lifetime as a medicine man."[97]

TRIAL AND ERROR, COINCIDENCE AND CURARE

The broad ascription of coincidence or trial and error to the attainment of either actual medicine or knowledge regarding its preparation or location is a tempting one, and certainly one with some reasonable precedent. In the case of inventions such as *curare*, a muscle relaxant developed deep in the Amazon and later used as a general anesthetic, it may not be so simple. As experimental psychologist and former professor of psychology at the Hebrew University of Jerusalem Benny Shanon noted, while this may well account for certain processes, "at another level it is a euphemism disguising the fact that we actually have very little idea of how Indian people come up with their insights."[98]

By no means do we suggest that trial and error, human observation, and intellect are not often a reasonable explanation. We might easily, in fact, furnish such examples. Our opening and archetypal doctor, Asclepius himself, observed, in one version, the passing of an herb from one snake to another and learned his skills in this way. An Ojibway woman in Ontario, too, well known for her skills as a midwife, told of how she discovered one of the medicines she used, seemingly some form of analgesic or anesthetic. She noticed where a moose had chewed the bark off a tree. Her husband told her that the moose seemed to be doing this in order not to feel pain and that it was "nature's ways of healing animals." This gave her the idea to begin using it on human patients.[99]

In other words, even where there has been a reasonable suggestion that humans observing animal behavior around plants to learn their properties informed the myths and explains why, in so many of them, it is an animal who offers this knowledge, there is often no mention of the altered states that have first been induced in many of the myths. This important distinction is spoken to strongly among the likes of the Northern Shoshone Indians. Some of their specialists acquired their knowledge of herbs not just by one or the other means, but both by "experience *or* through dreams" [emphasis added].[100]

In other cases, the anthropologist or ethnologist, particularly those of the first half of the twentieth century, will simply ignore the claims made. Frances Densmore, for example, noted that the Chippewa Indians "say that they received this knowledge in dreams," continuing skeptically, however, to say, "but the response of the physical organisms was the test of the plant as a remedy." The two, of course, are by no means mutually exclusive. Doubtlessly, such dream references could be a mythologization of the brain's capacity to retain information during sleep; however, the distinction is important all the same. To assume, for example, that all dreams of animals were contrived tales related to the observation of literal animals toward medicinal ends ignores a significant number of accounts, particularly because in the previous case (Chippewa), the dreamers are not shamans but something closer to general practitioners. They, therefore, do not attain their powers from dream animals, spirits, or deceased persons at all. More specifically, among these people, fairies, jinn, or even dwarfs might come in dreams, generally during childhood, and "prescribe equipment, behavior, including taboos, and songs which were his most potent instrument."[101]

Indeed, among some groups, these distinctions are drawn rather sharply. Consider the boreal Canadian Dene, among whom the animal has a dual existence as both a natural and supernatural being. They encounter the supernatural aspect during dreams and visions, as opposed to the literal animal. This dichotomy, in fact, "dominates traditional Dene thought, experience, and interaction with animals."[102] Pliny himself, as we have seen, while justifiably and even with open reverence describing the hard work, passion, and dedication of man in gradually understanding the properties of plants, also gave some mention of dreams for their ostensible part.

To question the nature of curare's origins, however, and the many examples like it, is by no means to question the intellect of the medicine man or other Indigenous individuals in that way; it is, in fact, to listen to their own words and claims. As Canadian anthropologist Jeremy Narby noted, having lived among the South American Tukano, "When one asks these people about the invention of curare, they almost invariably answer that it has a mythical origin" and that "the creator of the universe invented curare and gave it to them." Narby further noted that "innumerable other tribes claim their botanical knowledge derived from plant-induced hallucinations."[103] These people, in other words, are very clear that it was during altered states of consciousness that they claimed to have communicated quite literally with the plants as opposed to later anthropomorphizing or mythologization of the plant. Narby opines the extent to which the credit for such discoveries is not rightfully attributed to those Amazonians. "According to the usual theory," he wrote, "Indians stumbled on nature's useful molecules by chance experimentation. In the case of curare, this explanation seems improbable." Narby goes on to explain the complexities, noting that to produce it, "it is necessary to combine several plants and boil them for seventy-two hours, while avoiding the fragrant but mortal vapors emitted by the broth. The final product is a paste that is inactive unless injected under the skin. If swallowed, it has no effect. It is difficult to see how anybody could have stumbled on this recipe by chance experimentation."[104]

Swiss medical historian Henry Sigerist noted the same long before in his illuminating study *Primitive Medicine*. "We should remember," he reminds the reader, "that we owe many effective drugs to primitive and folk medicine, such as *opium, coa, cinchonaa, ephedrine, caffeine, cascara sagrada, chaulmoogra, digitalis, ipecacuancha, podphyllum, pyrethrum*, and *squill*, to mention only a few."[105] Appeals to incredulity, of course, rarely fly; however, their initial usefulness is often overlooked, and the broader context in which they might arise, such as our own collection of tales, must be remembered in as much as they might bolster the validity of such appeals.

Many more examples of complex concoctions could be furnished. A Brazilian tribe of the Waiká language group, for example, had to be similarly careful in preparing the psychoactive *Virola*. The outer bark of a tree is removed, and the inner bark is then stripped into a number of 50 x 5 cm pieces before they are heated. This releases a red sap, which is mixed with the ash of another tree (*Caesalpiniaceae*) and the dried leaves of another herb (*Acanthaceae*). The shaman then kneads the three between his legs, toasts the mixture, grinds it to a powder, and stores it carefully on a palm leaf for use the next day. Even with careful and successful adherence, the resulting snuff can kill a shaman. Not that the explanation is wrong, but authors such as Balick seemingly attribute this to trial and error without any relevant testimony.[106]

PLACEBO, HEALING NEAR DEATH, AND THE OTHERWORLD

However romantically and in whatever guise the legend or folktale might speak, particularly as they arise around the important man's life, the fundamental idea that nonhuman or discarnate entities might impart healing or related secret knowledge is the wide river into which those tributaries all seem to flow: that contact with an invigorating otherworld may promote physical and mental healing. The visionary, attempting to shamanize with their fasting and other techniques of ecstasy, pursues altered states and seeks to enter a covenant with the dead and other forces to attain their power for the good of the community. The medieval man or woman might encounter the saintly martyr and receive his or her aid in this manner, and, as we have seen, similar encounters and similar effects are reported on an ongoing basis.

Health Near Death

Considering how widespread we have found contact with the otherworld and with its inhabitants as healing to be, a further note should be offered here in reference to those who have and who still make contact with those realms, those who undergo, for example, a near-death experience (NDE). During a 1907 NDE, White Bull, a Sioux Indian warrior, leaves his body and meets a man in white and four others. The skull of a buffalo emerges from the ground and tells him, "Observe what I eat: I eat these. They make me strong. These four roots I eat. Do likewise." After he and the five men located those roots during the experience, the chief sent his wife to find them in the real world after describing them to her. "She found them. He ate them, and he was cured."[107]

A legend attached to El Santuario de Chimayo chapel in New

Mexico seems to speak to something similar. Bernardo Abeyta, the region's landowner, was apparently "divinely cured when perilously near death." In one version, as he was close to dying, his wife prayed and saw a vision. This vision "bade her take the dirt from this spot to her husband. [. . .] Obeying, she saw Don Abeyta rise from his death bed completely cured."[108]

Just as the shaman might attain the capacity to heal from other worlds, so too, the suggestion seems to be, do those who themselves still come close to or fully experience death. "A significant number of NDErs," wrote American psychologist Kenneth Ring, "do seem to develop healing gifts of one sort or another following their experiences."[109]

The shaman becomes a healer by myriad means, one of which is an encounter with death, whether induced or spontaneous. Relatedly, humanistic psychologist and founder of the International Association for Near-Death Studies, Margot Grey, like Ring, noted in her work on British near-death experiences that the "gift of healing" seems to be a "spectacular manifestation" bestowed upon experiencers.[110] In one of Grey's accounts, a patient with leukemia meets an old man radiating light whom he seems to interpret as Jesus but leaves room for other possibilities. The man tells him "the germ is gone," which the individual notes meant to him, "I no longer have leukemia." Despite having been given two years to live prior to the experience, at the time of the sample, there had been no recurrence of the cancer for six years.[111]

Some of these comparisons are rather striking. The shaman is commonly supposed to have the ability to literally look at or otherwise "see" inside the body of another while in a trance in order to diagnose illness. Among the !Kung, for example, who live mostly at the edge of the Kalahari Desert, their most advanced healers, "can see illness or fetuses inside the body."[112] As relayed by Ring, a near-death experiencer relates that she had similarly learned how to "scan" a body for aberrant energy patterns.[113] These are not uncommon refrains among near-death experiencers. In 1974, Hans Holzer spoke to the "most illusive of all California mediums," Bill Corrado, with whom he was very impressed and who claimed related skills. Corrado told Holzer he can "tell people what their illnesses are" and "where they are" before sending them to a medical doctor to "have it verified and treated."[114]

Coming back to the healed rather than the healers, though, British neuropsychologist and neuropsychiatrist Peter Fenwick wrote that some people from his own samples "describe a more dramatic and more permanent effect. For them, the NDE brought a resolution to their illness, which usually seems to have been quite unexpected and caused doctors and relatives some surprise."[115] Rivas, Dirven, and Smit presented a number of cases from across the literature, noting that in those examples, "a materialistic explanation involving a 'spontaneous remission' of some kind—an entirely natural, spontaneous cure—seems utterly implausible, at least according to people medically qualified to determine such things."[116]

Radiation oncologist Jeffrey Long spoke of Geralyn, whose Burkitt's lymphoma, after she was given a mere 1 percent chance of survival, simply disappeared after a near-death experience. Having died in the hospital, Geralyn rose from her body, observed her doctors and family, and continued to rise until she was "within something that resembled a cloud." Feeling the "total embrace of love," she met three beings before being sent back. "I knew I was healed," she wrote. The doctors were apparently "awestruck to find that after only one chemo treatment, the tumors were gone." Long wrote, "Time and again the people who write these case studies use words like *miracle* or *I was healed*."[117]

After her own contact with the beyond in 1967, Joan, who saw a distant light and felt a "tremendous peace," met with someone unknown to her and was told to return, but not before it was specifically made known to her that she would recover. Upon awakening, her fever had gone, and she improved rapidly through the night. "My doctor was amazed at such a dramatic recovery," were her words.[118]

Since birth, the right hand of one of Welsh nurse Penny Sartori's patients had essentially been stuck in a closed position due to cerebral palsy. After undergoing a cardiac-related NDE, the patient was suddenly capable of opening his hand. Despite some criticism, Sartori responded that, "On investigation of the possible reasons for this, it was established that such a contracture would be highly unlikely to resolve without some form of operation to the ligaments and tendons."[119]

Seventy-two hours after the NDE of one Dr. Parti, in which he traveled over meadows, met deceased relatives, and attained a higher purpose, his fever was down, his addiction to pain medicine and depression evaporated, and his prostate cancer and sepsis simply disappeared. The author called this not only remarkable but inexplicable.[120] Of paramount and perhaps prescient importance here, too, Grey noted that in cases where healing occurred after the NDE, the contents and events experienced within the NDE itself were causally connected to the later healing. Exactly as we have seen in the folktales and legends, "respondents," according to Grey, "assert that it was their guides or the being of light who healed them at that time."[121] A prime example was that of Richard Borutta, who, during his near-death experience, was guided into light by "feathery spirits," where he says he was healed of alcoholism and that his liver was restored. According to Atwater, once revived, his liver was found to be "miraculously healed and his addiction gone."[122] This is substantially similar to those dreams and visions in which the saint is encountered as a healer. There, too, the healing is attributed directly to the saint or to the saint as a mediary between himself or herself and God.

Placebo, Belief, and Truth

Professor of anthropology Thomas Csordas made the important point that in analyses that attempt to speak to the mechanisms of healing, very rarely is the imaginal world of the supplicant approached or described.[123] The healer is cross-examined, the methods are recorded, but the actual experiences of those undergoing ritual or nonordinary healing have been much less systematically explored. Krippner and Achterberg made the same point, referring to an anomalous healing database of 3,500 references collected from 800 journals. "This worthy effort," they maintained, "the largest of its kind in the world, contains little information on the patients themselves, and we know nothing of their experience or the related biological correlates."[124]

Near-death experiences are absolutely fertile, if not unchallenging, ground for such research, not in the least because the experiences occur at a time of reduced or unrecordable brain function; hence, if healing occurs during those periods, as commonly claimed, it would be hard to attribute physiological factors to the spontaneous healing. While outside the stated scope of the work, that some external force independent of a functioning physiology might, in some cases, be involved should certainly remain on the table until more is known. The extent to which the experiences, however initially dissimilar, seem to converge on the question of the beyond, too, should remain a point of interest. Furthermore, during the near-death experience, the encounters are often so novel that the belief required to elicit a placebo explanation could not reasonably have the context within which to form. This, of course, is without mention of the fact that, regarding hypnotism, there is no functioning brain to be hypnotized. As a final note, it is important to observe that in cases where placebos are patently inviable (i.e., Sartori's patient) versus those with less complex effects, such as the reduction of elevated physiological markers, they are often both tied to contact with another world. Instances of healing in which the individual either travels to or is visited by the beyond, in other words, are independent of the type of affliction.

It should be remembered, too, that, while many a traveler has sought healing from healers around the world and been met with trickery or charlatanism, the broader dismissal of comparable cases of anomalous healing recorded in a professional medical setting is an unhelpful approach. At the very least, we have here a genuine collection of comparable experiences and traditions worthy of ongoing inquiry, even if psychosomatic processes are, in the end, the ultimate explanation in many examples.* Indeed, even where scholars have deemed certain cases among

---

*An excellent starting point in this regard for those interested is James McLenon's *Wondrous Healing: Shamanism, Human Evolution, and the Origin of Religion.*

traditional or folk healers as involving placebo, they have not always spoken strongly enough to the mystery that is placebo itself and, indeed, its limitations. One, of course, cannot explain a mystery with another mystery, at least not in any sense that closes a conversation. This is without mentioning that, in cases where the healer attempts to deceive the patient into believing something psychical or magical is occurring, there seems to be an open attempt at leveraging this effect in the patient. "It can't help everybody," were the words of a female healer practicing her magic in the Bosnian countryside, before continuing on to note that it was "only for those who believe that I have such a capacity to help."[125]

Josephina Sison, a Filipino healer, claimed similarly when she said, "I do not heal. The surgeries do not heal. Jesus heals, using your faith."[126] The healer, Joao Fernandes de Carvalho also noted that as his understanding increased, he came to realize his "medications were not what necessarily cured people. It was their faith that cured more than any combination of chemicals."[127] In such cases, of course, a form of healing is still technically occurring, and a certain amount of credit can therefore rightfully be afforded. Some anthropologists, such as Wendell Oswalt, speak this in passing, noting that among the Cree, the patient might be cured, as often they seemed to be, "through faith in a shaman's abilities."[128]

As early as 1823, revolutionary John Hunter noted that among certain tribes west of the Mississippi, he had "no doubt that the effect of this kind of practice on the imagination has wrought some cures and helped to establish the influence and authority they generally exercise."[129] Even in more recent accounts, the same theme emerges: Sutherland relayed the case of Morris, who, after his NDE, claimed to have attained the ability to heal by laying on hands; however, according to Morris, "the person has to be willing to help."[130]

In the broader sense too, of course, such generalizations regarding charlatanism are unwarranted or at least require some caveats. Consider just a couple of examples: the Shoshone doctor, who, being unsuccessful, "refused fees."[131] While, more recently, in Steward's time, some of them began to accept fees, those doctors would soon be considered "false doctors" among their own people. In other cases too, such as among certain tribes of central Australia, there is no monetary compensation at all, even for the successful medicine man.[132] Likewise, among the Elema of the Papuan Gulf, their *Kariki-haera* uses magic and dream communications to give warnings and tips related to hunting, for which he receives "no extra portion of the catch or other tangible reward."[133]

ALIENS, TIME, AND THE MAGIC IN THE MIND

Finally, although further still beyond the scope of this work, a small mention should be made of particular other events in which people claim to encounter entities from "otherworlds" and attain healing. Ostensible encounters with extraterrestrials, in many ways, fulfill the kinds of criteria we have set ourselves here. After all, in those cases, beings from another world seem to be involved in the imparting of secret healing or related knowledge. A young girl, for example, suffering gravely from cancer, encountered two figures with long yellow-red hair and small green slanted eyes emerging from an object, who apparently "used a device producing a bluish-white light and another instrument, in what appeared to be radiation treatment of the patient." This strange procedure left her apparently "completely cured."[134]

Jacques Vallée, the author of *Passport to Magonia*, whose work speaks perhaps most strongly to these connections, speculatively, although not without foundation, pointed out that in relation to these cases, "Clearly we are dealing here with a pattern reminiscent of medieval mystics."[135] Certain authors, such as Preston Dennett, have compiled hundreds of related cases, noting that "people reported their bodies being opened and closed with lasers that left no scars. They told how various organs were removed and put back again. They reported instantaneous cures of wounds and injuries. They reported healings of serious conditions like pneumonia or liver disease. They even reported healings of serious diseases, such as cancer."[136]

Others, such as psychologist Edith Fiore, wrote, in fact, that one of the most interesting findings to emerge from her case studies related to such seemingly extraterrestrial contact were "the many healings and attempts to heal on the part of the visitors."[137] Among others, Fiore gave the case of one of her patients, Linda, who came into her office and told Fiore of a dream in which she was taken into a spaceship where her yeast infection was healed with a blue gel. "The next morning," the author writes, "the yeast infection was gone."[138]

PLANTING THE SEEDS

While the likes of the ethnobotanist or the anthropologist would generally sidestep such questions, appealing often and not unreasonably to literary, diffusionist, or "culture pattern" explanations, these are strikingly similar tales found so disparately and in such ubiquity that the extent to which knowledge of this kind may actually have been imparted in this manner must, in our opinion, remain an open question. Furthermore, the extent to which, during altered states, individuals report contact with nonhuman entities and claim to attain novel information even today should give pause in concluding the solely romantic or otherwise contrived nature of such tales.

Perhaps greater distinction and specificity could have been made and offered between some of these account types; however, the particular utility of seeing them together in all their idiosyncratic particulars would be lost. With these limits in mind, and while any conclusions are tentative, particularly with regard to cases of ostensible "spontaneous" healing, it might be the case that the sleepers in those old dream temples were not wishing upon nothing, that the shamans with their psychoactive brews were engaging not in flights of fancy but in veridical and ontologically pertinent endeavors, and that our own contemporaries, too, just maybe, find themselves in the presence of a real and genuine mystery. Something, perhaps, truly out of this world.

EIGHT

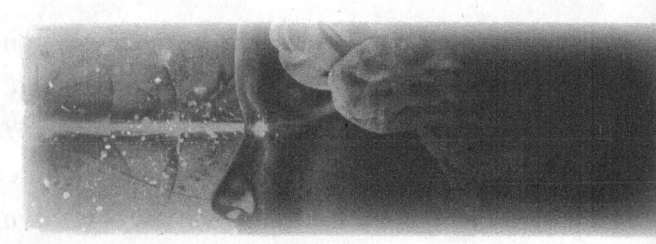

I Know What You Dreamed

Shared Visions, Double Revelations, and Ultimate Truth

> *Spontaneous human experiences provide the core motivation for studying psychic phenomena. While there is always some distortion and exaggeration when recalling unusual incidents, sufficient similarity appears in reports from different people, in tens of thousands of case studies around the world, to form basic categories for the phenomena. The scientific challenge is to take these raw experiences and try to figure out what they mean. Are they what they appear to be, genuine phenomena that transcend the usual boundaries of space and time, or are they better understood as conventional psychological and physical effects?*
>
> DEAN RADIN, *THE CONSCIOUS UNIVERSE*, 23

The Greek orator Aelius Aristides gave a healing dream in which one Philadelphus, rather ill, was in a sacred theater among a crowd of people all dressed in white, to whom he was delivering a speech. He was told by a god to drink wormwood diluted in vinegar in order to relieve his complaint. When he awoke, he called for his temple warden, Asclepiacus, in whose house he stayed, and told him his dream. Asclepiacus, as it happened, had had the very same dream. "Since our dreams agreed," he said, "we applied the remedy, and I drank more of it than anyone had ever drunk before," later noting that it would be "impossible to describe the relief the potion brought or how good it made me feel."[1]

Again, in an old Irish tale, it was the dreamers' shared experience that fundamentally suggested its truth. The tale has the dreamer, a young woman named Mary, telling of her dream, the likes of which she had apparently never had before [a stipulation often still made of the veridical dream] to Nona, a wise woman. She witnessed a raven killing her beautiful hound, tearing out his bowels, and flying away with his heart. When she arrived home, still in the dream, her lover, Ulick, was presented to her, dead in a coffin, his heart similarly torn out. A young man, Paudien, who lived with her, after some encouragement from Nona, told her his own dream, and he told it in verse:

> *His beak was dropping with warm gore,*
> *The bowels from out the good hound he tore;*
> *With his raven wing he flapped his prey,*
> *Then he croaked and flew with the heart away.*
> *Then there came a coffin and pall,*
> *With a crowd, and bearers, and keeners, and all,*
> *And blood was sprinkled on all around,*
> *And streamed from the coffin along the ground.*

"My very dream," Nona exclaims in reply, before suggesting that the fact it was a shared dream meant there was "something in such dreaming." In this case, despite her husband's disbelief, he was killed later that same day, and Paudin later dreamed of the body's location, which was therefore soon found.[2]

While, in our journey so far, we have seen in all ages how powerful the veridical vision can be—that the individual might be moved, that discoveries might be made, and that action might be taken in its light—there are yet other kinds in which even further corroboration is afforded to the visionaries. If the attestations of legend, lyric, and lore are to be believed, certain individuals, at certain times, share the same dream or broader visionary/experiential space. While greatly affecting the individual, these experiences, too, either as literary devices, anecdotes, or folkloric memorates seem to play a powerful and perhaps less appreciated role in supporting or engendering social and even metaphysical cohesion between individuals and groups. As British historian Emma Wilby put it, at least in terms of early modern perceptions, "a single meeting dream, if it were powerful enough, could have convinced two dreamers that they had genuinely encountered each other in the otherworld and generated the emotional resonance to nurture cult identity."[3]

While glaringly little work has been done in this area, particularly of a syncretic nature, the shared dream remains a significant historical and literary entity. Many people, in fact, still claim to have dreamed the same dream or experienced the same vision. They are still moved to action, and they are still brought closer together. The veridical value and force of these experiences in the minds of those involved are often great. "Since our dreams agreed," after all, was the reasoning given in our opening visions for taking them seriously. These are conclusions that have been drawn widely. While some of the same ground will be covered as has been by others, many other accounts will be offered. Furthermore, with the inclusion of certain related experiences, the shared visionary space and, hopefully, the presence of the shared vision as a significant entity will be deepened and widened. Here, and in our final chapter, a small contribution is offered toward that end, and, considering a number of the visions here are effectively shared versions of some of those from the previous chapters, we come full circle, in a sense, and fittingly approach the end of our journey in this way.

SINCE OUR DREAMS AGREED

Coordinated Revelations

Historian Titus Livius (known as Livy) recorded that, during the Samnite Wars, fought between the Roman Republic and the Samnites (of what is now modern south-central Italy), a consul from each army shared the same dream. Both men saw a man "more imposing than any ordinary human." This dream stated that during the coming battle, one of the two armies that devoted themselves to certain schools of thought would be victorious. Importantly, here, the dreams were known to have been the same, as the consuls later "compared their nocturnal visions."[4]

According to an old medieval legend, around the late eleventh or early twelfth century, two minstrels who lived in different regions of France also shared a revelation. A girl clad in white appeared to the jongleur of Brabant in a dream and urged him to go to the church of Notre Dame and speak to a Bishop Lambert and recount the vision to him. She also gave him specific instructions regarding how to cure illnesses that were plaguing the people. "In the same night," this woman, ostensibly the Virgin Mary, "appeared to the other minstrel who lived in Saint-Pol-sur-Ternoise, all in such clothing and in like form and in such appearance as she had shown herself to the first," before repeating her instructions word for word. Of interest here, too, both men, clearly inspired to action, come to the bishop at different times and give him their accounts. The tales remember the same impacts and effects that still occur regarding reports of shared dreams. It is the shared nature of the experiences that convinces the bishop of their reality after he learns both men are enemies and would therefore not have colluded at his expense. Realizing this, he "reflected, and his heart said to him that this vision came from God, by whom there would be peace and concord between these two mortal enemies."[5]

From a famed collection of Chinese marvel tales, we read in *The Two Brides* that Chi-Sheng is arranged to meet with a potential suitor, Wu'k'o, but falls ill around that time. Wu'k'o offers to bring him medicine, and despite his refusal, she turns up at his door. He immediately recognized her beauty, regretted his decision, and pledged himself to her. After taking her hand, however, he woke up and found himself with his mother. Hearing his dream, she goes and confirms that Wu'k'o looked "exactly as he had seen her in his dream." Wu'k'o later confesses, "When I was ill I dreamt that I went to your house and saw you, but I looked upon it only as a dream until I heard that you had dreamt that I had actually been there, and then I knew that my spirit must have been with you." Chi-sheng confirms that the particulars of the vision "coincided exactly with her own": The dream was credited with bringing about their matrimonial alliance.[6]

A much older example of such a coordinated revelation relates to the *Iliad* and is an example in which the goddesses Thetis and Iris visit both Achilles and Priam, respectively, and toward the same end, which is later carried out.[7] Reading again from Rabo's *Syriac Chronicle*, after the plundering of Mor Barsoum's monastery in Turkey, he appeared in the exact same dream, not to two but to three different soldiers. All three men saw the saint's monastery shining with light, with the man himself standing at its highest point in "indescribable glory." He said to them, "Go and tell your king that I am angry at my monks because they sinned and enraged my master." When one of these men woke up, sure this was a true dream, he went to the other two, and "all of them related to each other that they had seen the same vision."[8]

Holy Ground

The fact that the shared dream inspires action and real-world effects is particularly apparent in the tales related to the founding of holy sites. One example from 1079 was related to the founding of the Benedictine monastery of Anchin in France. The knight and lord of Courcelles, having become distracted while on horseback, separates from his brothers and finds himself in a more remote region of the forest. Thankfully, he finds shelter after coming upon a state castle. The following morning, when Walter, lord of Montigny, owner of the castle, enters his chamber to pay him his morning civilities, Sohier thanks him for his courtesy but notes that his sleep was broken by disturbing dreams. "Methought," he went on, "I was upon an islet near this castle, when I met a white stag of a marvelous size and beauty; the beast came towards me, threw me on the ground, tore out my bowels, and trailed them round the island." For such a specific dream, Sohier can only have been surprised to hear Walter exclaim, "Strange, I also had exactly the same dream."[9]

One of Islam's eighth-century saints, Sirrin, also made pragmatic use of the knowledge procured during such a dream. He once purchased a horse from a man who was initially glad to be rid of it due to it being injured. That man dreamed he saw the horse in heaven on a beautiful plot of land and was raised up. Going before Sirrin, he asked to go back on the bargain, as he now understood it was noble to be kind to animals. The saint, however, "had seen the same dream that night" and so refused the request, understanding the man's true intentions.[10]

The extent to which the shared dream might precipitate action comes through, even in the more exaggerated fairy and folktales. In an Italian story, "The Wildwood King," two sons of a king tell their father that "they both had a dream: their sister would run away from the home with a common soldier." The king, therefore, ordered her to be killed.[11]

Regarding something entirely less morbid, Freudian psychiatrist Dr. Jule Eisenbud, among his impressive and pioneering contributions, demonstrated clearly that such "dream telepathy" may be practically applied in the process of a patient's recovery. In one case, one of Eisenbud's patients seemed to report a dream that was connected with that of another patient whom he had been with the previous day. While the two patients had never met, when they became aware of the very specific associations Eisenbud had observed, one of them "was able to break through a long-standing block" tied directly to the contents of the dream, which brought some information she had forgotten to light.[12]

Shared Bonds

That the shared dream, then, and with Wilby's earlier words in mind, may at the very least deepen or assist relationships between people, is an idea supported not just by these relatively "ordinary" anecdotes but by the perennial tales. The twelfth-century Islamic scholar, Ibn Asakir, recorded an example in which a slave girl, Mahbiibah, owned by the caliph al-Mutawakkil, falls out of his graces. He dreams, happily, however, that they reconcile and later tells Asakir, "Come with us and let us see what she is about." When al-Mutawakkil calls her to him, she tells him, "O my Lord, I dreamt of thee this night that thou wert reconciled with me," to which he replied, "and I too, by Allah, dreamt of thee." For this reason, he then restored her to her former place in his favor.[13]

More recently, Brenda CampbellJones, who more than once shared dreams with her husband, in fact, wrote that whenever this occurred, she "felt a sense of awe" and felt that they had "just stepped onto sacred ground." And sacred ground, as it happens, is exactly how shared visionary spaces were characterized by many traditional communities that actively engaged with them.[14]

Saint Gobhan, who Baring Gould separates from the sixth-century Celtic saint Gobhan and who was a disciple of the renowned Saint Fursey, is said to have beheld, along with his two brothers, a "vision by night." The experience has Christ apparently appearing to them and telling them to come to him, that they will be refreshed in some way, that they should come and "inherit the kingdom prepared for you from the beginning of the world." The next day, they told Fursey they had "all seen the same vision, and heard the same words." Together, they set off from Ireland to Britain at the visions' behest.[15]

Double Dreams

If the historians of antiquity and the folklorists of recent centuries attest to the age and reach of the shared dream, the Babylonians and Assyrians speak once more to its even longer-recognized reality. In the ancient city of Uruk, located in modern-day Iraq, if a dreamer was unsure as to the meaning of a dream, someone else would go with them to the place where the dream unfolded. A certain tablet describing this process references this person as "one who lies at a person's head," the hope seeming to be to potentially "intercept" or "share" the dream with the dreamer.[16] Something more particular of this kind involved the dream of Xerxes, the fifth-century Achaemenid. After he dreams more than once of a "tall and beautiful man" who urges him to war, his uncle Artabanus decides to "wear the king's clothes and sleep in his bed with the hope of receiving the same dream." Very pertinently here, the result is an agreement regarding military policy.[17]

Other kinds of shared dreams have a dreamer understanding, *even within the dream*, that another is experiencing something alike. This is found among the old Greek and Latin fictions, which are home to a number of shared visionary spaces. Stavros Frangoulidis refers to this space, shared in the first and last books of Apuleius's *Metamorphoses*, as that of the "double dream"[18] in the tradition of German theologian Alfred Wikenhauser, who, in 1948, coined the term *doppeltraume*, or "double dreams."[19] In one of those, Isis appears to Lucian in a dream in order to prescribe a certain treatment. Isis herself makes it known, however, that she is, at that very moment, appearing to her priest, Mithras, in his sleep. "For at this very moment," were her words, and in relation to the same problem, "when I come to you I am present there too and am instructing my priest in his sleep about what he must do next."[20] Many others of this type exist, such as the dream between a Serapeum scribe and his mother recorded on a second-century Greek Egyptian papyrus in which, while Asclepius appears to the dreamer, offering gestures he should perform, his mother dreams of Asclepius in fact appearing to her son.[21]

Given the extent to which such literary proclamations seem to have the reader in mind and the fact that the scholar might not mention the shared dream as a phenomenon outside of that literature, one would be forgiven for assuming that such dreams were only found there. This, of course, is not the case. Robin Royston and Annie Humphreys gave the far more recent experience of Rachel, who dreamed, or more specifically, had a vision of her dead grandfather at the foot of her bed looking "suntanned" and "as he did a while before he died." Two weeks later, at her yoga class, when she was about to tell her friend of her strange experience, he said, "Was it about Grandpa?" before reciting the very same experience, including describing the same clothing. This experience, apparently, was powerful enough to convince Rachel of its reality, while before the confirmation, she was somewhat nonplused.[22]

Recorded in the early twentieth century, a Scottish account seems to give the same credence to such an experience based on its being shared. Two men, James McGeorge and John Goodfellow, are killed in a storm while doing their duty on a mail coach. Four days later, after "great bands of men had searched everywhere about, and always without success," Robert, the local toll-keeper, told his father, Kirk, "Do you know, I dreamed last night I saw John Goodfellow walking bareheaded with a shepherd at Tweedshaws Cross!" His father replies, "Well that is strange; I had a dream, and I saw the guard at the same place." Later, both set off from the search party to their dreamed-of locations and found the bodies. It is stipulated that Kirk "was not a man who believed in dreams, but he seems to have been impressed by this one."[23]

While commenting on how rare such experiences are and explaining that they most commonly occur between those close to each other, Virtanen gives a very similar account from rural Finland. One night, her informant dreamed that her father came to her bed, and she said to him, "I'll manage all right in the world, but how will Hilli and Toivo [her siblings] get on?" Unable to forget this dream, when she next went home to visit her parents, her father told her that one night he had a dream in which she told him those exact words.[24]

UNREMARKABLE MAGIC

Meshing Dreams

Dreams being the same clearly impresses; however, they do not need to be so stringently akin to being categorized as mutual. At times, the shared dream involves a more general correspondence—dreams that author Linda Lane Magallón calls "meshing dreams." Emma Wilby, whose nuanced analysis of the shared dream as a historical and especially early modern European entity deserves attention, gave the account of a husband and wife sleeping in the same bed, with one dreaming the following: "I am with my two sons and we are scrambling along a sea shore, over big boulders. I can sense a cliff rising beside me, to my right. The waves are crashing onto the rocks and there is a feeling of menace. My eldest son has gone in front and I cannot see him and am worried." The other dreamed as follows: "I am walking with my two sons near the edge of a cliff, on a barren peninsula. My sons run ahead. I see my eldest son clambering down the rocky cliff and I am scared."[25]

The singular work of Professor Montague Ullman bears mention here in that he and his colleagues, by any objective marker, successfully induced extrasensory dreams in individuals in carefully crafted laboratory experiences. The experiments were a fascinating exercise involving a combined experimental approach in which famous paintings were intended to be "sent" to the dreamer, with at times startling results. In just one of those, a particularly sensitive subject of theirs, Erwin, achieved "remarkable success" for his part. While the entirety of the studies and their detractors should of course be taken into account, in this case, the researchers concluded that the results "supported the telepathy hypothesis against odds on the order of a thousand to one that it could have happened by chance."[26]

Interestingly, Ullman himself, before the more carefully controlled experiments, recorded his dreams systematically with Laura Dale, later the editor of the *Journal of the American Society for Psychical Research*, and achieved a number of seeming "hits." One of those had Dale dreaming of a girl to whom she had previously given piano lessons. In the dream, she handed Dale a written analysis of a popular piece of music, apparently unusual in form. She then gave multiple analyses of several typical forms before speaking of the song in question. Ullman, within twenty-four hours, dreamed that he was in a theater attending a concert. His former piano teacher, in the dream, was giving a concert—a vocal concert—instead of playing the piano. Ullman noted that "the odd twist in both dreams was of piano players concerning themselves with vocal music."[27]

Relatedly, author and designer Nina Jun Yuchi wrote in 2021 that she dreamed of a friend in Hong Kong she hadn't seen for two years returning to her school. The next morning, she messaged her friend and discovered "she had also dreamt about returning to school the night before."[28] Gini Graham Scott gives an example of this, writing that a couple from one of her workshops dreamed together and that the man, Roger, dreamed of being in the desert, seeing a snake, and feeling his wife's joy with him. He killed the snake for her and later discovered that she dreamed the same night of being in a hot environment, feeling scared, noticing her husband behind her, and being comforted by him.[29]

At times, in fact, the dream content does not have to relate directly to the waking world in order to impress; it simply has to be shared with others. Andrew Lang was given an example by one Mrs. Ogilvie of Drumquaigh. She dreamed that her dog, Fanti, went mad. "Well, that is odd," said her brother. "So did I." Fanti, as Lang clarified with his tongue in cheek, lived sanely and harmlessly for the rest of his years.[30]

Lucid Dreaming and Active Participation

Other kinds of dreams have the dreamers participating in each other's dreams in a way that exactly corresponds to how they were seen acting by the other dreamer. As with most of what we have explored through these pages, this is as much an ancient reality as it is an ongoing one. An ancient Near Eastern dream tells that, after the Assyrian ruler Ashurbanipal prays to and receives a visit from the Mesopotamian goddess of love, war, and fertility, Ishtar, a priest reports having seen the entire encounter in a dream. He later recounts his experience in more detail than the king himself could.[31]

Similarly, in 1974, James Donahoe shared a dream between himself and his research partner, Pamela Yellen, in which he had just come down from the foot of a mountain and met Pamela outside a small house before going inside and sitting on the wooden floor. For her part, Pamela writes that she was "waiting for Jim at the foot of a mountain" before sitting on the floor of the house with other people. Jim's journal records that he wanted to do something with his lucid state before the dream ended, so he asked them to consciously watch him leave, while Pamela writes in her journal that one of the people "told us to observe him, since he was tired and was going to leave the dream state."[32]

In 1892, a Dr. Gleason of New York State dreamed she was in the dark woods, afraid that a man whom she knew might arrive, afraid for some reason that he would shake the leaves of a certain tree and set it alight. When she bumped into him four days later, he told her simply that he knew he had dreamed the same thing before she could begin to tell him. The dream, which occurred around the same time on that night, had him seeing a woman he knew paralyzed by fear in the bushes, after which he came up to her, shook the bush, and set it on fire.[33]

DREAMTIME BATTLES AND SHARED VISIONARY SPACES

These mutual visionary experiences seem to be a less often reported, if not necessarily rare, phenomenon. That two individuals would even assume they might have shared such an experience seems unlikely, and in a culture where the sharing of dreams, something practiced among many traditional communities, is less common, the likelihood falls even further. It seems that only a select few people, often closely bonded and at rare times, report such things, which might include "physically" sharing the same dream "space," simply dreaming of the same event, or receiving the same information around the same time and confirming with each other later. There seem to be those, however, who might experience such things far more often, and one of those is the shaman. Shirokogorov found this to be the case among the Siberian Tungus. "The Tungus," he wrote, "in the dream may have a talk with other persons and those persons would know about it. It is true not all men can do it, but many of them, and particularly shamans can do it easily."[34]

Among Shoshone Indians, a shaman might dream that his grandchild had the same kind of shamanic skills as he (though often the skill was different). Importantly, during these times, the grandchild might end up "dreaming the same." Similarly, among the Goshute Indians, their shamans "might give a power to his son, both having the same dream."[35] Once more, we see that such a truthful vision might, in and of itself, suggest a mystical path for the individual. The shared dream itself becomes the focal point around which the transfer of sacred power from one to another may unfold. This is brought out particularly strongly among many of the Aboriginal Australians. Their firm belief was not only that one might "rendezvous with other dreamers and embark on shared journeys" in that space, but some of their shamans too, in fact, "received their calling in this way."[36]

In a more pointed example from among the California Yuki, a boy much younger than those who would usually become doctors dreamed of On-wha'knamlikiat, a creator deity. "I did not see his face or body," the boy said, "but I was in the sky, and saw many colors, like a mass of flowers. In the morning I was bleeding from mouth and nose and badly frightened." Such an experience was known to mark a potential doctor, although not usually so early in life. In this case, however, it was the fact that, as it turned out, the boy's brother had "also dreamed of On-uhuknamlikiat" and witnessed the visionary events himself, which assured him and allowed for such an exception.[37]

Among the Canelos-Quichua of Ecuador, lovers sleeping on opposite sides of the house might frequently wake and speak of their dreams. They may agree to meet at a certain place within those dreams and continue their visionary adventures together. Such an excursion falls under the category of *muscuna*. Likewise and conversely, during an important and socially bonding annual festival called *jisa*, these Ecuadorians might take their time not to sleep, but to drink gallons of alcoholic beverages, and engage in hours of drumming in order to "collectively dream and sing to themselves for seventy-two hours."[38]

Shared Visions of Battles

The other worlds traversed by the shaman are not without danger or threat; they are not realms within which he or she might lightly tread. Among certain competing Siberian tribes, shamans are known to meet or intercept each other while they are retrieving the soul of another. Battles between shamans, in fact, "often take place in dreams," ranging from benign competition to more serious confrontations with potentially mortal consequences.[39] Such deathly duels were not unknown among the Quichua of the Ecuadorian jungle either. There, the dwelling of a powerful shaman named Orlando came under duress when a large *apapa* (a shaman in the form of an owl) entered through the window and came at him. Orlando, however, immediately awakened, "having seen the apapa coming in his dream." An hour-long battle ensued until Orlando prevailed.[40]

Even near the world's farthest end, the shared dream was an inherently assumed possibility. The South American Selk'nam shamans of Patagonia engaged in dream contests, sharing the same dream space to challenge one another and report the details later. In one more specific example, Onkolkxon, a great shaman, accurately "saw" the death of another shaman farther south during just such a shared encounter.[41]

Similarly, among the Yámana, traditionally from the islands south of Isla Grande de Tierra del Fuego and farther to Cape Horn, two rival shaman brothers dream the same dream: they meet on a certain shore and begin to fight. In this tale, both shamans die around the same time after the dream in which they had met and fought, therefore confirming their power to their respective groups.[42]

Something surprisingly comparable brings us again to the pages of the Icelandic *Landnámabók*, or *Book of Settlements*, and a certain man gifted with second sight. He saw a large bear leaving one town and a bull leaving another. They met in a field and engaged in a furious battle, with the bear getting the upper hand. The next morning, it was seen that in the valley where they met it was as if the ground had been turned over, and both of the men who these animals represented were injured, those being Dufthak of Dufthaksholt and Storolf, son of Salmon.[43]

Returning to the Americas, the Huichol of northwest Mexico, who speak to some truly archaic shamanic practices, given their lack of Spanish influence, speak of "telepathic group projections" as part of the knowledge imparted to them by sacred plants.[44] On the planet's other end, the Lotha Naga tribe of northeast India likewise believe that if a man fights with another man in his dreams, the two souls "really meet."[45] Anthropologist Gilbert Herdt claimed that the Sambia of Papua New Guinea, too, "genuinely believe that others have had some of the same dreams," this being an "important sign of their sense of community."[46]

Visionaries in Shared Spaces
Such specifically shared visionary spaces have their analogues far distant in time and space, suggestive of similar methods, ideas, and even ecstasies. The *benandanti* of Northern Italy between the fifteenth and sixteenth centuries were a group of primarily women who seemed to have likewise battled in similar states. "The spirits of the benandanti," wrote Italian historian Carlo Ginzburg, "left the inanimate body for a space of time, sometimes in the shape of a mouse or a butterfly, sometimes astride hares, cats or other animals, to journey in ecstasy to the procession of the dead or the battle against male and female witches."[47]

In the seventeenth century, too, Monsignor G. F. Tommasini remarked that on the Adriatic Peninsula, in Istria, people believe that there are those who go by night in spirit on the crossroads toward different ends and that they often meet together in this altered state at certain crossroads.[48] Folklorist Gustav Henningsen likewise noted that "the Italian witch-trial records and demonological writings of the fifteenth and sixteenth centuries teem with accounts of orgiastic nocturnal gatherings that people took part in while their bodies remained in their beds."[49]

That the shaman and the witch might share the same capacities in this regard is made particularly clear as far away from the Mediterranean as Chile. Some of the witches, or *kalku*, of the Mapuche are said to have the very same "power" as their shamans, who meet in caves or deep in the woods, later telling stories about their adventures. This, according to Faron, is not at all a fabrication and "probably is a dream experience."[50]

While numerous modern scholars consider at least some of the meetings of witches to have taken place in ecstatic states, as early as 1611, Pedro de Valencia, a Spanish humanist and literary critic, had already postulated that witches used certain ointments in order to produce their dream visions.[51]*

Not being just the purview of secret societies or shadowy sects, certain groups still attempt such things. Author and occultist Oliver Fox carried out a related experiment with two friends, Slade and Elkington. They were to attempt to literally meet on Southampton Common in their dreams that night. When they conferred the following day, Fox and Elkington both claimed to have indeed dreamed of that location, and both dreamed of the other *at* that location; although, both claimed that Slade had not turned up. They discovered later, however, that Slade "had not dreamed at all" that night, "which perhaps accounted for his inability to keep the appointment."[52]

THE DEAD, NEAR DEATH, AND SHARED DEATH

We have seen how often the dead might impart knowledge of another's

---

*It should be noted that the author, Henningsen, seems to consider that many efforts to ascribe the visionary witches phenomenon to hallucinogen salve constitute a "pseudo-scientific attempt to give the witch phenomenon a rational explanation."

death to the individual. In many cases where the individual comes to know of their death, we are not told *how* they know. It seems reasonable, however, to assume that many of them had such a visit and simply didn't share the details. One can imagine, then, how solidified the "dead as messengers" theme might become if more than one person were to witness such a thing. Death, as it happens, is a subject around which many shared visions tend to gather.

A Scottish story given in an 1898 issue of *Folklore* has a man of Bragar on the Outer Hebrides asleep while his brother "saw the form and likeness of another brother, who was lately deceased, enter the mill, and stoop over the sleeping brother, as if in the act of kissing him." When the man awoke, he said he had the same vision in his sleep, with his brother telling him, "I saw it at the same time while I was perfectly awake." The dreamer died very shortly after that.[53]

During the third-century persecution of Christians by Valerian, we read of the deaths of the martyrs James and Marian. Marian, having been tortured and imprisoned, was "consoled with a vision," which likewise recalls those of our earlier chapter on nearing-death awareness, in which he found himself in a heavenly realm where the dead Saint Cyprian brought him to understand he would be dying soon. When he tells James, Marian hears that he has had the same message. While their fate makes the suggestion seem inevitable, James is given a specific date when his deceased brother Agapius visits him in a vision with that information. And, accordingly, "so it happened."[54]

Returning to Apuleius's *Metamorphoses* for an example of such an experience relating to the death of another, Aristomenes of Messenia, while staying at an inn, supposes he has seen his friend, Socrates, being murdered by witches in the night. He saw his friend's neck being pierced, and his heart removed. Socrates shows up later, however, and reports having himself dreamed of being murdered in exactly the same manner.[55] In this case, the dream offered truth, although Aristomenes, with his advice to Socrates that he should leave lest the dream be fulfilled, sent him to his death at the hands of the witches.

British scholar Ernest Bennett gave us one of those "collective apparitions" in which three separate individuals, in 1926, witnessed an old man somehow crossing a lake near his house. A doctor who had just been to check on him asked another if he, too, could see the man, which he did. Three people had seen the vision, and as it turned out, the man had just died, unbeknownst to them.[56] Coming again to our crisis visions, they have also been reported by more than one person. Something of this kind comes from the Orokaiva people of Papua New Guinea, who strongly hold that the dead might return to visit their living friends. One man named Dasiga dreamed of a fleet of steamers and canoes filled with spirits of the dead cruising offshore at night. Three other men, including two from another village, were later "favoured with the same vision."[57]

Recalling our second chapter, James Monroe, the fifth president of the United States from 1817 to 1825, gave a shared account from among a number of other prophetic dreams he was sure were sufficient to establish "that dreams do show action of spirit." A lady living with her son on the East Coast of the United States dreamed that her daughter, living in New York, had suddenly fallen ill. "Her son," wrote Monroe, "had the same dream on the same night." They compared the dreams, and "they tallied exactly." Soon they found the girl had fallen ill, just as they had dreamed.[58] Perhaps the archetypal collective apparitions, though, were the appearances of Jesus to his apostles while walking on the sea in Mark 45–50. They, after all, "thought it was a ghost and cried out, for they all saw him and were terrified."

Another shared dream comes to us from the Western Highlands of Scotland and was recorded in a late nineteenth-century issue of *Folklore*. When the death of a certain outgoing laird occurred while away from his home, a servant living in the home while one of his relatives stayed there dreamed she had seen a *dreag** and was "quite sure" the new laird

---

*A dreag is a type of portentous meteor, fireball, or falling star that, among the ancient Britons, was a vehicle by which the soul of some departed Druid would make their way to paradise.

had died on his way there. "At the same time," his relative dreamed that a large river was running past his house and that the new laird was on the opposite side of it. It turns out a son of the lord died just about the date of the dream and the appearance of the dreag.[59]

Returning to the folklore of Illinois, a boy at play suddenly points to the ceiling and says, "Dada, look there!" His father looks up and sees, "with perfect clarity," his own father meeting his gaze. According to the author Isaac Funk, "a comparison of time showed that this was three hours before the death of the elder father in Kentucky, the son being wholly ignorant of the illness of the father."[60]

In a Hungarian Magyar folktale, a man named Paul the Handsome and a maid stayed in the same town, though unaware of each other's presence there. Paul dreamed that a bay stallion died, and this lady's maid, at the same time, dreamed that a mare was dying and soon died. When they met, they told each other their dreams, and they "knew" that her father and mother were represented by the mare and stallion and must have died the previous night. Next morning, an official proclaimed that the king and queen had suddenly died; the tale specifies this occurred "at the very moment they had their dreams."[61]

In what has been called perhaps the best known and, in fact, oldest of all Vietnamese legends, placed during the ancient Hồng Bàng dynasty (2879–2524 BCE), one of two brothers called Tan and Lang disappears. This brother, Lang, having fallen in love with the woman he met for Tan, took himself out of the picture, departed from the house they shared, came to a river, and there "death overtook him." The legend says that, in turn, both Tan and his wife follow him in grief and come to the same fate. Of interest here, however, is that all the inhabitants of the district were "alerted by a dream" of all three deaths and soon erected a pagoda in their honor.[62]

Rather than two or even three visionaries, as we have previously seen, at other times, many more people are said to have shared the same vision. Such accounts are often collected around the deaths of saints and other important figures. It is said of the early Egyptian

Muslim mystic and ascetic Dhu'l-Nun al-Misri, for example, that on the night of his departure from the world, seventy different people saw him in a dream.[63]

These after-death communications, or ADCs, which are general experiences of contact with the deceased after their death are, in fact, still reported as being shared by multiple people. An account from just two years ago comes to us again from the work of Evelyn Elsaesser. In her *Spontaneous Contacts with the Deceased*, she gave one of the cases in which, one night, a woman perceived her husband's dead son coming across the room to greet her. "He felt so real," were her words. "Even while asleep, I leaned back to kiss him." She then awoke to find her husband crying; he had just dreamed of his dead son too. Neither, as they clarified, had ever dreamed of him before or since.[64] In July 2018, a few weeks after the death of the informant's niece's nine-year-old son, Nicolas, they suddenly felt "a presence filled with well-being, love, and serenity. A voice, without being a voice," told her that "all is well. Everything is fine." The following day, while speaking to her niece, she found that her niece "had experienced the same thing in the same night, but twice and probably longer."[65]

Many of the most fascinating visionary spaces that may be shared are those around the deathbed. The "shared death experience" involves the individual seemingly experiencing some of the NDE of another. One of those related by Raymond Moody in one of the earlier works dedicated to the topic involved five members of a family from Atlanta. They were around the deathbed of their mother when a "bright light appeared in the room," which was "unlike any kind of light on this earth." All members of the family confirmed to each other they had seen the same thing, followed by her mother seeming to depart through an entranceway formed by the light, all agreeing later as to its appearance.[66] Another of Moody's cases had two women sharing the life review of a dying loved one. They saw her first boyfriend, her heartbreak, small things that meant a lot to her, acts of kindness, and secrets relating to her love life. "What we saw was so real that we thought we had died too," one of them said.[67]

LOVERS COLLIDE AND MEETINGS CONTRIVED

Love at Second Sight

Returning to the continent, the shared dream is a long-recognized trope in Eastern European folklore and often relates to the matters of love. Such a dream, or *hikaye*, "has two lovers meeting in a dream before later meeting in life."[68] A similar example from a Scottish wonder tale, "The Coming of Angus and Bride," is that Angus dreams of her being held captive by Queen Beira and later finds that she is a real person and learns where to locate her. "Beautiful princess, I beheld you in a dream," Angus tells her when they finally meet. "Mighty prince, I beheld you in a dream riding over bens and through glens in beauty and power," was her reply. They had both dreamed of each other.[69]

Something comparable was given in the *Kathāsaritsāgara*, an eleventh-century collection of Indian legends. Padmavati told her friends that while staying in Meghavana, she dreamed of a man wearing matted hair coming from a certain temple and telling her that she should be reunited with her husband soon. Later that morning, she saw, with astonishment, her husband, Muktaphaladhvaja, bathing at the temple she had seen. Muktaphaladhvaja was later heard describing that he, too, had seen this temple in all its features in his dream and, upon seeing her, was told that she was the very woman he had seen in the dream.[70]

A sixth-century French minstrel, Hyvarnion, dreamed for three nights of a beautiful maiden picking flowers in a meadow, picking him one, and offering it. Hyvarnion, gripped and infatuated, set out and found that meadow and that very woman, to whom he began to sing. According to the tale, "she too had had a dream, three times. And it was of golden-haired Hyvarnion that she had dreamed."[71] Perhaps most pointedly of this kind, and speaking to its antiquity, is the story of *Daphnis and Chloe*, an ancient Greek novel in which both lovers, sleeping apart, simultaneously dream of making love. Moxon makes the point that the dream serves the function of mediating a growing sense of mutuality. Of course, here, the shared dream is treated not just as a literary device but as a legitimate historical entity.[72]

The *Histories of Alexander*, quoted in Athenaeus's *Deipnosophists* 13:35, have Odatis, a girl of the Marathi people, dreaming of Zariadres, the younger brother of the ancient Persian monarch, Hystaspes. She becomes infatuated with this stranger, who, in the meantime, had also dreamed of her; descriptions of their dreams to their respective families, according to Moxon, seemed distinct enough "for the two families to realize who they are and enter into correspondence."[73]

More recently, Linda Lane Magallón relayed just such an example as given to her by an acquaintance. We read of a woman, Alison, who dreams of a strange and handsome young man entering her room, to whom she later makes love. The dream had a great impact on her and seemed unlike others. Two weeks later, Alison tells us that she met this very man and that, when they became closer, they eventually "each described the same vivid precognitive love dream." Lane speculates that such things might occur "rather frequently."[74]

Something more incidentally recorded, although entirely relevant, can be seen in the life of German botanist Georg Wilhelm Steller, a man who, after extended travels through Siberia during the eighteenth century, was said to know more of that land than anyone else. In 1728, he abruptly ended his studies and became obsessed with one Birgitta Helena, a woman "whom he believed to be the very woman he had seen in a dream while in Solikamsk" (an eastern Russian town).[75] Likewise, Anthea, a near-death experiencer from the sample of Cherie Sutherland, reported having a clairvoyant experience of her future husband when she was a child and, in her words, "when I saw him in real life I recognized him straightaway."[76]

While clearly, definitive statements as to the possibility are beyond our remit, it can certainly be speculated that such seemingly ongoing experiences gave rise to some of the folktales and that further work in this area might bear fruit. The double dream, again, has most often been approached as a purely literary device. A less singular approach might open the doors necessary for further exploration in this regard.

New Life

Wilby relayed a Scottish account, this time from 1878, in which a sixty-year-old woman, Elizabeth, dreams that she is crying near a window, as she is eight months pregnant, apparently something she was not happy about. In the morning, before she had a chance to relate this to anyone, her daughter, Molly, told her, "Oh, mother! I had a dream about you this morning! You were crying in front of a mirror. And when I looked at you, I knew you were pregnant."[77]

Something of interest that arises here is that the dream foretelling a birth, often that of someone destined to be great, is a common literary device among biographers, historians, storytellers, and others. Dozens could be quoted; however, those involving shared dreams are harder to find. We could look to the time of Aidan or Máedóc of Ferns, a sixth-to-seventh-century Irish saint. Eithne, the wife of Setna, a rich nobleman of the province of Connaught, had a vision in which she saw a star falling from heaven into her mouth. Setna, however, had the same vision, seeing a star fall into his wife's mouth. When they awoke, they confirmed the dream with each other. They told this to a certain wise man, and he told them that they would give birth to a "noble and worshipful son" who would be "filled with the grace of the holy spirit." That same night, this boy, Máedóc, was conceived.[78]

It seems very clear that many legends around the conception of saints relate to or attempt to tie themselves to the immaculate conception. As is something of our theme, this has no bearing on whether or not such shared experiences are actually reported to occur; as we know, in fact, they still are. Speaking to this, Patricia Maybruck, while rightly noting a lack of quantitative evidence, spoke to the surprisingly powerful anecdotal evidence for dreams symbolic of conception occurring "on the same night the dreamer had intercourse and was convinced she had conceived."[79]

While premonitions of birth are absolutely still recorded and by no means the sole remit of the so-inclined historical biographer or the storyteller, shared accounts have been, again, less forthcoming. Those such as Elizabeth's, however, are at least suggestive in that way and offer interested parties further avenues of inquiry.

SHARED RICHES AND FAMILIAR THINGS

Shared Treasures

In chapter 6, "Treasure, Tombs, and Visionary Boons," we referenced a case given by Louis Rogers in which, after the death of a woman's mother, she dreamed that the dead woman came to her and revealed the location of some lost bonds. Of interest here, the woman's sister "also dreamed that her dead mother came to her during the night, recounting the same story of the lost bonds with the same minute instructions for recognizing them."[80] As noted, in fact, many of the kinds of visions and dreams we have seen have their variants among the shared dreams. A North Carolina story given in 1926, which the authors noted had surprising parallels with a Baltic tale, has three brothers dreaming of hidden treasure, each dream being like the others "in all respects." They were each told the treasure was under a certain tree in a field. Two brothers failed to find the treasure; the third, however, found the correct spot and dug it up.[81]

Helen Creighton tells us that people have "always dreamed there was treasure buried at Kraut Point, Nova Scotia." In one case, certain people dreamed that money was buried at a certain spot. When a stranger arrived there, he told them, "He too had dreamed where the treasure was buried."[82] Similarly, and speaking again to the ubiquity of such tales in Ireland, two brothers in the 1830s were both said to have "dreamt for three consecutive nights that there was gold in the field."[83] For anyone wishing to compile further shared dreams, the shared treasure dream would most certainly bear fruit. Coming once more to the Irish saint Bairre, an angel "came to converse with him" and told him where to find the relics he wanted for his cemetery. When Bairre arrived, however, Finama, son of Eogan, was already there and carrying the relics away. Finama explained that he had the same vision of an angel who told him the very same thing.[84]

Warnings of Danger

In our opening chapter, we saw that warnings of danger—that someone or some group, perhaps a war party, were coming—are common in the Irish myths. Returning now to the rich Ulster Cycle, Cormac Conloingeas, while spending the night at Sleamhain of Meath, started out of his sleep and exclaimed that he had a warning dream and that there was a terrible battle about to come to them. After some time, Dubthach, the "Beetle of Ulster," a warrior known for his fiery disposition, started out of his sleep similarly and "called out the same thing: that there had been a warning dream coming to him and that it would not be long till there would be a great clashing of shields." Later, they sent messengers across the land and found the dreams told true.[85]

A very similar warning may be found in an old Chinese myth. Two brothers, Ahemang and Galemang, lived in the city of Samarqand during the Yuan Dynasty (1279–1368). Someone jealous of their increasing wealth and fame complained to the king and told him they were devils in disguise. "The only way for the country to remain at peace is if the brothers are dead," he told the ruler. It was decided that they would be arrested the following day. That same night, Ahemang dreamed that a wise scholar spoke to him, saying, "Those in high positions are often attacked, you should not stay here, but instead gather your people and travel to the east. Be sure to take a white camel with you." When Ahemang awoke in a cold sweat, he stirred his brother from sleep, who told him, "But I've had the same dream too!" They left the city immediately, successfully evading capture.[86]

Another shared warning, this time not of a mortal enemy but of an elemental one, comes from a man among California's Hupa Indians. He was sleeping in a sweathouse and once dreamed that a famine was coming. "I too dreamed that," his sister told him later that morning, and, accordingly, there was, apparently, a famine for several years.[87]

Unannounced Arrivals

These shared visions bring us full circle to our vardogers and "arrival visions," as the authors of *Phantasms of the Living* referred to them before giving an example in which more than one person mysteriously perceived the visitor's coming. The case is given by a then-Boston minister and reverend "of repute" who was visiting intimate friends. One March afternoon, the man stood at the window in one of their houses and, looking up the road, said to his host, "Here is your brother coming." "Oh yes, here he is; and see, Robert has got Dobbin out at last," was the man's reply. (Dobbin was a horse previously injured.) A third lady watched with them as they witnessed their visitors move "at a gentle pace along the front of the window, and then turning with the road round the corner of the house, they could no longer be seen." Fifteen minutes later, the minister looks out the window and sees them actually coming with the same horse. All three of them, and another who had arrived and apparently also seen the visitors pass, were "much amazed at this incident."[88]

Similar visions are found around the life of Saint Brigid. When one Bishop Bran and his brothers were on their way to Kildare, all three that night had the same dream. Through the darkness and cold, they saw a blaze of light shining across the moor. When they sought out its source, they found Brigid in a white robe, welcoming them into her home. When they awoke, they saw the same road in front of them, hurried on, and at the end they found Brigid, who apparently had been coming to find them.[89]

Mysterious Meetings

In the psychical literature, many cases could be excavated in which the individual seemingly presents themselves as an apparition to another while in an out-of-body state, often during dreams that are either spontaneous or intended. One of those that jives with both our crisis visions and our vardogers came in 1885, when a man, Jno. T. Milward Pierce, was kicked in the face by a horse in Nebraska. At that time, he saw his fiancée close, "looking perfectly material and natural," despite her being twenty-five miles away in Dakota at the time. Pierce was so struck that he left to see her the next morning. She told him, "Why, I expected you all yesterday afternoon. I thought I saw you looking so pale, and your face all bleeding." Her vision was found to coincide exactly with his.[90]

Japan's folklore seems particularly rife with visions of this kind, and they range from the fantastical to the relatively mundane. The Japanese, in fact, have the term *Yume no idu de aru*, meaning "to meet in the dream."[91] In one of those dreams from the *Dainihonkoku Hokkegenki*, an eleventh-century collection of Buddhist tales and folklore, a priest named Shuncho, concerned with the sufferings of prisoners in his town, is arrested. One night, many of his jailers had the very same strange dream: that the prison was filled with hundreds of white elephants and various deva kings who were speaking to this man, Shuncho.[92] In another old Japanese tale, a person called Tsunekiyo Yasunaga dreams that he sees his wife at the capital with another man. He saw them boiling rice and eating together. Although he knew this was a dream, he couldn't help but become anxious, so at dawn, he rushed to the capital and found his wife alone and all well. Before telling her his dream, she told him she dreamed that a strange boy enticed her away with him and that they had eaten boiled rice together. Yasunaga told her that they had the same dream, a happenstance that the translator called an "extraordinary thing."[93]

Dreamtime Connections

The seemingly semifictional Indian trickster and wizard Muladeva, once staying in a traveler's house at Bennayada, dreamed of the moon with a full disc, bright and brilliant, entering his body, which was later interpreted to mean he would be king in seven days. According to the tale, "another tramp had the very same dream."[94]

At the beginning of the twentieth century, Rougemont relayed the account of a Parisian tradesman who dreamed of hearing a voice say to him, "I have now finished forty years, seven months, and twenty-nine days of labor, and I am happy." His wife, at his side, had the very same dream. According to the tale, she won the lottery using this sequence.[95] In cases such as these, such a rapport might be common between two people. In a communication read to the Psychological Society in 1877, for example, we read of a Mr. E. P. Toy who stated that he and his wife were "in the habit of dreaming upon the same subject at the same time," including very mundane experiences. On one occasion, he dreamed of being at his child's funeral but not grieving. His wife dreamed the same thing. They had both dreamed he was charged by a bull on the same night as well.[96]

Hungarian psychoanalyst and anthropologist Géza Róheim gave a curiosity of enough relevant particularity that its inclusion is warranted nearer the end here. In 1932, a very disturbed patient of his dreamed that she entered the therapist's room and told him she had a dream of a white dove alighting upon a pink cloud with a blue sky behind. Still in the dream, before she gets the chance to tell Géza, he tells her he had the very same dream. In other words, as Géza states it, "she dreamed of having dreamed the same thing that I had." Of interest here, Géza had just heard a lecture on telepathy delivered in the Hungarian Psychoanalytical Society regarding such episodes between patient and psychoanalyst, a subject which, according to Géza, he had "never been interested in before."[9] For our final connection, such special types, given to psychiatrists in earnest, echo an ancient dream between Athenian statesman Aristides and a temple official who likewise dreamed a double dream *inside* a dream. They *dreamed*, in other words, like Róheim's patient, of dreaming the same. Even here, the dream results in real-world action; in this case, Aristides continued incubation at the temples.[98]

MAGIC AND TRUTH

While it cannot be said that the veridical value of the shared dream is inherently greater than the individuals' singular experience, we can say that, in both the old tales and in our own times, this is often the case. Furthermore, the shared dream as a literary device, at the very least, performs this very function for the reader. The reader, as it happens, is often similarly impressed with these accounts in their literal anecdotal form as opposed to those more singular. The shared dream, double dream, or double vision is found among many typical kinds of extrasensory dream types in legend, lyric, and lore and deserves more extensive treatment. These visions and dreams are found in relation to all of the phenomena covered here and opening up the inquiry as one into more general and shared visionary spaces may allow for otherwise unattainable insights. Near-death experiences, shared death experiences, shared psychic journeys, etc.—these strange and otherworldly things are not just the property of the individual but often occur to many at once. This, like so many of the subjects we have explored, attains particular importance in light of their evidently continued existence.

EPILOGUE

The Magic in the Mind

To deny that the dream, the vision, or the otherwise prophetical intimation can impart accurate information to the visionary, which they may then make use of, which might change them—which might inspire art and craft, legend, lyric, and lore—would be to deny the surprisingly consistent and multivarious testimonies of disparate men and women at all times and in all corners of the globe. While this has been no scientific inquiry, and the reader would be encouraged to corroborate or disprove for themselves just how similar and relevant these chosen tales have been to those collected using far stricter methods,* such ventures are not the sole arbiters of progress, an equation into which the inner world of the individual and its meaningful and potentially veridical coherence with that of others is perhaps less often factored, and my own sense is that there is a contribution to be made regarding the present dataset, although much more remains to be done.

If one begins to take the notions entertained within these pages, admittedly entirely antithetical to pervasive cultural paradigms, rather more seriously, the realization that we are and have always been connected in stranger and more mysterious ways than we have supposed begins to dawn. Despite cultural and temporal disparities, despite the waxing and

---

*For overviews regarding the empirical evidence for ESP, the reader would be directed to the likes of Dean Radin's *The Conscious Universe* or the work of Pratt Gaither, such as *Extra-Sensory Perception After Sixty Years.*

waning of interests in magic and the occult, these "extrasensory" capacities have been (and continue to be) attested to in all their very particular idiosyncrasies, far and wide. Both generally and in this broader psychical context, their presence, pedigree, and interrelatedness are frequently overlooked by anthropologists, ethnologists, folklorists, explorers, and others alike.

We have seen, sometimes for the first time, that even the most neglected areas of and related to parapsychology, such as the vardoger and its visionary relatives, the shared dream, nearing-death awareness, and visions of a distant crisis unrelated to death, are ubiquitously found in the records, and in numbers far greater than could be represented here. Stories related to discoveries of lost things are certainly known, but here, it is made clear that they are *everywhere* known, relate to more than just treasure, ongoing, and still come even with all their idiosyncrasies such as the connection with the deceased. Others, such as crisis apparitions and deathbed visions, are similarly widespread and evergreen, and while perhaps the most speculative chapter, it is clear that reported contact with other worlds, whether spontaneous or induced, often comes with the very same curative effects and results across greatly disparate cultures right through to our own times. Even in all their synchronicities, these experiences remain comparable, often even in their minutiae, across vast swaths of time and space and therefore demand attention.

Despite the issues with attempting to obtain evidence from the past, the tales nevertheless share undeniable and surprising similarities and seem, in light of the modern accounts, to be a testament to something perennial. They appear to fundamentally resist the morphing and diffusion of traditions, stories, people, and things and seem rather, in some meaningful way, to bind them, and therefore, us, together. This, of course, like love and hate, life and death, elation and melancholy, would be expected if such things were an entirely natural part of the human experience. If there *is* magic in the mind, after all, then all things are inherently magical, mysterious, and imbued with the heady aroma of possibility.

Notes

FOREWORD

1. Hufford, *The Terror that Comes in the Night*.

CHAPTER 1. *I KNEW YOU WERE COMING.*

1. Virtanen, *That Must Have Been ESP!*, 92.
2. Sitwell, *The Scarlet Tree*, 137.
3. Ullman et al., *Dream Telepathy*, 7.
4. Leiter, "The Vardøgr, Perhaps Another Indicator of the Non-Locality of Consciousness," 621.
5. Toelken, "The Moccasin Telegraph and Other Improbabilities," 45–8.
6. Freuchen, *It's All Adventure*, 321.
7. Hill-Tout, *British North America*, 228.
8. Miller, *Nurturing Doubt*, 132.
9. Miller, *Nurturing Doubt*, 124.
10. Miller, *Nurturing Doubt*, 165.
11. Keeney, *Shaking Out the Spirits*, 4.
12. McDowell, *Sayings of the Ancestors*, 62.
13. DeVita, *Stumbling toward Truth*, 145.
14. Scholes, *The First Decade of the Inquisition in Mexico*, 210.
15. Schwab, *Tribes of the Liberian Hinterland*, 405.
16. Leland, *Legends of Florence*, 69.
17. Boas, *The Religion of the Kwakiutl Indians*, 24.

18. Parker, *Seneca Myths and Folk Tales*, 340.
19. Parker, *Seneca Myths and Folk Tales*, 259.
20. Merriam, *The Dawn of the World*, 164.
21. Tikalsky et al., *The Sacred Oral Tradition of the Havasupai*, 177.
22. Dorsey, *The Pawnee Mythology (Part 1)*, 262–3.
23. Brinton, *The Myths of the New World*, 289.
24. Siffredi, "Confrontation with Kixwet," 233–4.
25. Bogoras, "The Folklore of Northeastern Asia," 596.
26. Speck, *Naskapi*, 172.
27. Routledge, *The Mystery of Easter Island*, 142.
28. David-Neel, *With Mystics and Magicians in Tibet*, 308–9.
29. MacDougall, *History of Inverness County*, 332–3.
30. O'Farrell, *Irish Saints*, 15–6.
31. Green, *These Wonders to Behold*, 79.
32. Handy, *Polynesian Religion*, 60.
33. Rhine, *The Invisible Picture*, 121–2.
34. Gaster, *Ma'aseh Book*, 390.
35. Shaw, "Dreaming as Accomplishment," 45.
36. Barker and Mathews, *The Two Worlds of Jimmie Barker*, 71.
37. Shirokogorov, *Pyschomental Complex of the Tungus*, 118.
38. Shirokogorov, *Pyschomental Complex of the Tungus*, 118–9.
39. Jochelson, *The Yakut*, 56.
40. Ruppert and Bernet, *Our Voices*, 100.
41. Golomb, *An Anthropology of Curing in Multiethnic Thailand*, 261.
42. Brinton, *The Myths of the New World*, 289–90.
43. Paterson, *Weird Tales*, 230–1.
44. White, *A Picture of Pioneer Times in California*, 428.
45. Beaumont, *An Historical, Physiological and Theological Treatise*, 85.
46. Rougemont, *The National Dream Book*, 27.
47. Hand and Talley, *Popular Beliefs and Superstitions from Utah*, 84.
48. Seklemian, *The Golden Maiden*, 147.
49. Dalgairns, *Life of St. Stephen Harding*, 110–1.
50. Waldron, *The History and Description of the Isle of Man*, 75–6.
51. Krohn, *Suomalaisten Runojen Uskonto*, 164.
52. Sheldrake, *Dogs That Know When Their Owners Are Coming Home*, 89.
53. Jacobson, *Life without Death?*, 41–2.
54. Spencer, *Powers of the Mind*, 253.

55. Steiger, *The Psychic Feats of Olof Jonsson*, 31.
56. Humphreys, *The Fetch*, 357.
57. Hofberg, *Swedish Fairy Tales*, 97–8.
58. Lang, "Andrew Lang on More Coincidences and Dream-Warnings," 588.
59. Leiter, "The Vardøgr, Perhaps Another Indicator of the Non-Locality of Consciousness," 621–34.
60. Myers, *Human Personality and Its Survival of Bodily Death*, 272.
61. Steiger, *Real Ghosts, Restless Spirits and Haunted Minds*, 116.
62. Craigie, "The Norwegian Vardogr," 305.
63. Kvideland and Sehmsdorf, *Scandinavian Folk Belief and Legend*, 64.
64. Dodds, "Two Concordant Experiences Coinciding with a Death," 337–8.
65. Sabine, *Second Sight in Daily Life*, 108–9.
66. Sabine, *Second Sight in Daily Life*, 109.
67. Krohn, *Suomalaisten Runojen Uskonto*, 165.
68. Virtanen, *That Must Have Been ESP!*, 93.
69. Virtanen, *That Must Have Been ESP!*, 93.
70. Rainwater, *Grandma Speaks*, 44.
71. Bennett, *Traditions of Belief*, 134.
72. Dégh, *Folktales of Hungary*, 151.
73. Ramsay, *Folklore*, 17.
74. Savage, *Miramichi*, 9.
75. Collins, *Cistercian Legends of the Thirteenth Century*, 109.
76. Sheldrake, *The Sense of Being Stared At*, 89.
77. MacLeod, *Celtic Myth and Religion*, 78.
78. Plutarch, *Lives, vol. 5*, 303–7.
79. Rabb, *National Epics*, 133.
80. Dodds, "Telepathy and Clairvoyance in Classical Antiquity," 306–7.
81. Plutarch, *Lives, vol. 7*, 196–97.
82. Hodges, *The Early Church from Ignatius to Augustine*, 95.
83. Tyler, *Japanese Tales*, 253–62.
84. Sun, *Chinese Myths*, 111.
85. Clouston, *A Group of Eastern Romances and Stories*, 138–9.
86. Orbelean, *History of the State of Sisakan, vol. 1*.
87. Lang, *Lives and Legends of the Georgian Saints*, 139.
88. Feather, *The Gift*, 7.
89. Jones, *Thirty-Seven Tales from the Konjaku Monogatari Collection*, 35.
90. Ryder, *The Panchatantra of Vishnu Sharma*, 428–29.

91. Swami, *Lives of the Vaishnava Saints*, 147.
92. Keith-Falconer, *Kalilah and Dimnah, or The Fables of Bidpai*, xxxi–i.
93. Gordon, *Before the Bible*, 64.
94. Rae, *The White Sea Peninsula*, 184–85.
95. Mackenzie, *Teutonic Myth and Legend*, 326.
96. Davidson, *Myths and Symbols in Pagan Europe*, 143.
97. Rand, *Legends of the Micmacs*, 372.
98. Elliott, *The Apocryphal New Testament*, 702.
99. Gibbs, *Holy Land Travel Diary*, 40.
100. Wallace, *Celtic Saints*, 17.
101. Gurney, Myers, and Podmore, *Phantasms of the Living Vol. 2*, 100.
102. Deans, "Cases," 58–64.
103. Nedelec, *Cambria Sacra, or, The History of the Early Cambro-British Christians*, 378–79.
104. Wells, *Untold Stories and Unknown Saints*, 140.
105. Carroll, *The Life of St. Alphonsus Liguori*, 194.
106. Fitzsimon, *Words of Comfort to Persecuted Catholics*, 20.
107. Stokes, *Three Months in the Forests of France*, 110.
108. Stokes, *The Birth and Life of St. Moling*, 25.
109. Ó hÓgáin, *Myth, Legend & Romance*, 49.
110. Kirk, *The Secret Commonwealth of Elves, Fauns, & Fairies*, 27–28.
111. Adamnan, *Life of Saint Columba, Founder of Hy*, 85.
112. O'Hanlon, *The Life of St. David*, 69–70.
113. Carletti, *Life of St. Benedict*, 136.
114. Rabb, *National Epics*, 308.
115. O'Donaghue, *Brendaniana*, 212.
116. Lynch, *Knights of God*, 146–47.
117. Colum, *A Treasury of Irish Folklore*, 104–12.
118. McNamara et al., *Sainted Women of the Dark Ages*, 129.
119. Mango, *The Chronicle of Theophanes Confessor*, 135–36.
120. Cline et al., *The Sinkaietk or Southern Okanagon of Washington*, 163.
121. Giles, *Strange Stories from a Chinese Studio*, 380–4.
122. Rose, *Living Magic*, 152.
123. Parker, *The Euahlayi Tribe*, 135.
124. Wissler and Duval, *Mythology of the Blackfoot Indians*, 280.
125. Savage, *Life Beyond Death*, 90–1.
126. Turner, *The Spirit and the Drum*, 107.

127. Ingham, *Tales with a Texas Twist*, 18–23.
128. Stokes, *Lives of Saints, from the Book of Lismore*, 265.
129. Plummer, *Bethada Náem nÉrenn*, 36–37.
130. Gregory, *A Book of Saints and Wonders*, 162–3.
131. Baring-Gould and Fisher, *The Lives of the British Saints*, 146.
132. Plummer, *Bethada Náem nÉrenn*, 17.
133. Michael the Syrian, *Michael Rabo's Chronicle, The 4th through 6th Centuries*, 593–4.
134. Calmet, *The Phantom World*, 78–9.
135. Ury, *Tales of Times Now Past*, 116.
136. Horne, *The Sacred Books and Early Literature of the East*, 82.
137. Bosworth, et al., *The Encyclopedia of Islam*, 210.
138. Lingwood, *Politics, Poetry and Sufism in Medieval Iran*, 136–37.
139. Maulana Jalalu-'d-Din Muhammad I Rumi, *Masnavi I Ma'navi*, 181.
140. Shah, *The Sufis*, 47.
141. Carpenter, "Chaitanya, an Indian St. Francis," 666.
142. Plummer, *Bethada Náem nÉrenn*, 310.
143. Moxon, *Peter's Halakhic Nightmare*, 492.
144. Wilhelm, *The Chinese Fairy Book*, 82.
145. Werner, *Myths and Legends of China*, 130–31.
146. Thompson, *The Life and Glories of St. Joseph*, 17–18.
147. Hutchinson, *The Golden Porch*, 71.
148. Moxon, *Peter's Halakhic Nightmare*, 475.
149. Dillon, "The Story of the Finding of Cashel," 61–73.
150. McGrew, *Sturlunga Saga, Vol. 2*, 365.
151. Grousset, *Conqueror of the World*, 37.
152. Visser, *The Dragon in China and Japan*, 182.
153. Brown, *Three Elema Myths*, 175–6.
154. Howitt, *The Native Tribes of South-East Australia*, 401.
155. Taylor, *Te Ika a Maui, or New Zealand and its Inhabitants*, 335.
156. Booss, *A Treasury of Irish Myth, Legend, and Folklore*, 462.
157. Plummer, *Bethada Náem nÉrenn*, 310.
158. Virtanen, *That Must Have Been ESP!*, 94.
159. Skinner, *Myths and Legends Beyond Our Borders*, 41.
160. Hobley, *Ethnology of A-Kamba and Other East African Tribes*, 116.
161. Park, *Africa and Its Exploration as Told by Its Explorers, vol. 2*, 213.
162. Wallace and Hoebel, *The Comanches*, 334.

163. Moss, *Dreamways of the Iroquois*, 42–43.
164. Steward, *Northern and Gosiute Shoshoni*, 285.
165. VanStone, *Athapaskan Adaptions*, 68.
166. Herdt, *Guardians of the Flute*, 46.
167. Brabrook, "Presidential Address," 22.
168. Rand, *A Short Statement of Facts*, 8–9.
169. Plutarch, *Morals*, 318–19.
170. Moss, *The Secret History of Dreaming*, 146.
171. Dorsey, *The Pawnee Mythology (Part 1)*, 417.
172. Fraser, "The First Battle of Moytura," 1–63.
173. Dentan, *The Semai*, 19.
174. Roseman, *Healing Sounds from the Malaysian Rainforest*, 56.
175. Thwaites, *The Jesuit Relations and Allied Documents, vols. 1–10*, 171.
176. Lowie, *The Crow Indians*, 238.
177. Sheldrake, *Dogs That Know When Their Owners Are Coming Home*, xiii.
178. Sheldrake, *Dogs That Know When Their Owners Are Coming Home*, 16.
179. Sheldrake, *Dogs That Know When Their Owners Are Coming Home*, 22.
180. Sheldrake, *Dogs That Know When Their Owners Are Coming Home*, 245–71.
181. Venkataswami, *Folktales from India*, 31.
182. Gusinde, *Folk Literature of the Yamana Indians*, 195.
183. Leigh, *Ballads & Legends of Cheshire*, 75–77.
184. Craigie, "The Norwegian Vardogr," 305.

CHAPTER 2. I KNEW YOU WERE IN TROUBLE

1. Centerwall, "A Strange Premonition," 27.
2. De Peyer, "Uncanny Communication and the Porous Mind," 167.
3. De Peyer, "Uncanny Communication and the Porous Mind," 160.
4. Flammarion, *The Unknown*, 278–9.
5. Freud, "Dreams and the Occult," 108.
6. Laskow, "The Role of the Supernatural in the Discovery of EEGs."
7. Ullman et al., *Dream Telepathy*, 74.
8. Jung, *Memories, Dreams, Reflections*, 302–3.
9. Eisenbud, "Psychiatric Contributions to Parapsychology," 8.
10. Jacobson, *Life without Death?*, 39.
11. Luck, *Arcana Mundi*, 46.
12. Philostratus, *Lives of the Sophists*, 415–16.

13. Ramsay, *Tales from Turkey*, 202.
14. Callaway, *Nursery Tales, Traditions, and Histories of the Zulus*, 146–7.
15. Harrington, *Religion and Ceremonies of the Lenape*, 308–09.
16. Tikalsky et al., *The Sacred Oral Tradition of the Havasupai*, 163–4.
17. Ingham, *Tales with a Texas Twist*, 18–23.
18. Afanas'ev, *Russian Fairy Tales*, 262–3.
19. Jenness, *The Life of the Copper Eskimos*, 200.
20. Faurot, *Asian-Pacific Folktales and Legends*, 189–90.
21. Terada, *The Magic Crocodile and Other Folktales from Indonesia*, 120.
22. Burnouf, *Legends of Indian Buddhism*, 74–93.
23. Menon, *Folk Tales of Kerala*, 76.
24. Kracke, "To Dream, Perchance to Cure," 107.
25. Hoffmann, *The Menominee*, 93.
26. De Voragine (Ryan translation), *The Golden Legend*, 188.
27. Tyler, *Japanese Tales*, 129.
28. Green, *These Wonders to Behold*, 46–7.
29. Feather, *The Gift*, 217–8.
30. Boratav, "The Tale and the Epico-Novelistic Narrative," 18.
31. Pliny, *Natural History, vol. 2*, 149.
32. Valerius Maximus, *His Collections*, 40.
33. Fansler, "Metrical Romances in the Philippines," 226.
34. Rabb, *National Epics*, 323.
35. Arnot, *Armenian Literature*, 57.
36. Walker and Uysal, *Tales Alive in Turkey*, 208–9.
37. Newell, "The Legend of the Holy Grail," 41.
38. Steiger and Steiger, *Amazing Moms*, 170–1.
39. Burton, *The Land of Midian (Revisited)*, 12–13.
40. Hamon, *Mysteries and Romances of the World's Greatest Occultist*, 78–79.
41. Kvideland and Sehmsdorf, *Scandinavian Folk Belief and Legend*, 63–4.
42. Rhine, *The Invisible Picture*, 58.
43. Glass-Coffin, *The Gift of Life*, 69.
44. Leach, *The Rainbow Book of American Folk Tales and Legends*, 259.
45. Haynes, *The Hidden Springs*, 62.
46. Kramer, *Literature Among the Cuna Indians*, 89.
47. Curtin and Hewitt, *Seneca Fiction, Legends, and Myths*, 113–4.
48. Jacobs, *Coos Narrative and Ethnologic Texts*, 56–7.
49. Thompson, *Pitch Woman and Other Stories*, 71–72.

244   Notes

50. Jacobs, *Kalapuya Texts Part 1: Santiam Kalapuya Ethnologic Texts*, 51.
51. Schaefer, "Crossing of the Souls," 162–3.
52. Brown, "Shamanism and It's Discontents," 111.
53. Schwartz, *Lilith's Cave*, 28.
54. Salo, *Roles of Magic and Healing*, 16.
55. McFadden, *Profiles in Wisdom*, 89–90.
56. Felgar and Moser, *People of the Desert and Sea*, 201.
57. Hendricks, *Roosters, Rhymes, and Railroad Tracks*, 51.
58. Cowell, *The Jataka, or Stories of the Buddha's Former Births*, 108.
59. McCulloch, *Bengali Household Tales*, 73–80.
60. Dineshchandra, *The Folk-Literature of Bengal*, 207–8.
61. Greey, *The Golden Lotus, and Other Legends of Japan*, 177.
62. Douglas, *Scottish Fairy and Folk Tales*, 147–8.
63. Hutchinson, *The Golden Porch*, 30.
64. Gaster, *Ma'aseh Book*, 238.
65. Curtin and Hewitt, *Seneca Fiction, Legends, and Myths*, 352.
66. Moss, *Dreamways of the Iroqois*, 41.
67. Barbeau, *Huron and Wyandot Mythology*, 399.
68. Rand, *Legends of the Micmacs*, 40.
69. Geoffrey, *Coronation Commentary*, 322.
70. Inglis, *The Paranormal*, 175–76.
71. Khan et al., *Neo-Aramaic and Kurdish Folklore from Northern Iraq*, 550.
72. Wadley, "Folk Literature of South Asia," 2.
73. Riordan, *A World of Folk Tales*, 66.
74. Hartland, "The Voice of the Stone of Destiny," 43.
75. Yoder, *Discovering American Folklife*, 224.
76. Pedroso and Consiglieri, *Portuguese Folk-Tales*, 41–44.
77. Nicholson, *Studies in Islamic Mysticism*, 164–65.
78. Podmore, *Apparitions and Thought-Transference*, 181.
79. Rhine, *The Invisible Picture*, 64–65.
80. Creighton, *Bluenose Ghosts*, 15.
81. Rhine, *Hidden Channels of the Mind*, 72–73.
82. Garrett, *Telepathy*, 69–72.
83. Kepelino, *Kepelino's Traditions of Hawaii*, 122.
84. Beckwith, *The Hawaiian Romance of Laieikawai*, 371–2.
85. Edmundson, *A Journal of the Life*, 21–22.
86. Curtin, *Myths of the Modocs*, 60–7.

87. Munro, *Life of St. Columban by the Monk Jonas*, 12.
88. Nunn, *Nova Scotia History with a Twist*, 151.
89. Hope, *Franciscan Martyrs in England*, 11–12.
90. De Voragine (Granger and Ripperger translation), *The Golden Legend*, 242.
91. Gomme, *English Traditions and Foreign Customs*, 182.
92. Lang, "Andrew Lang on More Coincidences and Dream-Warnings," 599.
93. Nicolson, *Shetland Folklore*, 72–3.
94. Ramsay, *Folklore*, 17.
95. Dalyell, *The Darker Superstitions of Scotland*, 473–4.
96. Defoe, *The Secrets of the Invisible World Disclos'd*, 263–4.
97. Holzer, *Hidden Meanings in Dreams*, 39.
98. Ahmed, *Discovering Islam*, 37.
99. Head, *Hagiography and the Cult of Saints*, 39.
100. Benn, *Daily Life in Traditional China*, 273–4.
101. Ahern, *The Cult of the Dead in a Chinese Village*, 183.
102. De Paor, *Saint Patrick's World*, 266.
103. Head, *Hagiography and the Cult of Saints*, 141.
104. Vigfusson and Powell, *Origines Islandicae*, 417.

CHAPTER 3. A DATE WITH DESTINY

1. Ariès, *The Hour of Our Death*, 9.
2. Frankl, *Man's Search for Meaning*, 70–71.
3. Clarke, "Brief Lives," 307.
4. Bronkhorst, *Dreams at the Threshold*, 110.
5. Fenwick and Fenwick, *The Art of Dying*, 43.
6. Pearson, *At Heaven's Door*, 24–25.
7. Phillips, "Medicine," 45.
8. Exton-Smith, "Terminal Illness in the Aged," 305–8.
9. Ngeh, "The Phenomenon of Premonition of Death in Older Patient," 1672.
10. Parkes, "Accuracy of Predictions of Survival in Later Stages of Cancer," 29–31.
11. Reichard, *Navaho Religion*, 41.
12. Dorsey, *A Study of Siouan Cults*, 569.
13. Lowie, *The Northern Shoshone*, 225.
14. Shaw, "Dreaming as Accomplishment," 42.
15. Schwab, *Tribes of the Liberian Hinterland*, 241.
16. Exton-Smith, "Terminal Illness in the Aged," 305–8.

17. Schwab, *Tribes of the Liberian Hinterland*, 241.
18. Humphreys, *The Southern New Hebrides*, 147.
19. Hyatt, *Folk-Lore from Adams County, Illinois*, 569.
20. Creighton, *Bluenose Ghosts*, 2.
21. Ariès, *The Hour of Our Death*, 5–10.
22. Creighton, *Bluenose Ghosts*, 13–14.
23. Weisman and Hackett, "Predilection to Death," 232–56.
24. Schouppe, *Purgatory*, 277.
25. Tylenda, *Jesuit Saints & Martyrs*, 384.
26. Farnum, *The Wool Merchant of Segovia*, 26.
27. Kerr, *The Life of Cesare Cardinal Baronius of the Roman Oratory*, 407–13.
28. Carletti, *Life of St. Benedict*, 136.
29. Butler, *Butler's Lives of the Saints*, 125.
30. Taylor, "Is It Possible to Foresee Death?"
31. Bolshakoff, *Russian Mystics*, 69.
32. Charles, *The Book of Jubilees*, 207–10.
33. Smyth, *Aeschylus*, 111.
34. Valerius Maximus, *His Collections*, 39.
35. Shakespaere, *Julius Caesar*, 75.
36. Ariès, *The Hour of Our Death*, 6.
37. Elton and Powell, *The Nine Books of the Danish History of Saxo Grammaticus*, 48–49.
38. Arnold, *Stories of Ancient Peoples*, 112.
39. Forty, *Classic Mythology*, 34–35.
40. Plutarch, *Lives, vol. 4*, 441–43.
41. Valerius Maximus, *Memorable Deeds and Sayings*, 30.
42. Feather, *The Gift*, 50.
43. Rougemont, *The National Dream Book*, 12.
44. Pliny, *The Letters of the Younger Pliny*, 151–51.
45. Ury, *Tales of Times Now Past*, 100–101.
46. Dykstra, "Tales of the Compassionate Kannon," 137.
47. Terada, *Under the Starfruit Tree*, 83.
48. Michael the Syrian, *Michael Rabo's Chronicle, The 4th through 6th Centuries*, 254.
49. Collins and Fishbane, *Death, Ecstasy, and Other Worldly Journeys*, 346–7.
50. Davidson, *Myths and Symbols in Pagan Europe*, 66.
51. O'Grady, *Silva Gadelica (I-XXXI)*, 443.
52. ÓCuiv, "Miscellanea," 116–7.

53. Gillespie, *Devoted People*, 130.
54. Mac'Manus, "Folk-Tales from Western Ireland," 339.
55. Plummer, *Bethada Náem nÉrenn*, 183.
56. Van Braght, *The Bloody Theatre, or Martyr's Mirror of the Defenceless Christians*, 1068.
57. Nora Chadwick, *Stories and Ballads of the Far Past*, 77–78.
58. Jalal al-Din al-Suyuti, *History of the Caliphs*, 196.
59. Reichel-Dolmatoff, *The Shaman and the Jaguar*, 49.
60. Knight, "The Psychiatrist Who Believed People Could Tell the Future."
61. Fearn-Wannan, *Australian Folklore*, 193.
62. Lawrence-Smith, *Tales of Old Worcestershire*, 23–24.
63. Krausmüller, "Can Human Beings Know the Hour of Their Own Death or of the Death of Others?, 63.
64. Curtis, *Persian Myths*, 34–36.
65. Flower, *The Seer in Ancient Greece*, 93.
66. Herbermann et al., *The Catholic Encyclopedia*, 80.
67. Nedelec, *Cambria Sacra; or, The History of the Early Cambro-British Christians*, 234.
68. Windham, *Sixty Saints for Boys*, 60–65.
69. Cave, *A Complete History*, 458.
70. Consitt, *Life of Saint Cuthbert*, 26–8.
71. Liguori, *Victories of the Martyrs*, 222.
72. Plutarch, *Morals*, 157.
73. Liguori, *Victories of the Martyrs*, 204–7.
74. D'Aguilers, *Historia Francorum Qui Ceperunt Iherusalem*, 88–89.
75. Giles, *The Venerable Bede's Ecclesiastical History of England*, 186.
76. Hanauer, *Folk-Lore of the Holy Land*, 161–62.
77. Greenhouse, *Premonitions*, 154.
78. Taylor, *Te Ika a Maui, or New Zealand and its Inhabitants*, 334.
79. Trautmann, *Legends and Tales of Old Munich*, 51.
80. Timbs, *Signs Before Death*, 102–3.
81. Sinclair, *Satan's Invisible World Discovered*, 251–53.
82. Jones, *Things That Go Bump in the Night*, 92.
83. Olden, *The People of Tipi Sapa (The Dakotas)*, 71.
84. Luraghi, *The Ancient Messenians*, 470.
85. Savage, *Life Beyond Death*, 45–6.
86. Jones, "The Ghosts of New York," 245.

87. Batthyány, *Threshold*, 122.
88. Batthyány, *Threshold*, 122–3.
89. Fenwick and Fenwick, *The Art of Dying*, 42.
90. Roscoe, *The Bakitara or Banyoro*, 49.
91. Kachhawa, "Do Some People Have Premonitions About Their Death?," 2020.
92. Madigan, *Ordained Women in the Early Church*, 59.
93. Aflaki, *Legends of the Sufis*, 118–21.
94. Talbot, *Holy Women of Byzantium*, 61.
95. Gregory of Tours, *Life of the Fathers*, 61–62.
96. Gregory of Tours, *Life of the Fathers*, 120.
97. Callanan and Kelley, *Final Gifts*, 16.
98. Callanan and Kelley, *Final Gifts*, 14.
99. Osis and Haraldsson, *At the Hour of Death*, 162–83.
100. Brou, *Saint Madeleine Sophie Barat*, 86–87.
101. Guerber, *Legends of the Rhine*, 59.
102. Rougemont, *The National Dream Book*, 19.
103. Forbes, *Lives of S. Ninian and S. Kentigern*, 114–15.
104. Tedlock, *The Beautiful and the Dangerous*, 51.
105. Herbermann et al., *The Catholic Encyclopedia*, 201.
106. Talbot, *Holy Women of Byzantium*, 151–52.
107. Hull, *Early Christian Ireland*, 122–23.
108. Valerius Maximus, *His Collections*, 33–34.
109. Osis and Haraldsson, *At the Hour of Death*, 46.
110. Osis and Haraldsson, *At the Hour of Death*, 66–67.
111. Giles, *The Venerable Bede's Ecclesiastical History of England*, 190–91.
112. Guerber, *Legends of the Middle Ages*, 298–99.
113. Leland, *Legends of Florence*, 160.
114. McNamara et al., *Sainted Women of the Dark Ages*, 324–25.
115. Caesarius of Heisterbach, *The Dialogue on Miracles, vols. 1–2*, 535–36.
116. Herbermann et al., *The Catholic Encyclopedia*, 294.
117. Brown, *The Little Flowers of Saint Francis*, 204.
118. Ramsay, *Everyday Life in Turkey*, 183.
119. Ariès, *The Hour of Our Death*, 10.
120. Sartori, *The Near-Death Experiences of Hospitalized Intensive Care Patients*, 102.
121. Whitney, "A Terrible Ordeal," 14.
122. Seton, *The Arctic Prairies*, 57–58.

123. Hamon, *Mysteries and Romances of the World's Greatest Occultist*, 96–97.
124. Sadeh, *Jewish Folktales*, 180.
125. McNamara et al., *Sainted Women of the Dark Ages*, 162.
126. Herbermann et al., *The Catholic Encyclopedia*, 407.
127. Herbermann et al., *The Catholic Encyclopedia*, 507.
128. Tabor, *The Saints in Art*, 75.
129. Ariès, *The Hour of Our Death*, 6–7.
130. Ariès, *The Hour of Our Death*, 8.

CHAPTER 4. DISCOVERIES AT THE DEATHBED

1. Blum and Blum, *The Dangerous Hour*, 301.
2. Mesegeur, *The Secret of Dreams*, 129.
3. Krause, *The Tlingit Indians*, 199.
4. Jackson, *The Fish People*, 201.
5. Osis and Haraldsson, *At the Hour of Death*, 31.
6. Osis and Haraldsson, *At the Hour of Death*, 31.
7. Batthyány, *Threshold*, 124.
8. Batthyány, *Threshold*, 125.
9. Lu, *Encounters with the World of Spirits*, 143–46.
10. Cobbe, *The Peak in Darien*, 261.
11. McNamara et al., *Sainted Women of the Dark Ages*, 85.
12. Camm, *Forgotten Shrines*, 228.
13. Dennys, *The Folk-Lore of China*, 73.
14. Augear, *letter to the editor*, 274–5.
15. Duncan and Harris, *The Troll Tale and Other Scary Stories*, 155.
16. Osis and Haraldsson, *At the Hour of Death*, 166.
17. Moody, *Glimpses of Eternity*, 15–18.
18. Coffin, *Death in Early America*, 57.
19. Schouppe, *Purgatory*, 285.
20. Steele, *The Little Flowers of Saint Francis*, 393.
21. Mesegeur, *The Secret of Dreams*, 129–30.
22. Calmet, *The Phantom World*, 210.
23. Rogo, *An Experience of Phantoms*, 164.
24. Barrett, *Death-Bed Visions*, 19–20.
25. Barrett, *Death-Bed Visions*, 12–13.
26. Colgrave and Mynors, *Bede's Ecclesiastical History of the English People*, 359.

27. Kalmus, "Doorway to Another World," 29–31.
28. Caesarius of Heisterbach, *The Dialogue on Miracles*, vol. 2, 234.
29. Savage, *Life Beyond Death*, 234.
30. Kieckhefer, *Unquiet Souls*, 162.
31. Gregory, *Visions and Beliefs in the West of Ireland*, 77.
32. Lecouteux, *The Pagan Book of the Dead*, 71–72.
33. Caesarius of Heisterbach, *The Dialogue on Miracles*, vol. 1, 535–36.
34. Thurston, *The Church and Spiritualism*, 214.
35. Harris, *Essays in Occultism, Spiritism, and Demonology*, 72.
36. Anonymous, *Tales of Superstition: or Relations of Apparitions*, 18.
37. Tylenda, *Jesuit Saints & Martyrs*, 50.
38. Tuckett, *The Evidence for the Supernatural*, 82.
39. M. L'Abbé Janvier, *Life of Sister Mary St. Peter, Carmelite of Tours*, 440.
40. Nagarajan, *Jewish Tales from Eastern Europe*, 101–3.
41. Cluness, *Told Round the Peat Fire*, 226.
42. Henderson, *Notes on the Folk-Lore of the Northern Counties of England and the Borders*, 47.
43. Robe, *Hispanic Legends from New Mexico*, 43.
44. Kroeber, *Yurok Myths*, 382–84.
45. Sutter, *Tell Me, Grandmother*, 137–38.
46. Pearson et al., "Crisis Impressions," 2.
47. Bois, *Le Miracle Moderne*, 22.
48. Funk, *The Widow's Mite and Other Psychic Phenomena*, 28.
49. Collins, *Cistercian Legends of the Thirteenth Century*, 14–17.
50. Jarvis, *Haunted Shores*, 77–79.
51. Creighton, *Bluenose Ghosts*, viii.

CHAPTER 5. REVENANTS, WRAITHS, AND DISINTERESTED SHADES

1. Hopkins, *Chuj (Mayan) Narratives*, 66.
2. Summers, *The Vampire in Europe*, 84.
3. Collison-Morley, *Greek and Roman Ghost Stories*, 71.
4. Felton, *Haunted Greece and Rome*, 26.
5. Apuleius, *The Golden Ass*, 264.
6. Belsey, *Tales of the Troubled Dead*, 16.
7. Gale, *Korean Folk Tales*, 36–37.

8. Landtman, *The Kiwai Papuans of British New Guinea*, 292.
9. Dorson, *Folktales Told around the World*, 539.
10. Hansen, *The Types of the Folktake in Cuba, Puerto Rico, the Dominican Republic, and Spanish South America*, 89.
11. Baylor, "Folklore from Socorro, New Mexico," 93.
12. Parsons, *Mitla, Town of the Souls, and other Zapoteco-Speaking Pueblos of Oaxaca*, Mexico.
13. Brewster, "Stories of the Supernatural from Southern Indiana," 227–34.
14. Garcez, *American Indian Ghost Stories of the Southwest*, 7–11.
15. Elsaesser, *Spontaneous Contacts with the Deceased*, 89–90.
16. Collins, *Cistercian Legends of the Thirteenth Century*, 143–4.
17. Macaulay, *The History of Herodotus*, 298–9.
18. Green and McCreery, *Apparitions*, 98.
19. John Blake, "Do Loved Ones Bid Farewell from beyond the Grave?"
20. Gordon Smith, *Ancient Tales and Folk-Lore of Japan*, 2–9.
21. Martin, *Mysterious Tales of Japan*, 69.
22. Nakamura, *Miraculous Stories from the Japanese Buddhist Tradition*, 194–97.
23. Benn, *Daily Life in Traditional China*, 279.
24. Masters, *The Natural History of the Vampire*, 53–55.
25. Calmet, *The Phantom World*, 262–3.
26. Summers, *The Vampire in Europe*, 46.
27. Calmet, *The Phantom World*, 171–2.
28. Lecouteux, *The Pagan Book of the Dead*, 96–97.
29. Ralston, *Russian Folk-Tales*, 10–12.
30. Pedroso and Consiglieri, *Portuguese Folk-Tales*, 29–32.
31. Philostratus, *The Life of Apollonius of Tyana*, 217–20.
32. Konstantinos, *Vampires*, 21.
33. Hobley, *Ethnology of A-Kamba and Other East African Tribes*, 90.
34. Brunvand, *The Vanishing Hitchhiker*, 33.
35. Arnason, *Icelandic Legends*, 173–7.
36. Adams, *Ghost Stories of the Lehigh Valley*, 87.
37. Li, "Two Chinese Ghosts," 279–80.
38. Owen, *Footfalls on the Boundary of Another World*, 367.
39. Allred, "Notes on the Appearance of a Spectral Death Messenger," 197–9.
40. J. L. L., "Popular Tales and Legends," 342.
41. Lysaght, "Traditional Beliefs and Narratives of a Contemporary Irish Traditions Bearer," 291.

42. Hogg, "Adam Bell," 125–31.
43. Elsaesser, *Spontaneous Contacts with the Deceased*, 156–7.
44. Hyatt, *Folk-Lore from Adams County, Illinois*, 548.
45. Inglis, *The Paranormal*, 166.
46. Lang, *The Making of Religion*, 113–4.
47. Leach, *Whistle in the Graveyard*, 64–65.
48. Dance, *Shuckin' and Jivin'*, 32.
49. Vigfusson and Powell, *Origines Islandicae*, 561–2.
50. Arnason, *Icelandic Legends*, 191–2.
51. Craigie, *Scandinavian Folk-Lore*, 290–2.
52. Hutchinson, *The Golden Porch*, 243.
53. Lame Deer and Erdoes, *Lame Deer*, 130–1.
54. Lame Deer and Erdoes, *Lame Deer*, 151.
55. Russell, *The Pima Indians*, 57.
56. Tedlock, *The Beautiful and the Dangerous*, 288–90.
57. Carletti, *Life of St. Benedict*, 108–9.
58. Butler, *Butler's Lives of the Saints*, 125.
59. Plummer, *Bethada Náem nÉrenn*, 40.
60. Steiger, *The Psychic Feats of Olof Jonsson*, 31–2.
61. Chadwick and Chadwick, *The Growth of Literature*, 161–8.
62. Jones, "Some Historic Ghosts of New York," 186.
63. Thurston, *The Life of Saint Hugh of Lincoln*, 565–66.
64. Spencer, *The Encyclopedia of Ghosts and Spirits*, 181–2.
65. Baring-Gould, *Early Reminiscences*, 24.
66. Ottway, *News from the Invisible World*, 65–67.
67. Lecouteux, *The Return of the Dead*, 12.
68. Price, *Noted Witnesses for Psychic Occurrences*, 70.

CHAPTER 6. TREASURE, TOMBS, AND VISIONARY BOONS

1. Creighton, *Bluenose Ghosts*, 42.
2. Creighton, *Bluenose Ghosts*, 43.
3. Creighton, *Bluenose Ghosts*, 44.
4. Ramsay, *Folklore: Prince Edward Island*, 67.
5. Skinner, *Myths and Legends of Our Own Land*, 276.
6. Gale, *Miscellanea*, 330.

7. Applegate, *Native Tales of New Mexico*, 113–4.
8. Porter, *Road To Heaven*, 182.
9. Dennys, *The Folk-Lore of China*, 42.
10. Pausanias, *Messenia*, 20–36.
11. Rougemont, *The National Dream Book*, 14.
12. Westropp, "A Folklore Survey of County Clare," 208.
13. O'Reilly, "Now You See It, Now You Don't," 199–200.
14. Leach, *Dictionary of Folklore, Mythology and Legend*, 376.
15. Leland, *Legends of Florence*, 104–5.
16. Finucane, *Appearances of the Dead*, 20.
17. Hofberg, *Swedish Fairy Tales*, 28–30.
18. Spence, *Legends and Romances of Spain*, 330.
19. Shenhar-Alroy, *Jewish and Israeli Folklore*, 64.
20. Radcliffe, *Fiends, Ghosts, and Sprites*, 248–49.
21. Hoogasian-Villa, *100 Armenian Tales*, 351–52.
22. Arcangel, *Afterlife Encounters*, 73.
23. Feather, *The Gift*, 48.
24. Jones, "The Ghosts of New York," 245.
25. Jones, "The Ghosts of New York," 238.
26. Heikkinen and Kervinen, "Finland: The Male Domination," 203.
27. Arcangel, *Afterlife Encounters*, 74–82.
28. Bennett, *Traditions of Belief*, 73.
29. Guggenheim and Guggenheim, *Hello from Heaven*, 244.
30. Guggenheim and Guggenheim, *Hello from Heaven*, 244.
31. Rogers, *Dreams and Premonitions*, 39–41.
32. Hutchinson, *Dreams and Their Meanings*, 239–40.
33. Fansler, *Filipino Popular Tales*, 304–9.
34. Bracciolini, *The Facetiae*, 14–15.
35. Skinner, *Myths and Legends of Our Own Land*, 288.
36. Craigie, "Some Highland Folklore," 373.
37. Hankey, "California Ghosts," 166.
38. Willard, "Paviotso Shamanism," 109.
39. Willard, "Paviotso Shamanism," 109–10.
40. Scholes, "The First Decade of the Inquisition in New Mexico," 219–20.
41. Jenness, *The Life of the Copper Eskimos*, 200.
42. Laubscher, *Sex, Custom and Psychopathology*, 41.

43. Ó hÓgáin, *Myth, Legend & Romance*, 390.
44. Dodds, *The Ancient Concept of Progress*, 175.
45. Pliny, *Natural History*, 625.
46. Plutarch, *Morals*, 10.
47. Schwartz, *Lilith's Cave*, 95–96.
48. Kahk, "Estonia II: The Crusade against Idolatry," 274.
49. Mayer, *Extraordinary Knowing*, 1–10.
50. Harrington, *Religion and Ceremonies of the Lenape*, 162–63.
51. Kroeber, *Yurok Myths*, 56.
52. Maulana Jalalu-'d-Din Muhammad I Rumi, *Masnavi I Ma'navi, The Spiritual Couplets of Maulana Jalalu-'d-Din Muhammad I Rumi*, 312.
53. Parsons, *Folklore of the Antilles, French and English*, 334.
54. Bell, *Lives and Legends of the English Bishops and Kings*, 61–2.
55. Duckett, *The Wandering Saints of the Early Middle Ages*, 240.
56. Wilby, *Cunning Folk and Familiar Spirits*, 38.
57. Maxwell-Stuart, *An Abundance of Witches*, 113.
58. Velimirovic, *Stories of Saints from the Prologue*, 64.
59. Carey, *King of Mysteries*, 176.
60. Gillespie, *Devoted People*, 129–30.
61. Seymour, *Irish Witchcraft and Demonology*, 78.
62. Guiley, *The Dreamer's Way*, 165.
63. Hazlitt, *Tales and Legends of National Origin*, 44–49.
64. Jones, "The Ghosts of New York," 245.
65. Elwin, *The Muria and Their Ghotul*, 475.
66. Dracott, *Folk Tales from Simla*, 3.
67. Davies, *Balm from Beyond*, 77–8.
68. Elsaesser, *Spontaneous Contacts with the Deceased*, 135–6.
69. Tedlock, *The Woman in the Shaman's Body*, 109.
70. Lecouteux, *The Pagan Book of the Dead*, 47.
71. Augustine, *Buddhist Hagiography in Early Japan*, 115–6.
72. Harvey, *The Mind of China*, 51.
73. O'Mara, *In Search of Irish Saints*, 17.
74. Baring-Gould, *The Lives of the Saints*, 571–2.
75. Iliowizi, *In the Pale*, 355–56.
76. Downey, *A History of Antioch in Syria*, 497.
77. Boas, *Folktales of Salishan and Sahaptin Tribes*, 47.
78. Elsaesser, *Spontaneous Contacts with the Dead*, 156–7.

79. Gomme, *English Traditions and Foreign Customs*, 179.
80. Beatty, *A Treasury of Australian Folk Tales and Traditions*, 83–4.
81. Kunow, *Maya Medicine*, 44.
82. Weaver, "An Extraordinary Clairvoyant and an Extraordinary Policeman."
83. Rogers, *Dreams and Premonitions*, 49–50.
84. Salo, *Roles of Magic and Healing*, 12.
85. Kahk, "Estonia II: The Crusade against Idolatry," 274.
86. Codrington, *The Melanesians*, 291.
87. Feather, *The Gift*, 48.
88. Evans-Pritchard, *Witchcraft, Oracles, and Magic Among the Azande*, 185.
89. Sigerist, *Primitive and Archaic Medicine*, 176.
90. Craigie, *Scandinavian Folk-Lore*, 291–2.
91. Green, *These Wonders to Behold*, 49–50.
92. Oppenheim, "The Interpretation of Dreams in the Ancient Near East," 197.
93. Aflaki, *Legends of the Sufis*, 99.
94. Dorsey, *The Pawnee Mythology (Part 1)*, 415.
95. Skinner, *Social Life and Ceremonial Bundles of the Menomini Indians*, 51.
96. Steward, *Northern and Gosiute Shoshoni*, 283.
97. Lindstrom, *Tanna Times*, 27.
98. Shaw, "Dreaming as Accomplishment," 48–49.
99. Nagarajan, *Jewish Tales from Eastern Europe*, 77.
100. Garnett, *Greek Folk Poesy*, 363–4.
101. Guerber, *Legends of Switzerland*, 37.
102. Hauff, *Fairy Tales*, 67–72.
103. Ó hÓgáin, *Myth, Legend & Romance*, 71.
104. Thompson, *Pitch Woman and Other Stories*, 103.
105. Davis and Leung, *Chinese Fables and Folk Stories*, 22–26.
106. Horne, *The Sacred Books and Early Literature of the East*, 81–82.
107. Abbot, *Notable Women in History*, 443.
108. Williams, *Orokaiva Magic*, 336.
109. Pinch, *Magic in Ancient Egypt*, 96.
110. Connor, *Women of Byzantium*, 349.
111. Minorsky, *A History of Sharvan and Darband in the 10th–11th Centuries*, 25.
112. Chamberlain, "Periodical Literature," 78.
113. Herbermann et al., *The Catholic Encyclopedia*, 359.
114. Lang, *The Book of Dreams and Ghosts*, 11.

CHAPTER 7. I KNEW THE CURE

1. Condos, *Star Myths of the Greek and Romans*, 143–4.
2. Luck, *Arcana Mundi*, 147.
3. Guiley, *The Dreamer's Way*, 169.
4. Kittredge, *Witchcraft in Old and New England*, 221.
5. Blacker, "Japan," 78.
6. Blacker, "Japan," 78.
7. Morriseau, *Legends of My People*, 53.
8. Lincoln, *The Dream in Native American and Other Primitive Cultures*, 22.
9. Rose, "Folk-Medicine in the Panjab," 85.
10. Head, *Hagiography and the Cult of Saints*, 182.
11. Kittredge, *Witchcraft in Old and New England*, 125.
12. Guiley, *The Dreamer's Way*, 162.
13. Head, *Hagiography and the Cult of Saints*, 13.
14. Crapanzano, "Saints, Jnun, and Dreams," 148–9.
15. Shaw, "Dreaming as Accomplishment," 47.
16. Shockey, *Reflections of Heaven*, 77–79.
17. Kunow, *Maya Medicine*, 33.
18. Willard, "Paviotso Shamanism," 101.
19. Morriseau, *Legends of My People*, 55.
20. Tedlock, *The Woman in the Shaman's Body*, 134.
21. Black, *Folk-Medicine*, 160.
22. Gregory, *Visions and Beliefs in the West of Ireland*, 29.
23. Skinner, *Social Life and Ceremonial Bundles of the Menomini Indians*, 147.
24. Boas, *The Religion of the Kwakiutl Indians*, 46–50.
25. Tedlock, *The Woman in the Shaman's Body*, 138.
26. Leach, *Dictionary of Folklore, Mythology and Legend*, 191.
27. Reichel-Domatoff, *The Shaman and the Jaguar*, 98.
28. Heucher, *Magic Plants*, 16.
29. Tedlock, *The Woman in the Shaman's Body*, 128.
30. Walker, *The Art of the Turkish Tale*, 188–90.
31. Kennedy, *Legendary Fictions of the Irish Celts*, 100–4.
32. Kahk, "Estonia II: The Crusade against Idolatry," 201.
33. Craigie, *Scandinavian Folk-Lore*, 140–1.
34. Kennedy, *Legendary Fictions of the Irish Celts*, 119–21.
35. Dennys, *The Folk-Lore of China*, 41–42.

36. De Onis, *The Golden Land*, 72–80.
37. Dykstra, "Tales of the Compassionate Kannon," 125.
38. Plutarch, *Lives, vol. 12*, 50–51.
39. Pliny, *Natural History, vol. 2, books 3–7*, 199.
40. Stannard, "The Plant Called Moly," 255.
41. Pliny, *Natural History, vol. 2, books 3–7*, 159–65.
42. Zosimus, *The History of Count Zosimus*, 35–36.
43. Guiley, *The Dreamer's Way*, 170–1.
44. Rougemont, *The National Dream Book*, 21.
45. Reilly, *Walking with Angels*, 87–89.
46. Shafton, *Dream-Singers*, 134.
47. Grey, *Return from Death*, 138.
48. Barasch, *Healing Dreams*, 1–3.
49. Gray, "The 'Crazy' Way Mark Ruffalo Discovered He Had a Brain Tumor."
50. Evans-Pritchard, *Witchcraft, Oracles, and Magic Among the Azande*, 99.
51. Firth, *Rank and Religion in Tikopia*, 276.
52. Hanauer, *Folk-Lore of the Holy Land*, 139.
53. Kracke, "To Dream, Perchance to Cure," 108.
54. Morriseau, *Legends of My People*, 50–51.
55. Bodding, "Studies in Santal Medicine and Connected Folklore," 138.
56. Golomb, *An Anthropology of Curing in Multiethnic Thailand*, 98.
57. Hilger, *Araucanian Child Life and Its Cultural Background*, 121.
58. Handy, *Polynesian Religion*, 61.
59. Carpenter, *Tales of a Korean Grandmother*, 81–82.
60. Rautman, *Daily Life in the Byzantine Empire*, 364.
61. Jameson, *Legends of the Monastic Orders as Represented in the Fine Arts*, 266.
62. Faraone and Obbink, *Magika Hiera*, 9.
63. Edgar and Henig, "Istikhara," 11.
64. Kunow, *Maya Medicine*, 50.
65. Kroeber, *Yurok Myths*, 409.
66. Lincoln, *The Dream in Native American and Other Primitive Cultures*, 25.
67. Hadas and Smith, *Heroes and Gods*, 117–18.
68. Virtue, *Angel Visions II*, 334.
69. Dorsey, *The Pawnee Mythology (Part 1)*, 388–89.
70. Maxfield and Millington, "Visayan Folk-Tales," 89.
71. Krippner, "Tribal Shamans and Their Travels Into Dreamtime," 187.
72. Whitten, *Sacha Runa*, 98–100.

73. Kunow, *Maya Medicine*, 36–38.
74. Siffredi, "Confrontation with Kixwet," 233.
75. Bower, *History of the Popes*, 144.
76. Gregory of Tours, *Life of the Fathers*, 59.
77. Collins, *Cistercian Legends of the Thirteenth Century*, 113–5.
78. Thwaites, *The Jesuit Relations and Allied Documents*, vol. 10, 127–29.
79. Skinner, *Notes on the Eastern Cree and Northern Saulteaux*, 259.
80. Handy, *Polynesian Religion*, 61.
81. Mayor, *Greek Fire, Poison Arrows and Scorpion Bombs*, 90–1.
82. Vernalaken, *In the Land of Marvels*, 303–309.
83. Oppenheim, "The Interpretation of Dreams in the Ancient Near East," 194.
84. Walker, *A Treasury of Turkish Folktales for Children*, 4–5.
85. Jack, "Maliseet Legends," 201.
86. Skinner, *Notes on the Eastern Cree and Northern Saulteaux*, 76.
87. Dorsey, *The Pawnee Mythology (Part 1)*, 296–7.
88. Moerman, *Geraniums for the Iroquois*, 2.
89. Phillips, *Ethnobotany of the Coos, Lower Umpqua, and Siuslaw Indians*, 23.
90. MacFarlan, *Native American Tales and Legends*, 304.
91. Knappert, *Pacific Mythology*, 180.
92. Sharp, *Loon*, 116.
93. Walker, *The Art of the Turkish Tale*, 222.
94. Rajketan and Mayanglambam, *A Collection of Essays in Manipuri Folklore*, 8.
95. Roseman, *Healing Sounds from the Malaysian Rainforest*, 29–30.
96. Roseman, *Healing Sounds from the Malaysian Rainforest*, 58.
97. Schultes and Raffauf, *Vine of the Soul*, 58.
98. Shanon, *The Antipodes of the Mind*, 28.
99. Morriseau, *Legends of My People*, 52.
100. Steward, *Northern and Gosiute Shoshoni*, 281–82.
101. Densmore, *Uses of Plants by the Chippewa Indians*, 322.
102. Sharp, *Loon*, 58.
103. Narby, *The Cosmic Serpent*, 40.
104. Narby, *The Cosmic Serpent*, 38.
105. Sigerist, *Primitive and Archaic Medicine*, 203–204.
106. Balick, *Plants, People, and Culture*, 154–55.
107. Vestal, *Warpath*, 249–50.
108. Bullock, *Living Legends of the Santa Fe Country*, 1–3.

109. Ring, *Lessons from the Light*, 218.
110. Grey, *Return from Death*, 134.
111. Grey, *Return from Death*, 137.
112. Singh, "Why Is There Shamanism?," 43.
113. Ring, *Lessons From the Light*, 220.
114. Holzer, *The Directory of the Occult*, 63–67.
115. Fenwick and Fenwick, *The Truth in the Light*, 28.
116. Rivas et al., *The Self Does Not Die*, 171.
117. Long, *Evidence of the Afterlife*, 185–86.
118. Fenwick and Fenwick, *The Truth in the Light*, 28.
119. Sartori, *The Near-Death Experiences of Hospitalized Intensive Care Patients*, 286–87.
120. Diamond, *Life after Near Death*, 70.
121. Grey, *Return from Death*, 136.
122. Atwater, *The Big Book of Near-Death Experiences*, 392.
123. Csordas, *The Sacred Self*, 3.
124. Krippner and Achterberg, "Anomalous Healing Experiences," 367.
125. Edgar and Henig, "Istikhara," 16.
126. McClenon, *Wondrous Healing*, 10.
127. Connor and Keeney, *Shamans of the World*, 61.
128. Oswalt, *Other Peoples, Other Customs*, 221.
129. Hunter, *Manners and Customs of Several Indians Tribes Located West of the Mississippi*, 354.
130. Sutherland, *Transformed by the Light*, 124.
131. Steward, *Northern and Gosiute Shoshoni*, 286.
132. Spencer and Gillen, *Across Australia*, 339–41.
133. Williams, *Orokaiva Magic*, 93–94.
134. Vallée, *Passport to Magonia*, 260–61.
135. Vallée, *Passport to Magonia*, 135.
136. Dennett, *UFO Healings*, xi.
137. Fiore, *Encounters*, 322.
138. Fiore, *Encounters*, 78.

CHAPTER 8. I KNOW WHAT YOU DREAMED

1. Luck, *Arcana Mundi*, 149–50.
2. Hardy, *Legends, Tales, and Stories of Ireland*, 99.

3. Wilby, *The Visions of Isobel Gowdie*, 516.
4. Hadas and Smith, *Heroes and Gods*, 182–83.
5. Ziolkowski, *Reading the Juggler of Notre Dame*, 97–100.
6. Giles, *Strange Stories from a Chinese Studio*, 359–64.
7. Moxon, *Peter's Halakhic Nightmare*, 7.
8. Michael the Syrian, *Michael Rabo's Chronicle, The 4th through 6th Centuries*, 682–3.
9. Burns and Lambert, *Tales and Traditions, Ecclesiastical and Miscellaneous*, 153–60.
10. Sayani, *Saints of Islam*, 19–20.
11. Calvino, *Italian Folktales*, 403.
12. Ullman et al., *Dream Telepathy*, 40.
13. Jalal al-Din al-Suyuti, *History of the Caliphs*, 369.
14. CampbellJones and CampbellJones, *Journey of Spirit Walk of Faith*, 12.
15. Baring-Gould and Fisher, *The Lives of the British Saints*, 145.
16. Gurney, "The Babylonians and Hittites," 158.
17. Moxon, *Peter's Halakhic Nightmare*, 465.
18. Frangoulidis, "Double Dreams in Apuleius' Metamorphoses," 363–6.
19. Moxon, *Peter's Halakhic Nightmare*, 273.
20. Frangoulidis, "Double Dreams in Apuleius' Metamorphoses," 368.
21. Moxon, *Peter's Halakhic Nightmare*, 481.
22. Royston and Humphreys, *The Hidden Power of Dreams*, 170–73.
23. Marchbank, *Upper Annandale*, 147–50.
24. Virtanen, *That Must Have Been ESP!*, 99.
25. Wilby, *The Visions of Isobel Gowdie*, 507–508.
26. Ullman et al., *Dream Telepathy*, 116.
27. Ullman et al., *Dream Telepathy*, 68.
28. Yuchi, "Mutual Dreaming: Rest as Political Resistance and Temporal Lucidity," 2021.
29. Scott, *Shamanism & Personal Mastery*, 9–10.
30. Lang, *The Book of Dreams and Ghosts*, 4.
31. Oppenheim, "The Interpretation of Dreams in the Ancient Near East," 249.
32. Donahoe, *Dream Reality*, 52.
33. De Bercker, *The Understanding of Dreams*, 394–5.
34. Shirokogorov, *Pyschomental Complex of the Tungus*, 117.
35. Steward, *Northern and Gosiute Shoshoni*, 282.

36. Moss, *The Secret History of Dreaming*, 9.
37. Kroeber, *Handbook of the Indians of California*, 197.
38. Whitten, *Sacha Runa*, 58–57.
39. Krippner, "Tribal Shamans and Their Travels into Dreamtime," 192.
40. Whitten, *Sacha Runa*, 152.
41. Gusinde, *Folk Literature of the Selknam Indians*, 104–6.
42. Gusinde, *Folk Literature of the Yamana Indians*, 183–4.
43. Thorgilsson, *The Book of the Settlement of Iceland*, 198.
44. Valadez, "Wolf Power and Interspecies Communication in Huichol Shamanism," 302.
45. Mills, *The Lhota Nagas*, 171.
46. Wilby, *The Visions of Isobel Gowdie*, 522.
47. Ginzburg, *Ecstasies*, 155.
48. Ginzburg, *Ecstasies*, 160.
49. Henningsen, "The Ladies from Outside," 204.
50. Faron, *The Mapuche Indians of Chile*, 83.
51. Henningsen, *The Witches' Advocate*, 6–9.
52. Fox, *Astral Projection*, 47.
53. MacPhail, "Giants in Pageants," 87–88.
54. Liguori, *Victories of the Martyrs*, 149–50.
55. Frangoulidis, "Double Dreams in Apuleius' Metamorphoses," 365–8.
56. Bennett, *Apparitions and Haunted Houses*, 48–51, Kindle.
57. Williams, *Orokaiva Magic*, 77.
58. Monroe, *The Dream Investigator and Oneirocritica*, 35.
59. Maclagan, "Ghost Lights of the West Highlands," 252.
60. Funk, *The Widow's Mite and Other Psychic Phenomena*, 28.
61. Kriza et al., *The Folk-Tales of the Magyars*, 34–35.
62. Sun, *Land of Seagull and Fox*, 31–32.
63. Attar, *Muslim Saints and Mystics*, 98.
64. Elsaesser, *Spontaneous Contacts with the Deceased*, 134–5.
65. Elsaesser, *Spontaneous Contacts with the Deceased*, 57.
66. Moody, *Glimpses of Eternity*, 13–14.
67. Moody, *Glimpses of Eternity*, 14–15.
68. Boratav, "The Tale and the Epico-Novelistic Narrative," 35.
69. Mackenzie, *Wonder Tales from Scottish Myth & Legend*, 33–39.
70. Tawney, *The Kathá Sarit Ságara or Ocean of the Streams of Story*, vol. 2, 553–54.

71. Brown, *The Book of Saints and Friendly Beasts*, 126–8.
72. Moxon, *Peter's Halakhic Nightmare*, 472.
73. Moxon, *Peter's Halakhic Nightmare*, 472.
74. Magallón, *Mutual Dreaming*, 17.
75. Bobrick, *East of the Sun*, 177.
76. Sutherland, *Transformed by the Light*, 117–8.
77. Wilby, *The Visions of Isobel Gowdie*, 514.
78. Plummer, *Bethada Náem nÉrenn*, 184.
79. Maybruck, "Pregnancy and Dreams," 151.
80. Rogers, *Dreams and Premonitions*, 39–41.
81. Thompson, "Folktales and Legends," 693–94.
82. Creighton, *The Best of Helen Creighton*, 24–5.
83. McBride, *Tipperary Folk Tales*, 99.
84. Plummer, *Bethada Náem nÉrenn*, 18.
85. Booss, *A Treasury of Irish Myth, Legend, and Folklore*, 599–60.
86. Xuegang, *Chinese Myths*, 153–55.
87. Goddard, *Hupa Texts*, 191–4.
88. Gurney, Myers, and Podmore, *Phantasms of the Living, vol. 2*, 97–98.
89. Lynch, *Knights of God*, 122.
90. Hart and Hart, "Visions and Apparitions Collectively and Reciprocally Perceived," 230–31.
91. Hoffmann, *A Japanese Grammar*, 188.
92. Dykstra, "Miraculous Tales of the Lotus Sutra," 200.
93. Jones, *Ages Ago*, 104–5.
94. Bloomfield, "The Character and Adventures of Muladeva," 645–6.
95. Rougemont, *The National Dream Book*, 15–6.
96. Gurney, Myers, and Podmore, *Phantasms of the Living, vol. 1*, 314.
97. Róheim, "Telepathy in a Dream," 154.
98. Moxon, *Peter's Halakhic Nightmare*, 482.

Bibliography

Abbot, Willis. *Notable Women in History*. John C. Winston, 1913.

Adamnan. *Life of Saint Columba, Founder of Hy*. Edited by William Reeves. Edmonston and Douglas, 1874.

Adams, Charles. *Ghost Stories of the Lehigh Valley*. Exeter House Books, 1993.

Afanas'ev, Aleksandr, comp. *Russian Fairy Tales*. Translated by Norbert Guterman. Folkloric commentary by Roman Jakobson. Pantheon Books, 1975.

Aflākī, Shams al-Dīn Aḥmad. *Legends of the Sufis*. Translated by James Redhouse. Theosophical Publishing House, 1976.

Africa and Its Exploration as Told by Its Explorers. Vol. 2. Russell E. Train Africana Collection (Smithsonian Libraries). Sampson Low, Marston, 1860.

Ahern, Emily. *The Cult of the Dead in a Chinese Village*. Stanford University Press, 1973.

Ahmed, Akbar. *Discovering Islam: Making Sense of Muslim History and Society*. Routledge & Kegan Paul, 1988.

Allred, Grover. "Notes on the Appearance of a Spectral Death Messenger." *Western Folklore* 19, no. 3 (1960): 197–9.

Anonymous. *Tales of Superstition: or Relations of Apparitions*. London, 1803.

Applegate, Frank. *Native Tales of New Mexico*. J. B. Lippincott, 1932.

Apuleius. *The Golden Ass*. Translated by E. J. Kennedy. Penguin Books Ltd., 1998. Kindle.

Aṛak'el of Tabriz. *Book of History*. Translated by George Bournoutian. Mazda Publishers, 2010.

Arcangel, Diana. *Afterlife Encounters*. Hampton Roads, 2005.

Ariès, Philippe. *The Hour of Our Death: The Classic History of Western Attitudes toward Death over the Last One Thousand Years*. Translated by Helen Weaver. Distributed by Random House, 1981.

Arnason, Jon. *Icelandic Legends*. Translated by George Powell and Eirikr Magnusson. R. Bentley, 1864.

Arnold, Emma. *Stories of Ancient Peoples*. American Book Company, 1901.

Arnot, Robert. *Armenian Literature, Comprising Poetry, Drama, Folklore, and Classic Traditions*. Rev. ed. Colonial Press, 1901.

Attar, Farid al-Din. *Muslim Saints and Mystics: Episodes from the Tadhkirat Al-Auliya (Memorial of the Saints)*. Translated by Arthur John Arberry. Routledge & Kegan Paul, 1966.

Attwater, Donald. *Martyrs: from St. Stephen to John Tung*. Sheed and Ward, 1957.

Atwater, P. M. H. *The Big Book of Near-Death Experiences*.

Augear, Robert. Letter to the editor. *Journal of the Society for Psychical Research* 7 (1895–6): 274–5.

Augustine, Jonathan. *Buddhist Hagiography in Early Japan: Images of Compassion in the Gyoki Tradition*. Routledge Curzon, 2005.

Balick, Michael. *Plants, People, and Culture: The Science of Ethnobotany*. Scientific American Library, 1996.

Barasch, Marc. *Healing Dreams: Exploring the Dreams That Can Transform Your Life*. Riverhead, 2001.

Barbeau, C. Marius. *Huron and Wyandot Mythology, with an Appendix Containing Earlier Published Records*. Canadian Government Printing Bureau, 1915.

Baring-Gould, Sabine. *Early Reminiscences 1834–1864*. John Lane (The Bodley Head), 1923.

Baring-Gould, Sabine. *The Lives of the Saints*. Vol. 12, part 2. J. C. Nimmo, 1897.

Baring-Gould, Sabine, and John Fisher. *The Lives of the British Saints*. Vol. 3. The Honourable Society of Cymmrodorion, 1911.

Barker, Jimmie, and Janet Mathews. *The Two Worlds of Jimmie Barker: The Life of an Australian Aboriginal 1900–1972, as told to Janet Mathews*. Australian Institute of Aboriginal Studies, 1977.

Barrett, William. *Death-Bed Visions*. Methuen, 1926.

Batthyány, Alexander. *Threshold: Terminal Lucidity and the Border of Life and Death*. Scribe, 2023. Kindle.

Baylor, Dorothy. "Folklore from Socorro, New Mexico." *Hoosier Folklore* 6, no. 3 (1947): 91–100.

Beatty, Bill. *A Treasury of Australian Folk Tales and Traditions*. Ure Smith, 1965.

Beaumont, John. *An Historical, Physiological and Theological Treatise of Spirits, Apparitions, Witchcrafts, and Other Magical Practices*. Printed for D. Browne, J. Taylor, R. Smith, F. Coggan, and T. Browne, 1705.

Beckwith, Martha, trans. "The Hawaiian Romance of Laieikawai." Reprinted from the Thirty-Third Annual Report of the Bureau of American Ethnology 1910–1911. U.S. Government Printing Office, 1918.

Bell, Arthur. *Lives and Legends of the English Bishops and Kings, Mediaeval Monks, and Other Later Saints*. George Bell & Sons, 1904.

Belsey, Catherine. *Tales of the Troubled Dead. Ghost Stories in Cultural History*. Edinburgh University Press, 2019.

Benn, Charles. *Daily Life in Traditional China: The Tang Dynasty*. Greenwood Press, 2002.

Bennett, Ernest, *Apparitions and Haunted Houses*. David & Charles, 2012. Kindle.

Bennett, Gillian. *Traditions of Belief: Women and the Supernatural*. Penguin Books, 1987.

Bhakti Vidhan Mahayogi Swami, trans. *Lives of the Vaishnava Saints*. Opensource, 2022.

Black, William. *Folk-Medicine: A Chapter in the History of Culture*. The Folk-Lore Society, 1883.

Blacker, Carmen. "Japan." In *Oracles and Divination*, edited by Michael Loewe and Carmen Blacker, 63–86. Shambhala, 1981.

Bloomfield, Maurice. "The Character and Adventures of Muladeva." *Proceedings of the American Philosophical Society* 52, no. 212 (1913): 616–50.

Blum, Richard, and Eva Marie Blum. *The Dangerous Hour: The Lore of Crisis and Mystery in Rural Greece*. Scribner, 1970.

Boas, Franz, ed. *Folk-Tales of Salishan and Sahaptin Tribes*. Collected by James A. Teit, Livingston Farrand, Marian K. Gould, and Herbert J. Spinden. American Folk-Lore Society, 1917.

Boas, Franz. *The Religion of the Kwakiutl Indians*. Columbia University Press, 1930.

Bobrick, Benson. *East of the Sun: The Epic Conquest and Tragic History of Siberia*. Poseidon Press, 1992.

Bodding, Paul. "Studies in Santal Medicine and Connected Folklore: The Santals and Disease." Vol. 10, no. 1 of *Memoirs of the Asiatic Society of Bengal*. Asiatic Society of Bengal, 1925.

Bogoras, Waldemar. "The Folklore of Northeastern Asia, as Compared with that of Northwestern America." *American Anthropologist* 4, no. 4 (1902): 577–683.

Bois, Jules. *Le Miracle Moderne*. Société d'éditions littéraires et artistiques, 1907.

Bolshakoff, Serge. *Russian Mystics*. Cistercian Publications, 1977.

Booss, Claire, ed., comp. *A Treasury of Irish Myth, Legend, and Folklore*. Avenel, 1986.

Boratav, Pertev. "The Tale and the Epico-Novelistic Narrative." Translated by Mona Fikry. In *Studies in East European Folk Narrative*, edited by Linda Dégh, 4–47. American Folklore Society and the Indiana University Folklore Monograph Series, 1978.

Bosworth, Edmund, Pellat, and E. J. van Donzel, eds. *The Encyclopedia of Islam*. Vol. 6, *Mahk-Mid*. E. J. Brill, 1991.

Bower, Archibald. *The History of the Popes*. Vol. 3. Griffith & Simon, 1845.

Brabrook, E. W. "Presidential Address." *Folklore* 13, no. 1 (1902): 12–28.

Bracciolini, Poggio. *The Facetiae:, or Jocose Tales of Poggio*. Vol. 2. Now Translated into English with the Latin Text in Two Volumes Vol. II. Paris: Isidore. Liseux, 1879.

Brand, John. *Observations on Popular Antiquities*. Newcastle Upon Tyne: J. Johnson, 1777.

Brewster, Paul. "Stories of the Supernatural Stories from Southern Indiana." *Southern Folklore Quarterly* 10, no. 4 (1946): 227–34.

Brinton, Daniel. *The Myths of the New World: A Treatise on the Symbolism and Mythology of the Red Race of America*. Henry Holt & Company, 1876.

Brou, Alexandre. *Saint Madeleine Sophie Barat*. Translated by Jane Saul. Desclee Company, 1925.

Brown, Abbie Farwell. *The Book of Saints and Friendly Beasts*. Houghton, Mifflin & Co., 1900.

Brown, Herbert, trans. *Three Elema Myths: Recorded in Toaripi*. Canberra, A.C.T.: Dept. of Linguistics, Research School of Pacific Studies, Australian National University, 1988.

Brown, Michael. "Shamanism and Its Discontents." *Medical Anthropology Quarterly* 2, no. 2 (1988): 102–20.

Brown, Raphael, trans. *The Little Flowers of Saint Francis*. Image Books, 1958.

Brunvand, Jan. *The Vanishing Hitchhiker: American Urban Legends and Their Meanings.* W. W. Norton, 1981.
Bullock, Alice. *Living Legends of the Santa Fe Country.* Sunstone Press, 1972.
Burnouf, Eugene. *Legends of Indian Buddhism.* Dutton, 1911.
Burns and Lambert. *Tales and Traditions, Ecclesiastical and Miscellaneous: Being a Second Series of Historical Tales and Legends.* Burns and Lambert, 1858.
Burton, Richard. *The Land of Midian (Revisited).* Vol. 1. Kegan Paul, 1879.
Butler, Alban. *Butler's Lives of the Saints.* Christian Classics, 1996.
Caesarius of Heisterbach. *The Dialogue on Miracles.* 2 vols. Translated by H. Von E. Scott and Charles Cook Swinton Bland. Harcourt, Brace & Company, 1929.
Callanan, Maggie, and Patricia Kelley. *Final Gifts: Understanding the Special Awareness, Needs, and Communications of the Dying.* Bantam Books, 1997.
Callaway, Henry. *Nursery Tales, Traditions, and Histories of the Zulus: In Their Own Words with a Translation into English, and Notes.* Vol. 1. Natal: John A. Blair; London: Trubner 1868.
Calmet, Augustine. *The Phantom World: or, The Philosophy of Spirits, Apparitions, etc.* vol 2. Philadelphia: A. Hart, Late Carey & Hart, 1850.
Calvino, Italo. *Italian Folktales.* Translated by George Martin. Harcourt Brace Jovanovich, 1980.
Camm, Bede. *Forgotten Shrines: An Account of Some Old Catholic Halls and Families in England, and of Relics and Memorials of the English Martyrs.* Macdonald & Evans, 1910.
CampbellJones, Brenda, and Franklin CampbellJones. *Journey of Spirit Walk of Faith: Our Relationship with God.* Authorhouse, 2010.
Carey, John. *King of Mysteries: Early Irish Religious Writings.* Four Courts Press, 1998.
Carletti, Giuseppe, trans. *Life of St. Benedict Surnamed "The Moor," The Son of a Slave, Canonized by Pope Pius VII, May 24th, 1807.* P. J. Kenedy, 1895.
Carpenter, Frances. *Tales of a Korean Grandmother.* C. E. Tuttle Co., 1973.
Carpenter, Joseph. "Chaitanya, An Indian St. Francis." *The Hibbert Journal* 19 (1920–1): 666–678.
Carroll, Austin. *The Life of St. Alphonsus Liguori.* P. O'Shea, 1886.
Cave, William. *A Complete History of the Lives, Acts, and Martyrdoms of the Holy Apostles, and the Two Evangelists, St. Mark and Luke.* Vol. 2. Solomon Wiatt, 1810.

Centerwall, A. "A Strange Premonition." *Journal of Christian Nursing* 17, no. 2 (2000): 27–29.

Chadwick, H. Munro, and N. Kershaw Chadwick. *The Growth of Literature.* Vol. 3. Cambridge University Press, 1940.

Chadwick, Nora Kershaw, trans. *Stories and Ballads of the Far Past.* Cambridge: At the University Press, 1921.

Chamberlain, Alexander. "Periodical Literature." *The Journal of American Folklore* 24, no. 91 (1911): 3–147.

Charles, R. H., ed., trans. *The Book of Jubilees.* Adam & Charles Black, 1902.

Clarke, Andrew, ed. *"Brief Lives," Chiefly of Contemporaries, Set Down by John Aubrey, Between the Years 1669 & 1696.* Volume I. Clarendon Press, 1898.

Cline, Walter, Rachel S. Commons, May Mandelbaum, Richard H. Post, and L. V. W. Walters. *The Sinkaietk or Southern Okanagon of Washington.* Edited by Leslie Spier. George Banta, 1938.

Clough, Hugh. *Plutarch's Lives 12.* P. F. Collier & Sons Company, 1909.

Clouston, William. *A Group of Eastern Romances and Stories from the Persian, Tamil, and Urdu.* Glasgow: Privately Printed [W. Hodge & Co.], 1889.

Cluness, Andrew. *Told Round the Peat Fire.* Robert Hale Ltd., 1955.

Cobbe, Frances. *The Peak in Darien, With Some Other Inquiries Touching Concerns of the Soul and the Body: An Octave of Essays.* Geo. H. Ellis, 1882.

Codrington, Robert. *The Melanesians: Studies in their Anthropology and Folk-Lore.* Clarendon Press, 1891.

Coffin, Margaret. *Death in Early America: The History and Folklore of Customs and Superstitions of Early Medicine, Funerals, Burials, and Mourning.* Nelslon, 1976.

Colgrave, Bertram, and R. A. B. Mynors, eds. *Bede's Ecclesiastical History of the English People.* Clarendon Press, 1969.

Collins, Henry, trans. *Cistercian Legends of the Thirteenth Century.* London: R. Washbourne, 1872.

Collins, John, and Michael Fishbane, eds. *Death, Ecstasy, and Other Worldly Journeys.* State University of New York Press, 1995.

Collison-Morley, Lacy. *Greek and Roman Ghost Stories.* Simpkin, Marshall Blackwell & Co. Limited, 1912.

Collum, Padraic, ed. *A Treasury of Irish Folklore: The Stories, Traditions, Legends, Humor, Wisdom, Ballads, and Songs of the Irish People.* Kilkenny Press: Distributed by Crown Publishers, 1989.

Condos, Theony, trans. *Star Myths of the Greek and Romans*. Phanes Press, 1997.
Connor, Carolyn. *Women of Byzantium*. Yale University Press, 2004.
Connor, Nancy, and Bradford Keeney, Bradford, eds. *Shamans of the World: Extraordinary First-Person Accounts of Healings, Mysteries, and Miracles*. Sounds True, 2008.
Consitt, Edward. *Life of Saint Cuthbert*. Burns & Oates, 1904.
Cowell, Edward, trans. *The Jātaka, or, Stories of the Buddha's Former Births*. Volume II & V: Translated from the Pali by Various Hands under the Editorship of Professor E. B. Cowell. Cambridge University Press, 1895.
Craigie, William, trans. *Scandinavian Folk-Lore: Illustrations of the Traditional Beliefs of the Northern Peoples*. A. Gardner, 1896.
Craigie, William. "Some Highland Folklore." *Folklore* 09 (1898): 372–79.
Craigie, William. "The Norwegian Vardogr." *Blackwood's Magazine* 191 (1912): 304–3134.
Craigie, William. "Just Like Ghosts: The Norwegian Vardogrs and Their Curious Warnings. A Study in Psychic Force." *Livingston Chronicle* 3, no. 48 (31 August 1912).
Crapanzano, Vincent. "Saints, Jnun, and Dreams: An Essay in Moroccan Ethnopsychology." *Psychiatry* 38, no. 2 (1975): 145–159.
Creighton, Helen. *The Best of Helen Creighton*. Edited by Rosemary Bauchman. Lancelot Press, 1988.
Creighton, Helen. *Bluenose Ghosts*. Nimbus, 1994.
Csordas, Thomas. *The Sacred Self: A Cultural Phenomenology of Charismatic Healing*. University of California Press, 1994.
Curtin, Jeremiah. *Myths of the Modocs*. Little, Brown & Company, 1912.
Curtin, Jeremiah, and John Hewitt, eds. *Seneca Fiction, Legends, and Myths*. Washington: Government Printing Office, 1918. Reprinted from the Thirty-Second Annual Report of the Bureau of American Ethnology 1910–1911. U.S. Government Printing Office, 1918.
Curtis, Vesta. *Persian Myths*. London: University of Texas Press, 1993. Digitized by the trustees of the British Museum Press, 2009.
D'Aguilers, Raymond. *Historia Francorum Qui Ceperunt Iherusalem*. Translated by John Hill and Laurita Hill. The American Philosophical Society, 1968.
Dalgairns, John. *Life of St. Stephen Harding, Abbot of Citeaux; and Founder of the Cistercian Order*. Edited by John Henry Newman. London: Art and Book; New York: Benziger, 1898.

Dalyell, John. *The Darker Superstitions of Scotland*. Waugh & Innes, 1834.

Dance, Daryl. *Shuckin' and Jivin': Folklore from Contemporary Black Americans*. Indiana University Press, 1978.

David-Neel, Alexandra. *With Mystics and Magicians in Tibet*. John Lane (The Bodley Head), 1931.

Davidson, Hilda. *Myths and Symbols in Pagan Europe: Early Scandinavian and Celtic Religions*. Manchester University Press, 1988.

Davies, Rodney. *Balm from Beyond: How the Departed Can Help Us*. Robert Hale, 2010.

Davis, Mary, and Chow-Leung. *Chinese Fables and Folk Stories*. American Book Co., 1908.

Deans, H. Cowan. "Cases." *Journal of the Society for Psychical Research* 11 (1903-4): 58-64.

De Bercker, Raymond. *The Understanding of Dreams and Their Influence on the History of Man*. Hawthorn Books, Inc., 1968.

Defoe, Daniel. *The Secrets of the Invisible World Disclos'd: or, An Universal History of Apparitions*. Printed for J. Watts and Sold by T. Worral, 1735.

Déegh, Linda. *Folktales of Hungary*. Translated by Judit Halász. Chicago: University Press, 1965.

Dennett, Preston. *UFO Healings: True Accounts of People Healed by Extraterrestrials*. Wild Flower Press, 1996.

Dennys, Nicholas. *The Folk-Lore of China, and Its Affinities with That of the Aryan and Semitic Races*. London: Trubner & Co.; Hong Kong: "China Mail" Office, 1876.

Densmore, Frances. *Uses of Plants by the Chippewa Indians*. From the Forty-Fourth Annual Report of the Bureau of American Ethnology. U.S. Government Printing Office, Washington: U.S. G.P.O., 1928.

Dentaon, Robert. *The Semai: a Nonviolent People of Malaya*. Holt, Rinehart & Winston, 1968.

De Onis, Harriet, ed. & trans. *The Golden Land: An Anthology of Latin American Folklore in Literature*. Knopf, 1961.

De Paor, Liam. *Saint Patrick's World: The Christian Culture of Ireland's Apostolic Age*. University of Notre Dame Press, 1996.

De Peyer, Janine. "Uncanny Communication and the Porous Mind." *Psychoanalytic Dialogues* 26, no. 2 (2016): 156-74.

DeVita, Philip. *Stumbling toward Truth: Anthropologists at Work*. Waveland Press, Inc., 2000.

De Voragine, Jacobus. *The Golden Legend: Part One*. Translated by Granger Ryan and Helmut Ripperger. Longmans, Green and Co., 1941.

De Voragine, Jacobus. *The Golden Legend: Readings on the Saints*. Vol. 1. Translated by William Granger Ryan. Princeton University Press, 1993.

Dewdney, Selwyn, ed. *Legends of My People: The Great Ojibway*. McGraw-Hill Ryerson, 1977.

Diamond, Debra. *Life after Near Death: Miraculous Stories of Healing and Transformation in the Extraordinary Lives of People with Newfound Powers*. New Page Books, 2016. Kindle.

Diamond, Jenness. *The Life of the Copper Eskimos*. Ottawa: F. A. Acland, Printer to the King's Most Excellent Majesty, 1922.

Dillon, Myles. "The Story of the Finding of Cashel." *Ériu* 16 (1952): 61–73.

Dineshchandra, Rai Sabeh. *The Folk-Literature of Bengal*. University of Calcutta, 1920.

Dodds, Eric. "Telepathy and Clairvoyance in Classical Antiquity." *Journal of Parapsychology* 10 (1946): 290–309.

Dodds, Eric. "Two Concordant Experiences Coinciding with a Death." *Journal of the Society for Psychical Research* 41, no. 713 (1962): 337–346.

Dodds, Eric. *The Ancient Concept of Progress and Other Essays on Greek Literature and Belief*. Clarendon Press, 1973.

Donahoe, James. *Dream Reality: The Conscious Creation of Dream and Paranormal Experience*. Bench Press, 1979.

Dorsey, George. *The Pawnee Mythology (Part 1)*. Carnegie Institution of Washington, 1906.

Dorsey, James Owen. *A Study of Siouan Cults*. Smithsonian Institution, Bureau of Ethnology, 1894.

Dorson, Richard, ed. *Folktales Told around the World*. University of Chicago Press, 1978.

Douglas, George. *Scottish Fairy and Folk Tales*. A.L. Burt Co., 1901.

Douglas, Mackenzie. *Wonder Tales from Scottish Myth & Legend*. Blackie & Son, 1917.

Downey, Glanville. *A History of Antioch in Syria: From Seleucus to the Arab Conquest*. Princeton University Press, 1961.

Dracott, Alice Elizabeth. *Folk Tales from Simla: Stories from the Himalayas*. Hippocrene Books, 1998.

"The Dream." *The Dublin Penny Journal* 2, no. 91 (1834): 305–6.

Duckett, Eleanor Shipley. *The Wandering Saints of the Early Middle Ages.* Norton, 1964.

Duncan, Birke, and Jason Marc Harris, comps. *The Troll Tale and Other Scary Stories.* Northwest Folklore, 2001.

Dykstra, Yoshiko. "Tales of the Compassionate Kannon: The *Hasedera Kannon Genki.*" *Monumenta Nipponica* 31, no. 2 (1976): 113–143.

Dykstra, Yoshiko. "Miraculous Tales of the Lotus Sutra: The *Dainihonkoku Hokkegenki.*" *Monumenta Nipponica* 32, no. 2 (1977): 189–210.

Edgar, Iain, and David Henig. "*Istikhara*: The Guidance and Practice of Islamic Dream Incubation through Ethnographic Comparison." *History and Anthropology* 21, no. 3 (2010): 251–262.

Edmundson, William. *A Journal of the Life, Travels, Sufferings, and Labour of Love in the Work of the Ministry.* 2nd ed. Edited by John Stoddart. Printed and Sold by M. Hinde, 1774.

Eisenbud, Jule. "Psychiatric Contributions to Parapsychology: A Review." In *Psychoanalysis and the Occult*, edited by George Devereaux, 3–15. International Universities Press, Inc., 1970.

Elliott, James. *The Apocryphal New Testament: A Collection of Apocryphal Christian Literature in an English Translation.* Clarendon Press, 1993.

Ellis, William. *Polynesia Researches.* Vol. 1. 2nd ed. Fisher, Son, & Jackson, 1831.

Elsaesser, Evelyn. *Spontaneous Contacts with the Deceased: A Large-Scale International Survey Reveals the Circumstances, Lived Experience and Beneficial Impact of After-Death Communications (ADCs).* IFF Books, 2023. Kindle.

Elton, Oliver, trans., and Frederick Powell. *The Nine Books of the Danish History of Saxo Grammaticus in Two Volumes.* Vol. 1. Norroena Society, 1905.

Elwin, Verrier. *The Muria and their Ghotul.* Calcutta: Oxford University Press, Bombay, 1947.

Evans-Pritchard, Edward. *Witchcraft, Oracles, and Magic Among the Azande.* Clarendon Press, 1976.

Exton-Smith, Arthur. "Terminal Illness in the Aged." *The Lancet* 278, no. 7197 (1961): 305–308.

Fansler, Dean. *Filipino Popular Tales.* American Folklore Society, 1921.

Fansler, Dean. "Metrical Romances in the Philippines." *The Journal of American Folklore* 29, no. 112 (1916): 203–234.

Faraone, Christopher, and Dirk Obbink, eds. *Magika Hiera: Ancient Greek Magic and Religion.* Oxford University Press, 1997.

Farnum, Mabel. *The Wool Merchant of Segovia (St. Alphonsus Rodriguez).* The Bruce Publishing Co., 1945.

Faron, Louis. *The Mapuche Indians of Chile.* Waveland Press, Inc., 1986.

Faurot, Jeanette, ed. *Asian-Pacific Folktales and Legends.* Simon & Schuster, 1995.

Fearn-Wannan (Bill Wannan). *Australian Folklore: A Dictionary of Lore, Legends and Popular Allusions.* Lansdowne, 1970.

Feather, Sally Rhine. *The Gift: ESP, the Extraordinary Experiences of Ordinary People.* St. Martin's Press, 2005.

Felgar, Richard, and Mary Beck Moser. *People of the Desert and Sea: Ethnobotany of the Seri Indians.* University of Arizona Press, 1985.

Felton, Debbie. *Haunted Greece and Rome: Ghost Stories from Classical Antiquity.* University of Texas Press, 2010. Kindle.

Fenwick, Peter, and Elizabeth Fenwick. *The Art of Dying.* Continuum, 2008.

Fenwick, Peter, and Elizabeth Fenwick. *The Truth in the Light.* Berkley Books, 1997.

Finucane, Ronald. *Appearances of the Dead: A Cultural History of Ghosts.* Junction Books, 1982.

Finucane, Ronald. *Appearances of the Dead: A Cultural History of Ghosts.* Junction Books, 1982.

Fiore, Edith. *Encounters: A Psychologist Reveals Case Studies of Abductions by Extraterrestrials.* Ballantine Books, 1990.

Firdoawsi, Abolqasem. *Shahnameh: The Persian Book of Kings.* Translated by Dick Davis. Penguin Books, 2016.

Firth, Raymond. *Rank and Religion in Tikopia: A Study in Polynesian Paganism and Conversion to Christianity.* Allen & Unwin, 1970.

Fitzsimon, Henry. *Words of Comfort to Persecuted Catholics.* Edited by Edmund Hogan. M. H. Gill & Son, 1881.

Flammarion, Camille. *L'inconnu.: The Unknown.* Harper, 1900.

Fletcher, Alice. "Giving Thanks: A Pawnee Ceremony." *The Journal of American Folklore* 13, no. 51 (1900): 261–266.

Flower, Michael. *The Seer in Ancient Greece.* University of California Press. 2008.

Forbes, Alexander, ed. *Lives of S. Ninian and S. Kentigern.* Edmonston & Douglas, 1874.

Forty, Jo, ed. *Classic Mythology.* Grange Books, 1999.

Fox, Oliver. *Astral Projection: A Record of Out-of-the-Body Experiences.* Carol Publishing Group, 1993.

Frangoulidis, Stavros. "Double Dreams in Apuleius' *Metamorphoses*." *Trends in Classics* 4, no. 2 (2012): 363–376.
Frankl, Viktor. *Man's Search for Meaning. Revised and Updated.* Beacon Press, 2014.
Fraser, John. "The First Battle of Moytura." *Ériu* 8 (1916): 1–63.
Freuchen, Peter. *It's All Adventure.* Farrar & Rinehart, Inc., 1938.
Freud, Sigmund. "Dreams and the Occult." In *Psychoanalysis and the Occult*, edited by George Devereaux, 91–109. International Universities Press, Inc., 1970.
Funk, Isaac. *The Widow's Mite and Other Psychic Phenomena.* Funk & Wagnalls Company, 1904.
Gale, James, trans. *Korean Folk Tales: Imps, Ghosts and Fairies.* J. M. Dent & Sons, 1913.
Garcez, Antonio. *American Indian Ghost Stories of the Southwest.* Red Rabbit Press, 2000.
Garnett, Lucy. *Greek Folk Poesy: Annotated Translations from the Whole Cycle of Romaic Folk-Verse and Folk-Prose* Vol. 1. Edited by John Stuart-Glennie. Printed for the Authors by Billing & Sons, 1896.
Garrett, Eileen. *Telepathy: In Search of a Lost Faculty.* Garrett Publications, 1968.
Gaster, Moses. *Rumanian Bird and Beast Stories.* Sidgwick & Jackson, 1915.
Gaster, Moses, trans. *Ma'aseh Book: Book of Jewish Tales and Legends. Vol. 1.* The Jewish Publication Society of America, 1934.
Geoffrey, Dennis. *Coronation Commentary.* William Heinemann Ltd., 1937.
Gibbs, Eddie. *Holy Land Travel Diary.* Lion Publishing, 1982.
Giles, Herbert, trans. *Strange Stories from a Chinese Studio.* 3rd ed. Kelly & Walsh, Limited, 1916.
Giles, J. A., ed. *The Venerable Bede's Ecclesiastical History of England.* 3rd ed. George Bell & Sons, 1903.
Gillespie, Raymond. *Devoted People: Belief and Religion in Early Modern Ireland.* Manchester University Press; New York, 1997. Distributed exclusively in the USA by St. Martin's Press, 1997.
Ginzburg, Carlo. *Ecstasies: Deciphering the Witches' Sabbath.* Translated by Raymond Rosenthal. Penguin Books, 1992.
Glass-Coffin, Bonnie. *The Gift of Life: Female Spirituality and Healing in Northern Peru.* University of New Mexico Press, 1998.
Goddard, Pliny. *Hupa Texts.* The University Press, 1904.
Golomb, Louis. *An Anthropology of Curing in Multiethnic Thailand.* University of Illinois Press, 1985.

Gomme, George Laurence, ed. *English Traditions and Foreign Customs: A Classified Collection of the Chief Contents of "The Gentleman's Magazine" from 1731–1868.* Elliot Stock, 62 Paternoster Row, 1885.

Gordon, Cyrus. *Before the Bible: The Common Background of Greek and Hebrew Civilizations.* Harper & Row, 1962.

Gordon Smith, Richard. *Ancient Tales and Folk-Lore of Japan.* A. & C. Black, 1908.

Gray, Lauren. "The 'Crazy' Way Mark Ruffalo Discovered He Had a Brain Tumor." *Best Life*, April 16, 2022.

Green, Celia, and Charles McCreery. *Apparitions.* Hamilton, 1975.

Green, Lawrence. *These Wonders to Behold.* H. Timmins, 1959.

Greenhouse, Herbert. *Premonitions: A Leap into the Future.* Warner Paperback Library, 1973.

Greey, Edward. *The Golden Lotus, and Other Legends of Japan.* Lee and Shepard; C. T. Dillingham, 1883.

Gregory, Lady. *A Book of Saints and Wonders.* Charles Scribner's Sons, 1907.

Gregory, Lady. *Cuchulain of Muirthemne: The Story of the Men of The Red Branch of Ulster.* London: J. Murray, 1907.

Gregory, Lady. *Visions and Beliefs in the West of Ireland Vol II.* G. P. Putnam's sons, 1920.

Gregory of Tours. *Life of the Fathers.* Translated by Edward James Edward. Liverpool University Press, 1991.

Grey, Margot. *Return from Death: An Exploration of the Near-Death Experience.* Arkana, 1985.

Grousset, Renée. *Conqueror of the World: The Life of Chingis-Khan.* Viking Press, 1972.

Guerber, Hélène. *Legends of the Middle Ages.* American Book Company, 1896.

Guerber, Hélène. *Legends of Switzerland.* Dodd, Mead & Co., 1899.

Guerber, Hélène. *Legends of the Rhine.* 6th ed. A. S. Barnes & Co., 1907.

Guggenheim, Bill, and Judy Guggenheim. *Hello from Heaven.* Bantam Books, 1996.

Guiley, Rosemary. *The Dreamer's Way: Using Proactive Dreaming to Heal and Transform Your Life.* Berkeley Books, 2004.

Gurney, Edmund, Frederic Myers, and Frank Podmore. *Phantasms of the Living.* 2 vols. Trübner and Co., 1886.

Gurney, Edmund, and F. W. H. Myers. "On Apparitions Occurring Soon after Death." *Proceedings of the Society for Psychical Research* 5 (1888–89): 403–485.

Gurney, O. R. "The Babylonians and Hittites." In *Oracles and Divination*, edited by Michael Loewe and Carmen Blacker, 142–173. Shambhala, 1981.

Gusinde, Martin. *Folk Literature of the Selknam Indians: Martin Gusinde's Collection of Selknam Narratives*. Edited by Johannes Wilbert. UCLA Latin American Center Publications, 1975.

Gusinde, Martin. *Folk Literature of the Yamana Indians: Martin Gusinde's Collection of Yamana Narratives*. Edited by Johannes Wilbert. University of California Press, 1977.

Hadas, Moses, and Joe P. Poe, trans. *Livy: A History of Rome—Selections*. The Modern Library, 1962.

Hadas, Moses, and Morton Smith. *Heroes and Gods: Spiritual Biographies in Antiquity*. Books for Libraries Press, 1970.

Hamon, Louis ("Cheiro"). *Mysteries and Romances of the World's Greatest Occultist*. Herbert Jenkins Limited, 1935.

Hanauer, James. *Folk-Lore of the Holy Land: Moslem, Christian and Jewish*. Edited by Marmaduke Pickthall. Duckworth & Co., 1907.

Hand, Wayland, and Jeannine Talley, eds. *Popular Beliefs and Superstitions from Utah: Collected by Anthon S. Cannon*. University of Utah Press, 1984.

Handy, Craighill. *Polynesian Religion*. Bernice P. Bishop Museum, 1927.

Hankey, Rosalie. "California Ghosts." *California Folklore Quarterly* 1, no. 2 (1942): 155–177.

Hansen, Terrence. *The Types of the Folktale in Cuba, Puerto Rico, the Dominican Republic, and Spanish South America*. University of California Press, 1957.

Hardwick, Charles. *Traditions, Superstitions, and Folk-Lore (Chiefly Lancashire and the North of England:)*. A. Ireland & Co., 1872.

Harrington, Mark. *Religion and Ceremonies of the Lenape Indians*. Museum of the American Indian, Heye Foundation, 1921.

Harrington, Mark. *The Indians of New Jersey: Dickon Among the Lenapes*. Rutgers University Press, 1963.

Harris, Richard Dean. *Essays in Occultism, Spiritism, and Demonology*. St. B. Herder, 1919.

Hart, Hornell, and Ella Hart. "Visions and Apparitions Collectively and Reciprocally Perceived." *Proceedings of the Society for Psychical Research* 41 (1932–3): 205–249.

Hartland, E. Sidney. "The Voice of the Stone of Destiny: An Enquiry into the Choice of Kings by Augury." *Folklore* 14, no. 1 (1903): 28–60.

Harvey, Edwin Deeks. *The Mind of China*. Hyperion Press, 1973.

Hauff, Wilhelm. *Fairy Tales.* Translated by L. L. Weedon. E. Nister, 1910.

Haynes, Renéee. *The Hidden Springs: An Enquiry into Extra-Sensory Perception.* Little, Brown and Company, 1973.

Hazlitt, William, ed. *Tales and Legends of National Origin or Widely Current in England from the Early Times.* Benjamin Blom, Inc., 1972.

Head, Thomas. *Hagiography and the Cult of Saints: The Diocese of Orleans, 800–1200.* Cambridge University Press, 1990.

Heikkienein, Antero, and Timo Kervinen. "Finland: The Male Domination." In *Early Modern European Witchcraft: Centres and Peripheries,* edited by Bengt Ankarloo and Gustav Henningsen, 319–338. Clarendon Press, 1993.

Henderson, William. *Notes on the Folk-Lore of the Northern Counties of England and the Borders.* Pub. for the Folklore Society by W. Satchell, Peyton & Co., 1879.

Hendricks, George. *Roosters, Rhymes, and Railroad Tracks: A Second Sampling of Superstitions & Popular Beliefs in Texas.* Southern Methodist University Press, 1980.

Henningsen, Gustav. *The Witches' Advocate: Basque Witchcraft and the Spanish Inquisition* (1609–1614). University of Nevada Press, 1980.

Henningsen, Gustav. "'The Ladies from Outside': An Archaic Pattern of the Witches' Sabbath." In *Early Modern European Witchcraft: Centres and Peripheries.*

Herbermann, Charles, Edward A. Pace, Condé B. Pallen, Thomas J. Shahan, and John J. Wynne, eds. *The Catholic Encyclopedia: An International Work of Reference on the Constitution, Doctrine, Discipline, and History of the Catholic Church.* Vols. 1–16. The Encyclopedia Press, 1907–1914.

Herdt, Gilibert H. *Guardians of the Flutes: Idioms of Masculinity.* McGraw-Hill, 1981.

Heucher, M. J. H. *Magic Plants; Being a Translation of a Curious Tract Entitled De Vegatalibus Magicis.* Edited by Edmund Goldsmid. Edinburgh: Privately Printed, 1886.

Hilger, M. Inez. *Araucanian Child Life and Its Cultural Background.* Smithsonian Institution, 1957.

Hill-Toute, Charles. *British North America: I. The Far West, The Home of the Salish and Déné.* A. Constable & Co., 1907.

Hobley, Charles. *Ethnology of A-Kamba and Other East African Tribes.* Cass, 1971.

Hodges, George. *The Early Church from Ignatius to Augustine.* Houghton Mifflin Company, 1915.

Hofberg, Herman. *Swedish Fairy Tales*. Translated by W. H. Myers. Belford-Clarke Co., 1890.

Hoffman, J. J. *Japanese Grammar*. E. J. Brill & A. W. Sythoff, 1868.

Hoffman, Walter. *The Menomini Indians*. Washington; From the Fourteenth Annual Report of the Bureau of Ethnology. U.S. Government Printing Office, 1896.

Hogg, "Adam Bell." In *Scottish Folk and Fairy Tales*, Edited by Gordon Jarvie, 125–31. Penguin, 1997.

Holzer, Hans. *The Directory of the Occult*. H. Regnery Co., 1974.

Holzer, Hans. *The Hidden Meanings in Dreams*. Dale Books Inc., 1979.

Hoogasian-Villa, Susie, ed. *100 Armenian Tales*. Wayne State University Press, 1966.

Hope, Anne Fulton. *Franciscan Martyrs in England*. Burns and Oakes, 1878.

Hopkins, Nicholas. *Chuj (Mayan) Narratives Folklore, History, and Ethnography from Northwestern Guatemala*. University Press of Colorado, 2021.

Horne, Charles. *The Sacred Books and Early Literature of the East; with a Historical Survey and Descriptions*. Volume 13, *Japan*. Parke, 1917.

Howitt, Alfred. *The Native Tribes of South-East Australia*. Macmillan & Co., Ltd, 1904.

Hufford, David. *The Terror that Comes in the Night: An Experience-Centered Study of Supernatural Assault Traditions*. University of Pennsylvania Press, 1982.

Hull, Eleanor. *Early Christian Ireland*. D. Nutt, 1905.

Humphreys, Chris. *The Fetch*. Knopf. 2007.

Humphreys, Clarence. *The Southern New Hebrides: An Ethnological Record*. AMS Press, 1978.

Hunter, John. *Manners and Customs of Several Indians Tribes Located West of the Mississippi*. J. Maxwell, 1823.

Hutchinson, Horace. *Dreams and Their Meanings*. Longmans, Green, 1901.

Hutchinson, Wilfred. *The Golden Porch: A Book of Greek Fairy Tales*. Longmans, Green & Co.; London: Edward Arnold, 1914.

Hyatt, Harry. *Folk-Lore from Adams County Illinois*. Alma Egan Hyatt Foundation, 1935.

Illiowizi, Henry. *In the Pale: Stories and Legends of the Russian Jews*. Jewish Publication Society of America, 1897.

Ingham, Donna. *Tales with a Texas Twist: Original Stories and Enduring Folklore from the Lone Star State*. Insiders' Guide, 2005.

Inglis, Brian. *The Paranormal: An Encyclopedia of Psychic Phenomena*. Granada, 1985.

Jack, Edward. "Maliseet Legends." *The Journal of American Folklore* 8, no. 30 (1895): 193–208.

Jackson, Blomfield, trans. *The Ecclesiastical History, Dialogues, and Letters of Theodoret*. Eerdmans, 1953.

Jackson, Jean. *The Fish People: Linguistic Exogamy and Tukanoan Identity in Northwest Amazonia*. Cambridge University Press, 1983.

Jacobs, Melville. *Coos Narrative and Ethnologic Texts*. The University of Washington, 1939.

Jacobs, Melville. "Kalapuya Texts Part 1: Santiam Kalapuya Ethnologic Texts." Vol. 11, *University of Washington Publications in Anthropology* 2 (1945): 3–83. University of Washington, 1945.

Jacobson, Nils-Olof. *Life without Death? On Parapsychology, Mysticism, and the Question of Survival*. Translated by Sheila La Farge. Delacorte Press, 1974.

Jalal al-Din al-Suyuti. *History of the Caliphs*. Translated by Major H. S. Jarrett. Printed by J. W. Thomas for the Asiatic Society, 1881.

Jameson, Anna. *Legends of the Monastic Orders as Represented in the Fine Arts: Forming the Second Series of Sacred and Legendary Art*. Longmans, Green, & Co., 1890.

Jarvis, Dale. *Haunted Shores: True Ghost Stories of Newfoundland and Labrador*. Flanker Press, 2004.

Jenness, Diamond. *The Life of the Copper Eskimos*. Vol. 12 of the *Report of the Canadian Arctic Expedition 1913–18*. F. A. Acland, 1922.

J. L. L. "Popular Tales and Legends." *The Dublin Penny Journal* 2, no. 95 (1834): 341–49.

J. L. L. "The Dream." *The Dublin Penny Journal* 2, no. 91 (1834): 305–312.

Jochelson, Waldemar. *The Yukut*. The American Museum of Natural History, 1933.

Jones, Louis. "The Ghosts of New York: An Analytical Study." *The Journal of American Folklore* 57, no. 226 (1944): 237–254.

Jones, Louis C. "Some Historic Ghosts of New York." *New York History* 26, no. 23 (1945): 177–88.

Jones, Louis. *Things That Go Bump in the Night: Haunted Trails and Ghostly Tales*. Hill & Wang, 1977.

Jones, S. W., trans. *Ages Ago: Thirty-Seven Tales from the Konjaku Monogatari Collection*. Harvard University Press, 1959.

Jung, Carl. *Memories, Dreams, Reflections*. Vintage Books, 1989.

Kachhawa, Indubala. "Do Some People Have Premonitions About Their Death?" *Medium*, December 24, 2020. Medium.com

Kahk, Juhan. "Estonia II: The Crusade against Idolatry." In *Early Modern European Witchcraft: Centres and Peripheries*.

Kalmus, Natalie M. "Doorway to Another World." *Coronet* 25, no. 6 (1949): 29–31.

Keeney, Bradford. *Shaking Out the Spirits: A Psychotherapist's Entry into the Healing Mysteries of Global Shamanism*. Station Hill Press, 1994.

Keith-Falconer, I. G. N. trans. *Kalilah and Dimnah, or The Fables of Bidpai*. Cambridge: At the University Press, 1885.

Kennedy, Patrick. *Legendary Fictions of the Irish Celts*. Macmillan & Co., 1866.

Kepelino, Keauokalaini. *Kepelino's Traditions of Hawaii*. Translated by Martha Warren Beckwith. Bishop Museum Press, 1932. New York: Reprinted, Kraus Reprint, 1971.

Kerr, Cowper Lady Amabel. *The Life of Cesare Cardinal Baronius of the Roman Oratory*. Art & Book Co., 1898.

Khan, Geoffrey, Masoud Mohammadirad, Dorota Molin, and Paul M. Noorlander et al. *Neo-Aramaic and Kurdish Folklore from Northern Iraq: A Comparative Anthology with a Sample of Glossed Texts*, Volume 2. Open Book Publishers, 2022.

Kieckhefer, Richard. *Unquiet Souls: Fourteenth-Century Saints and Their Religious Milieu*. University of Chicago Press, 1984.

Kirk, Robert. *The Secret Commonwealth of Elves, Fauns, and Fairies*. David Nutt, In The Strand, 1893.

Kittredge, George. *Witchcraft in Old and New England*. Harvard University Press, 1929.

Knappert, Jan. *Pacific Mythology: An Encyclopedia of Myth and Legend*. Aquarian/Thorsons, 1992.

Knight, Sam. "The Psychiatrist Who Believed People Could Tell the Future." *The New Yorker*, February 25, 2019, The New Yorker Website

Konstantinos. *Vampires: The Occult Truth*. Llewellyn Publications, 1996.

Kracke, Waud. "To Dream, Perchance to Cure: Dreaming and Shamanism in a Brazilian Indigenous Society." *Social Analysis: The International Journal of Social and Cultural Practice* 50, no. 2 (2006): 106–120.

Kramer, Fritz. *Literature Among the Cuna Indians*. Etnografiska Museet, 1970.

Krause, Aurel. *The Tlingit Indians: Results of a Trip to the Northwest Coast of*

America and the Bering Straits. Translated by Erna Gunther. University of Washington Press, 1970.

Krausmüller, Dirk. "Can Human Beings Know the Hour of Their Own Death or of the Death of Others? A Ninth-Century Controversy and Its Historical Context." *Zbornik Radova Vizantoloskog Instituta* (2016): 63–82.

Krippner, Stanley "Tribal Shamans and Their Travels into Dreamtime." In *Dreamtime and Dreamwork: Decoding the Language of the Night*, edited by Stanley Krippner. St Martin's Press, 1990.

Krippner, Stanley, and Jeanne Achterberg. "Anomalous Healing Experiences." In *Varieties of Anomalous Experience: Examining the Scientific Evidence*, edited by Etzel Cardeña, Steven Jay Lynn, and Stanley Krippner. American Psychological Association, 2014.

Kriza, Erdélyi, Pap, and others, comps. *The Folk-Tales of the Magyars.* Translated and edited by the Rev. W. Henry Jones and Lewis L. Kropf. The Folk-Lore Society, 1889.

Kroeber, Alfred. *Handbook of the Indians of California.* Dover Publications, 1976.

Kroeber, Alfred. *Yurok Myths.* University of California Press, 1976.

Krohn, Kaarle. *Suomalaisten Runojen Uskonto.* Suomalaisen Kirjallisuuden Seura, 1915.

Kunow, Marianna. *Maya Medicine: Traditional Healing in Yucatan.* University of New Mexico Press, 2003.

Kvideland, Reimund, and Henning Sehmsdorf, eds. *Scandinavian Folk Belief and Legend.* University of Minnesota Press, 1988.

Lame Deer, John (Fire), and Richard Erdoes. *Lame Deer, Seeker of Visions: The Life of a Sioux Medicine Man.* Washington Square Press, 1976.

Landtman, Gunnar. *The Kiwai Papuans of British New Guinea: A Nature-Born Instance of Rousseau's Ideal Community.* MacMillan, 1927.

Lang, Andrew. *The Book of Dreams and Ghosts.* Longmans, Green, 1897.

Lang, Andrew. *The Making of Religion.* Longmans, Green, 1900.

Lang, Andrew. "At the Sign of St. Paul's: Andrew Lang on More Coincidences and Dream-Warnings." *Illustrated London News*, April 20, 1912.

Lang, David, trans. *Lives and Legends of the Georgian Saints.* 2nd ed., rev. ed. St. Vladimir's Seminary Press, 1976.

Laubscher, Barend. *Sex, Custom and Psychopathology: A Study of South African Pagan Natives.* George Routledge & Sons, 1937.

Lawrence-Smith, Kathleen. *Tales of Old Worcestershire.* Countryside Books, 1989.

Leach, Maria. *Dictionary of Folklore, Mythology and Legend*. Vol. 1: A–I. Funk & Wagnalls, 1949.

Leach, Maria. *The Rainbow Book of American Folk Tales and Legends*. World Publishing, 1958.

Leach, Maria. *Whistle in the Graveyard: Folktales to Chill Your Bones*. Viking Press, 1974.

Lecouteux, Claude. *The Return of the Dead: Ghosts, Ancestors, and the Transparent Veil of the Pagan Mind*. Translated by Jon E. Graham. Inner Traditions, 2009.

Lecouteux, Claude. *The Pagan Book of the Dead: Ancestral Visions of the Afterlife and Other Worlds*. Inner Traditions, 2020. Kindle.

Leigh, Egerton. *Ballads & Legends of Cheshire*. Longmans & Co., 1867.

Leiter, L. D. "The Vardøgr, Perhaps Another Indicator of the Non-Locality of Consciousness." *Journal of Scientific Exploration* 16 (2002): 621–634.

Leland, Charles. *Legends of Florence: Collected from the People and Re-Told*. Second Series. Macmillan, 1896.

Li, Lillian. "Two Chinese Ghosts." *California Folklore Quarterly* 4, no. 3 (1945): 278–280.

Liguori, Alfonso Maria de. *Victories of the Martyrs*. Edited by Eugene Grimm. Benziger Brothers, 1888.

Lincoln, Jackson Steward. *The Dream in Native American and Other Primitive Cultures*. Dover Publications, 2003.

Lindstrom, Lamont. *Tanna Times: Islanders in the World*. University of Hawaii, 2021.

Lingwood, Chad. *Politics, Poetry, and Sufism in Medieval Iran*. Vol. 5. Brill, 2014.

Laskow, Sarah. "The Role of the Supernatural in the Discovery of EEGs." *The Atlantic*, November 23, 2014.

Long, Jeffrey. *Evidence of the Afterlife*. HarperOne, 2010.

Lowie, Robert. *The Northern Shoshone*. Vol. 2, part 2 of the Anthropological Papers of the American Museum of Natural History. Trustees of the Museum, 1909.

Lowie, Robert. *Dances and Societies of the Plains Shoshone*. Vol. 11, part 10 of the Anthropological Papers of the American Museum of Natural History. Trustees of the Museum, 1915.

Lowie, Robert. *The Crow Indians*. Farrar & Rinehart, 1935.

Lu Sheng-Yen. *Encounters with the World of Spirits*. Translated by Janny Chow. Purple Lotus Society, 1995.

Luck, George, trans. *Arcana Mundi: Magic and the Occult in the Greek and Roman Worlds: A Collection of Ancient Texts*. Johns Hopkins University Press, 1985.

Luraghi, Nino. *The Ancient Messenians: Constructions of Ethnicity and Memory*. Cambridge University Press, 2008.

Lynch, Patricia. *Knights of God: Tales and Legends of the Irish Saints*. Holt, Rinehart & Winston, 1969.

Lysaght, Patricia. "Traditional Beliefs and Narratives of a Contemporary Irish Tradition Bearer." In *Folk Belief Today*, edited by Mare Kõiva and Kai Vassiljeva. Estonian Academy of Sciences, Institute of Estonian Language, and Estonian Museum of Literature, 1995.

M. L'Abbé Janvier, trans. *Life of Sister Mary St. Peter, Carmelite of Tours*. n.p, 1884.

Macaulay, G. C., trans. *The History of Herodotus*. Vol. 1. Macmillan, 1914.

MacDougall, John. *History of Inverness County, Nova Scotia*. Mika Publishing, 1922.

MacFarlan, Allan. *Native American Tales and Legends*. Dover Publications, 2001.

Mackenzie, Donald. *Wonder Tales from Scottish Myth & Legend*. Blackie & Son, 1917.

Mackenzie, Donald. *Myths from Melanesia and Indonesia*. Gresham, 1930.

Mackenzie, Donald. *Teutonic Myth and Legend*. William H. Wise, 1934.

Maclagan, R. C. "Ghost Lights of the West Highlands" *Folklore* 8, no. 3 (1897): 203–256.

MacLeod, Sharon. *Celtic Myth and Religion: A Study of Traditional Belief, with Newly Translated Prayers, Poems, and Songs*. McFarland, 2012.

Mac'Manus, L. "Folk-Tales from Western Ireland." *Folklore* 25 (1890): 324–341.

Macphail, Malcolm, and Louise Kennedy. "Giants in Pageants." *Folklore* 9, no. 1 (1898): 84–93.

Madigan, Kevin, and Carolyn Osiek, eds., trans. *Ordained Women in the Early Church: A Documentary History*. Johns Hopkins University Press, 2005.

Magallón, Linda Lane. *Mutual Dreaming: When Two or More People Share the Same Dream*. New York: Simon & Schuster, 1997.

Mango, Cyril, and Roger Scott, eds., trans. *The Chronicle of Theophanes Confessor*. Clarendon Press, 1997.

Marchbank, Agnes. *Upper Annandale: Its History and Traditions*. J. & R. Parlane, Paisley, 1901.

Mark, Emily. "Ghosts in Ancient China." *World History Encyclopedia*, last modified April 20, 2016.

Martin, Rafe. *Mysterious Tales of Japan*. G.P. Putnam's Sons, 1996.

Masters, Anthony. *The Natural History of the Vampire*. Putnam, 1972.

Masters, Anthony. *The Natural History of the Vampire*. Putnam, 1972.

Maulana Jalalu-'d-Din Muhammad I Rumi. *Masnavi I Ma'navi: The Spiritual Couplets of Maulana Jalalu-'d-Din Muhammad I Rumi*. Translated by E. H. Whinfield. Trübner, 1887.

Maxfield, Berton, and W. H. Millington. "Visayan Folk-Tales." *The Journal of American Folklore* 20, no. 77 (1907): 89–103.

Maybruck, Patricia. "Pregnancy and Dreams." In *Dreamtime and Dreamwork: Decoding the Language of the Night*, edited by Stanley Krippner 143–151. Tarcher, 1990.

Mayer, Elizabeth. *Extraordinary Knowing: Science, Skepticism, and the Inexplicable Powers of the Human Mind*. Bantam Books, 2007.

Mayor, Adrienne. *Greek Fire, Poison Arrows and Scorpion Bombs: Biological and Chemical Warfare in the Ancient World*. Overlook Duckworth, 2009.

McBride, Aideen. *Tipperary Folk Tales*. The History Press Ireland, 2015.

McClenon, James. *Wondrous Healing: Shamanism, Human Evolution, and the Origin of Religion*. Northern Illinois University Press, 2002.

McCulloch, William, trans. *Bengali Household Tales*. Hodder and Stoughton, 1912.

McDowell, John. *Sayings of the Ancestors: The Spiritual Life of the Sibundoy Indians*. University Press of Kentucky, 1989.

McFadden, Steven. *Profiles in Wisdom: Native Elders Speak about the Earth*. Bear & Co., 1991.

McGrew, Julia, and R. George Thomas, trans. *Sturlunga Saga*. Vol. 2, *Shorter Sagas of the Icelanders*. Twayne Publishers, 1970.

McNamara, Jo Ann, John Halborg, and Gordon Whatley, eds. & trans. *Sainted Women of the Dark Ages*. Duke University Press, 1992.

Menon, I. K. K. *Folk Tales of Kerala*. Ministry of Information & Broadcasting (India), 1995.

Merriam, Clinton Hart, ed. *The Dawn of the World: Myths and Weird Tales Told by the Mewan Indians of California*. The Arthur H. Clark Company, 1910.

Mesegeur, Pedro. *The Secret of Dreams*. Newman Press, 1960.

Michael the Syrian. *The Syriac Chronicle of Michael Rabo (The Great): A Universal History from the Creation*. Translated by Matti Moosa. Beth Antioch Press, 2014.

Miller, Elmer. *Nurturing Doubt: From Mennonite Missionary to Anthropologist in the Argentine Chaco.* University of Illinois Press, 1995.

Mills, James. *The Lhota Nagas.* Macmillan, 1922.

Minorsky, Vladimir. *A History of Sharvan and Darband in the 10th–11th Centuries.* W. Heffer & Sons, 1958.

Moerman, Daniel. *Geraniums for the Iroquois: A Field Guide to American Indian Medicinal Plants:* Reference Publications, 1982.

Monroe, James. *The Dream Investigator and Oneirocritica.* Vol. 1. Peoria, IL, 1884.

Moody, Raymond. *Glimpses of Eternity: Sharing a Loved One's Passage from This Life to the Next.* Guideposts, 2010.

Morriseau, Norval. *Legends of My People: The Great Ojibway.* Edited by Selwyn Dewdney. McGraw-Hill Ryerson, 1977.

Moss, Robert. *Dreamways of the Iroqois: Honoring the Secret Wishes of the Soul.* Destiny Books, 2004.

Moss, Robert. *The Secret History of Dreaming.* New World Library, 2009.

Moxon, John. *Peter's Halakhic Nightmare: The "Animal" Vision of Acts 10:9–16 in Jewish and Graeco-Roman Perspective.* Mohr Siebeck, 2017.

Munro, Dana, ed. *Life of St. Columban by the Monk Jonas.* University of Pennsylvania Press, 1895.

Myers, Frederic W. H. *Human Personality and Its Survival of Bodily Death.* Vol. 1. Longmans, Green, 1903.

Nagarajan, Nadia Grosser. *Jewish Tales from Eastern Europe.* Jason Aronson, 1999.

Nakamura, Kyoko Motomuchi. *Miraculous Stories from the Japanese Buddhist Tradition: The* Nihon Ryoiki *of the Monk Kyokai.* Harvard University Press, 1973.

Narby, Jeremy. *The Cosmic Serpent: DNA and the Origins of Knowledge.* Jeremy P. Tarcher/Putnam, 1998.

Nedelec, Louis. *Cambria Sacra; or, The History of the Early Cambro-British Christians.* Burnes & Oates, 1879.

Newell, William. "The Legend of the Holy Grail." *The Journal of American Folklore* 11, no. 40 (1898): 39–54.

Ngeh, Joseph. "The Phenomenon of Premonition of Death in Older Patient." Letter to the editor. *Journal of the American Geriatrics Society* 51, no. 11 (2003): 1672–73.

Nicolson, James. *Shetland Folklore.* R. Hale, 1981.

Nicholson, Reynold Alleyne. *Studies in Islamic Mysticism.* Cambridge University Press, 1921.

Nunn, Bruce. *Nova Scotia History with a Twist: True and Unusual Stories.* Nimbus, 2008.

Ó Cuív, Brian. "Miscellanea." *Celtica* 18 (1986): 105–124.

O'Donoghue, Denis. *Brendaniana: St. Brendan the Voyager in Story and Legend.* Browne & Nolan, 1895.

O'Farrell, Padraic. *Irish Saints.* Gill & Macmillan, 2002.

O'Grady, Standish. *Silva Gadelica (I-XXXI): A Collection of Tales in Irish with Extracts Illustrating Persons and Places.* Williams & Norgate, 1892.

O'Hanlon, John. *The Life of St. David.* J. Mullany, 1869.

Ó hÓgáin, Dáithí. *Myth, Legend & Romance: An Encyclopaedia of the Irish Folk Tradition.* Prentice Hall Press, 1991.

Olden, Sarah. *The People of Tipi Sapa (The Dakotas).* Morehouse Publishing Co., 1918.

O'Mara, Roisin. *In Search of Irish Saints: The Peregrinatio Pro Christo.* Four Courts Press, 1994.

Oppenheim, A. Leo. "The Interpretation of Dreams in the Ancient Near East." *Transactions of the American Philosophical Society,* new series, 46, no. 4 (1956): 179–373.

Orbelean, Step'annos. *Step'annos Orbelean's History of the State of Sisakan.* Vol. 1. Translated by Robert Bedrosian. Sources of the Armenian Tradition, 2012.

O'Reilly, Barry. "Now You See It, Now You Don't: Irish Legends of Buried Treasure." *Béaloideas, The Journal of the Folklore of Ireland Society* 62/63 (1994–5): 199–207.

Osis, Kārlis, and Erlendur Haraldsson. *At the Hour of Death.* Distributed by Publishers Group West, 1986.

Oswalt, Wendell. *Other Peoples, Other Customs: World Ethnography and Its History.* New York: Holt, Rinehart & Winston, 1972.

Ottway, T., comp. *News from the Invisible World.* Barr, 1844.

Ozaki, Yei Theodora. *Warriors of Old Japan and Other Stories.* Translated by Mrs. Hugh Fraser. Houghton Mifflin, 1909.

Parker, Arthur. *Seneca Myths and Folk Tales.* Bison Books, 1989.

Parker, Katie. *The Euahlayi Tribe: A Study of Aboriginal Life in Australia.* Archibald Constable & Company, Ltd., 1905.

Parkes, Colin. "Accuracy of Predictions of Survival in Later Stages of Cancer." *British Medical Journal* 2 (1972): 29–31.

Parsons, Elsie Clews. *Folklore of the Sea Islands, South Carolina.* American Folk-Lore Society, 1923.

Parsons, Elsie Clews. *Mitla, Town of the Souls, and other Zapoteco-Speaking Pueblos of Oaxaca, Mexico*. University of Chicago Press, 1936.
Parsons, Elsie Clews. *Folklore of the Antilles, French and English*. Part 3. American Folk-Lore Society, 1943.
Paterson, William. *Weird Tales: Scottish*. William Paterson, 1888.
Pausanias. *Messenia*. Vol. 4 of *Description of Greece*. Translated by W. H. S. Jones and H. A. Ormerod. Published on Theoi website. Originally published by William Heinemann, 1918.
Pearson, Patricia. *Opening Heaven's Door: What the Dying Are Trying to Say*. Simon & Schuster UK, 2014. Kindle.
Pearson, Patricia, Julia Mossbridge, and Julie Beischel. "Crisis Impressions: A Historical and Conceptual Review." *Threshold: Journal of Interdisciplinary Consciousness Studies* 5, no. 2 (2023): 1–32.
Pedroso, Consiglieri, and Henriquetta Monteiro. *Portuguese Folk-Tales*. Folk-Lore Society, 1882.
Phillips, Patricia. *Ethnobotany of the Coos, Lower Umpqua, and Siuslaw Indians*. Oregon State University Press, 2016.
Phillips, John. "Medicine." In *Caring for the Dying Patient and His Family*, edited by Austin Kutscher and Michael Goldberg. Health Sciences Publishing, 1973.
Philostratus, trans. *The Life of Apollonius of Tyana*. With notes by Edward Berwick. J. M'Creery, 1809.
Philostratus. *Lives of the Sophists. Eunapius: Lives of the Philosophers and Sophists*. Translated by Wilmer Wright. Loeb Classical Library 134. William Heinemann, 1922.
Pinch, Geraldine. *Magic in Ancient Egypt*. University of Texas Press, 2009. Published in cooperation with the British Museum Press.
Pliny. *The Letters of the Younger Pliny*. Translated by John Delaware Lewis. Trubner, 1879.
Pliny. *Natural History*. Vol. 2, books 3–7. Translated by Harris Rackham. Loeb Classical Library 352. Harvard University Press, 1942.
Plummer, Charles, ed. *Bethada Náem nÉrenn: Lives of Irish Saints*, Vol. 2. Clarendon Press, 1922.
Plutarch. *Plutarch's Morals. Translated from the Greek by Several Hands*. Corrected and revised by William Goodwin. 5 vols. Little, Brown, 1874.
Plutarch. *Lives: Themistocles, Pericles, Aristides, Alcibiades and Coriolanus, Demosthenes and Cicero, Caesar and Antony*. Dryden's translation corrected

and revised by Arthur Hugh Clough. Vol. 12 of The Harvard Classics, edited by Charles W. Eliot. P. F. Collier & Sons, 1909.

Plutarch. *Lives: Alcibiades and Coriolanus. Lysander and Sulla.* Vol. 4. Translated by Bernadotte Perrin. Loeb Classical Library 80. Harvard University Press; Heinemann, 1916.

Plutarch. *Lives: Agesilaus and Pompey. Pelopidas and Marcellus.* Vol. 5. Translated by Bernadotte Perrin. Loeb Classical Library 87. Harvard University Press; Heinemann, 1917.

Plutarch. *Lives: Demosthenes and Cicero. Alexander and Caesar.* Vol. 7. Translated by Bernadotte Perrin. Loeb Classical Library 99. Harvard University Press; Heinemann, 1919.

Podmore, Frank. *Apparitions and Thought-Transference.* W. Scott, 1902.

Podmore, Frank. *Telepathic Hallucinations: The New View of Ghosts.* F. A. Stokes, 1909.

Porter, Bill. *Road to Heaven: Encounters with Chinese Hermits.* Mercury House, 1993.

Price, Walter. *Noted Witnesses for Psychic Occurrences.* Boston Society for Psychic Research, 1928.

Rabb, Kate. *National Epics.* A.C. McClurg, 1896.

Radcliffe, John. *Fiends, Ghosts, and Sprites.* R. Bentley, 1854.

Radin, Dean. *The Conscious Universe: The Scientific Truth of Psychic Phenomena.* HarperCollins, 1997.

Rae, Edward. *The White Sea Peninsula: A Journey in Russian Lapland and Karelia.* J. Murray, 1881.

Rainwater, Pearl. *Grandma Speaks.* Northwestern Pub. House, 1994.

Rajketan, Chirom, and Sadananda Mayanglambam, eds. *A Collection of Essays in Manipuri Folklore.* Cultural Research Centre Manipur, 2013.

Ralston, William R. Shedden. *Russian Folk-Tales.* Smith, Elder, 1873.

Ramsay, Allan, and Francis McCullagh. *Tales from Turkey: Collected and Done into English.* Simpkin, Marshall, Hamilton, Kent, 1914.

Ramsay, Sterling. *Folklore: Prince Edward Island.* Square Deal Publications, 1970.

Ramsay, Mrs. W. M. *Everyday Life in Turkey.* Hodder & Stoughton, 1897.

Rand, Silas. *A Short Statement of Facts Relating to the History, Manners, Customs, Language and Literature of the Micmac Tribe of Indians in Nova Scotia and P. E. Island.* James Bowes & Son, 1850.

Rand, Silas. *Legends of the Micmacs.* Longmans, Green, 1894.

Rautman, Marcus Louis. *Daily Life in the Byzantine Empire.* Greenwood Press, 2006.

Reichard, Gladys Amanda. *Navaho Religion: A Study of Symbolism*. Pantheon Books, 1950.

Reichel-Dolmatoff, Gerardo. *The Shaman and the Jaguar: A Study of Narcotic Drugs Among the Indians of Colombia*. Temple University Press, 1975.

Reilly, Carmel. *Walking with Angels: Inspirational Stories of Heavenly Encounters*. Constable, 2011.

Rhine, Louisa. *Hidden Channels of the Mind*. W. Sloane Associates, 1961.

Rhine, Louisa. *The Invisible Picture: A Study of Psychic Experiences*. McFarland, 1981.

Ring, Kenneth. *Lessons from the Light*. Perseus Books, 1998.

Riordan, James. *A World of Folk Tales*. Hamlyn, 1981.

Rivas, Titus, Anny Dirven, and Rudolf Smit. *The Self Does Not Die: Verified Paranormal Phenomena from Near-Death Experiences*. International Association for Near-Death Studies, 2016. Kindle.

Robe, Stanley, ed. *Hispanic Legends from New Mexico: Narratives from the R. D. Jameson Collection*. Vol. 31 of Folklore and Mythology Studies. University of California Press, 1980.

Rogers, Louis. *Dreams and Premonitions*. Theosophical Book Concern, 1916.

Rogo, Scott. *An Experience of Phantoms*. Taplinger Pub. Co, 1974.

Róheim, Géza "Telepathy in a Dream." In *Psychoanalysis and the Occult,* edited by George Devereux. International Universities Press, 1970.

Ronner, John. *Do You Have a Guardian Angel?* Mamre Press, 1985.

Roscoe, John. *The Bakitara or Banyoro: The First Part of the Report of the Mackie Ethnological Expedition to Central Africa*. Cambridge University Press, 1923.

Rose, H. A. "Folk-Medicine in the Panjab." *Folklore* 21, no. 1 (1910): 83–6.

Rose, Ronald. *Living Magic: The Realities Underlying the Psychical Practices and Beliefs of Australian Aborigines*. Rand McNally, 1956.

Roseman, Marina. *Healing Sounds from the Malaysian Rainforest: Temiar Music and Medicine*. University of California Press, 1993.

Rougemont, Claire. *The National Dream Book*. David McKay, 1901.

Routledge, Katherine. *The Mystery of Easter Island*. Adventures Unlimited Press, 1998.

Royston, Robin, and Annie Humphreys. *The Hidden Power of Dreams: An Essential Guide to Interpreting Your Dreams*. Bantam Press, 2006.

Ruppert, James, and John Bernet. *Our Voices: Native Stories of Alaska and the Yukon*. Bison Books, 2001.

Russell, Frank. *The Pima Indians*. University of Arizona Press, 1975.

Ryder, Arthur, trans. *The Panchatantra of Vishnu Sharma: English Translation*. University of Chicago Press, 1925.

Sabine, W. H. W. *Second Sight in Daily Life*. George Allen & Unwin, 1951.

Sadeh, Pinhas. *Jewish Folktales*. Translated by Hillel Halkin. Doubleday, 1989.

Salo, Matt. *Roles of Magic and Healing: The Tietäjä in the Memorates and Legends of Canadian Finns*. Publications in Folk Culture, no. 3. National Museums of Canada, 1973.

Sartori, Penny. *The Near-Death Experiences of Hospitalized Intensive Care Patients: A Five-Year Clinical Study*. Edwin Mellen Press, 2008.

Savage, Minot. *Life Beyond Death*. G. P. Putnam's Sons, 1899.

Savage, William T. *Miramichi*. Loring, 1865.

Sayani, Husain. *Saints of Islam*. Luzac, 1908.

Schaefer, Stacy. "Crossing of the Souls: Peyote, Perception, and Meaning among the Huichol Indians." In *People of the Peyote: Huichol Indian History, Religion, & Survival*, edited by Stacy Schaefer and Peter Furst. University of New Mexico Press, 1996.

Scholes, France. "The First Decade of the Inquisition in New Mexico." *New Mexico Historical Review* 10, no. 3 (1935): 195–241.

Schouppe, Francois. *Purgatory: Explained by the Lives and Legends of the Saints*. Tan Books, 1973.

Schultes, Richard Evans, and Robert Raffauf. *Vine of the Soul: Medicine Men, Their Plants and Rituals in the Colombian Amazonia*. Synergetic Press, 2004.

Schultes, Richard Evans, and Albert Hofmann. *Plants of the Gods: Origins of Hallucinogenic Use*. A. van der Marck Editions, 1987.

Schwab, George. *Tribes of the Liberian Hinterland*. Edited by George W. Harley. Peabody Museum Press, 1947.

Schwartz, Howard. *Lilith's Cave: Jewish Tales of the Supernatural*. Harper & Row, 1988.

Scott, Gini Graham. *Shamanism and Personal Mastery*. Paragon House, 1991.

Seklemian, A. G. *The Golden Maiden and Other Folk Tales and Fairy Stories Told in Armenia*. The Helman-Taylor Company, 1898.

Seton, Ernest Thompson. *The Arctic Prairies*. Scribner, 1920.

Seymour, St. John. *Irish Witchcraft and Demonology*. Hodges, Figgis, 1913.

Shafton, Anthony. *Dream-Singers: The African American Way with Dreams*. J. Wiley & Sons, 2002.

Shah, Idries. *The Sufis*. 2nd ed. Octagon Press, 1964.

Shakespeare, William. *Julius Caesar.* Edited by A. W. Verity. Cambridge University Press, 1907.

Shanon, Benny. *The Antipodes of the Mind: Charting the Phenomenology of the Ayahuasca Experience.* Oxford University Press, 2003.

Sharp, Henry. *Loon: Memory, Meaning, and Reality in a Northern Dene Community.* University of Nebraska Press, 2001.

Shaw, Rosalind. "Dreaming as Accomplishment: Power, The Individual and Temne Divination." In *Dreaming, Religion, and Society in Africa,* edited by M. C. Jedrej and Rosalind Shaw, 36–54. E. J. Brill, 1992.

Sheldrake, Rupert. *Dogs That Know When Their Owners Are Coming Home.* Hutchinson, 1999.

Sheldrake, Rupert. *The Sense of Being Stared At: And Other Aspects of the Extended Mind.* Crown, 2003.

Shenhar-Alroy, Aliza. *Jewish and Israeli Folklore.* South Asian Publishers, 1987.

Shirokogorov, Sergei. *Pyschomental Complex of the Tungus.* Kegan Paul, Trench, Trubner, 1935.

Shockey, Peter. *Reflections of Heaven: A Millennial Odyssey of Miracles, Angels, and Afterlife.* Doubleday, 1999.

Siffredi, Alejandra. "Confrontation with Kixwet." In *Folk Literature of the Chorote Indians,* edited by Johannes Wilbert and Karin Simoneau. UCLA Latin American Center Publications, 1985.

Sigerist, Henry. *Primitive and Archaic Medicine.* Vol. 1 of *A History of Medicine.* Oxford University Press, 1967.

Sinclair, George. *Satan's Invisible World Discovered.* Reproduced with permission of the British Museum. Scholars' Facsimiles & Reprints, 1969.

Singh, M. "Why Is There Shamanism? Developing the Cultural Evolutionary Theory and Addressing Alternative Accounts." *Behavioral and Brain Sciences* 41, no. 92 (2018): 1–62.

Sitwell, Osbert. *The Scarlet Tree.* Vol. 2 of *Left Hand, Right Hand!* Macmillan, 1946.

Skinner, Alanson. *Notes on the Eastern Cree and Northern Saulteaux.* Vol. 9, part 1 of the Anthropological Papers of the American Museum of Natural History. Trustees of the Museum, 1911.

Skinner, Alanson. *Social Life and Ceremonial Bundles of the Menomini Indians.* Vol. 13, part 1 of the Anthropological Papers of the American Museum of Natural History. Trustees of the Museum, 1913.

Skinner, Charles. *Myths & Legends of Our Own Land.* Vol. 1. Lippincott, 1896.

Skinner, Charles. *Myths and Legends Beyond Our Borders*. J. B. Lippincott, 1899.
Skinner, Charles. *Myths and Legends of Flowers, Trees, Fruits, and Plants in All Ages and Climes*. J. B. Lippincott, 1911.
Smyth, Herbert, trans. *Aeschylus*. Vol. 2. G.P. Putnam's Sons, 1930.
Spangler, Ann. *Dreams and Miracles: How God Speaks through Your Dreams*. Guideposts, 2000.
Speck, Frank. *Naskapi: The Savage Hunters of the Labrador Peninsula*. University of Oklahoma Press, 1935.
Spence, Lewis. *Legends and Romances of Spain*. The Oxford Society Ltd., 1920.
Spencer, Baldwin, and Francis Gillen. *Across Australia*. 2 vols. Macmillan, 1912.
Spencer, John and Anne. *The Encyclopedia of Ghosts and Spirits*. Headline, 1992.
Spencer, John and Anne. *Powers of the Mind*. TV Books, 1999.
Stannard, Jerry. "The Plant Called Moly." *Osiris* 14 (1962): 254–307.
Steiger, Brad. Real *Ghosts, Restless Spirits and Haunted Minds*. Award Books; Tandem Books, 1968.
Steiger, Brad. *The Psychic Feats of Olof Jonsson*. Prentice-Hall, 1971.
Steiger, Brad, and Sherry Steiger. *Amazing Moms*. Penguin Group, 1994.
Steward, Julian. *Northern and Gosiute Shoshoni*. University of California Press, 1943.
Stokes, Margaret. *Three Months in the Forests of France: A Pilgrimage in Search of Vestiges of the Irish Saints in France*. George Bell & Sons, 1895.
Stokes, Whitley, ed. and trans. *Lives of Saints, from the Book of Lismore*. Clarendon Press, 1890.
Stokes, Whitley, ed. *The Birth and Life of St. Moling*. Harrison and Sons, 1907.
Summers, Montague. *The Vampire in Europe*. Kessinger Publishing, 2003.
Sun, Ruth. *Land of Seagull and Fox: Folk Tales of Vietnam*. Tuttle, 1967.
Sun, Xuegang, and Cai Guoyun. *Chinese Myths*. Penguin, 2008.
Sutherland, A. "Ancient Ingenious Ideas of Transmitting Messages Over Long Distances." AncientPages.com, January 30, 2019.
Sutherland, Cherie. *Transformed by the Light: Life after Near-Death Experiences*. Bantam Books, 1992.
Sutter, Virginia. *Tell Me, Grandmother: Traditions, Stories, and Cultures of Arapaho People*. University Press of Colorado, 2004.
Tabor, Margaret. *The Saints in Art: With Their Attributes and Symbols Alphabetically Arranged*. E. P. Dutton, 1913.
Talbot, Alice-Mary, ed. *Holy Women of Byzantium: Ten Saints' Lives in English Translation*. Dumbarton Oaks Publishing Service, 1996.

Tawney, Henry, trans. *The Kathá Sarit Ságara, or Ocean of the Streams of Story.* Vol. 2. Calcutta, 1884.

Taylor, Richard. *Te Ika a Māui, or New Zealand and its Inhabitants.* William Macintosh; H. Ireson Jones, 1870.

Taylor, Steve. "Is It Possible to Foresee Death? The Strange Cases of People Who Predict the Date of Their Own Death." *Psychology Today*, December 3, 2023.

Tedlock, Barbara. *The Beautiful and the Dangerous: Dialogues with the Zuni Indians.* Penguin Books, 1993.

Tedlock, Barbara. *The Woman in the Shaman's Body.* Bantam Books, 2005.

Terada. Alice. *Under the Starfruit Tree: Folktales from Vietnam.* University of Hawaii Press, 1989.

Terada, Alice. *The Magic Crocodile and Other Folktales from Indonesia.* University of Hawaii Press, 1994.

Terada. Alice. *Under the Starfruit Tree: Folktales from Vietnam.* University of Hawaii Press, 1989.

Thomas, Patrick. *Celtic Earth, Celtic Heaven: Saints and Heroes of the Powys Borderland.* Gomer, 2003.

Thompson, Coquelle. *Pitch Woman and Other Stories: The Oral Traditions of Coquelle Thompson, Upper Coquille Athabaskan Indian.* Edited by William R. Seaburg. University of Nebraska Press, 2007.

Thompson, Edward. *The Life and Glories of St. Joseph.* Burns & Oates, 1888.

Thorgilsson, Ari. *The Book of the Settlement of Iceland.* Translated by Thomas Ellwood. T. Wilson, 1898.

Thurston, Herbert. *The Church and Spiritualism.* Bruce Publishing, 1933.

Thwaites, Reuben. *The Jesuit Relations and Allied Documents.* Vols. 1–10. Burrows Bros., 1896.

Tikalsky, Frank, Catherine Euler, and John Nagel, eds. *The Sacred Oral Tradition of the Havasupai: As Retold by Elders and Headmen Manakaja and Sinyella, 1918–1921.* University of New Mexico Press, 2010.

Timbs, John. *Signs Before Death: A Record of Strange Apparitions, Remarkable Dreams.* W. Tegg, 1875.

Toelken, Barre. "The Moccasin Telegraph and Other Improbabilities: A Personal Essay." In *Out of the Ordinary: Folklore and the Supernatural*, edited by Barbara Walker. Utah State University Press, 1995.

Trautmann, Franz. *Legends and Tales of Old Munich.* Lentner, 1912.

Tuckett, Ivor. *The Evidence for the Supernatural.* Watts, 1932.

Turner, Edith. *The Spirit and the Drum: A Memoir of Africa*. University of Arizona Press, 1987.

Tyler, Royall. *Japanese Tales*. Pantheon Books, 1987.

Tylenda, Joseph. *Jesuit Saints & Martyrs: Short Biographies of the Saints, Blessed, Venerables, and Servants of God of the Society of Jesus*. Jesuit Way, 1998.

Ullman, Montague, Stanley Krippner, and Alan Vaughan. *Dream Telepathy: Experiments in Nocturnal ESP*. Penguin, 1974.

Ury, Marion. *Tales of Times Now Past: Sixty-Two Stories from a Medieval Japanese Collection*. University of California Press, 1979.

Valadez, Susana. "Wolf Power and Interspecies Communication in Huichol Shamanism." In *People of the Peyote: Huichol Indian History, Religion, & Survival*, edited by Stacy Schaefer and Peter Furst. University of New Mexico Press, 1996.

Valerius Maximus. *His Collections of the Memorable Acts and Sayings of Orators, Philosophers, Statesmen, and Other Illustrious Persons*. Translated by Samuel Speed. London, 1684.

Valerius Maximus. *Memorable Deeds and Sayings: One Thousand Tales from Ancient Rome*. Translated by Henry Walker. Hackett, 2004.

Vallée, Jacques. *Passport to Magonia: On UFOs, Folklore, and Parallel Worlds*. Chicago: Contemporary Books, 1993.

Van Braght, Thieleman, comp. *The Bloody Theatre, or Martyr's Mirror of the Defenceless Christians*. Translated by Joseph F. Sohm. Mennonite Publishing Company, 1886.

Van Bronkhorst, Jeanne. *Dreams at the Threshold*. Llewellyn Publications, 2015.

VanStone, James. *Athapaskan Adaptions: Hunters and Fishermen of the Subarctic Forests*. Aldine Pub. Co., 1974.

Velimirovic, Nikolaj. *Stories of Saints from the Prologue: Based on the Prologue from Ohrid by Bishop Nikolai Velimirovich*. Compiled and adapted by Johanna Manley. Bishop Nikolai Resource Center, 1998.

Venkataswami, M. *Heerámma and Venkataswami, or Folktales from India*. Diocesan Press, 1923.

Vernalaken, Theodor. *In the Land of Marvels: Folk-Tales from Austria and Bohemia*. S. Sonnenschein & Co., 1889.

Vestal, Stanley. *Warpath: The True Story of the Fighting Sioux, Told in a Biography of Chief White Bull*. Bison, 1984.

Vigfusson, Gudbrand, and Frederick Powell, eds. and trans. *Origines Islandicae*. Clarendon Press, 1905.

Virtanen, Leea. *That Must Have Been ESP!: An Examination of Psychic Experiences.* Indiana University Press, 1990.

Virtue, Doreen. *Angel Visions II: More True Stories of People Who Have Had Contact with Angels, and How You Can, Too!* Hay House, 2006.

Visser, Marinus William De. *The Dragon in China and Japan.* J. Muller, 1913.

Vitale, Guido, trans. *Chinese Folklore: Pekinese Rhymes.* Pei-T'ang Press, 1896.

Vyasa. *The Mahābhārata.* Translated by John Smith. Penguin, 2009.

Wadley, Susan. "Folk Literature of South Asia." *Journal of South Asian Literature* 11, no. 12 (1975): 1–177.

Waldron, George. *The History and Description of the Isle of Man.* Manchester, 1744.

Walker, Barbara, and Warren Walker, eds. *Nigerian Folk Tales.* Rutgers University Press, 1961.

Walker, Barbara, ed. *A Treasury of Turkish Folktales for Children.* Linnet Books, 1988.

Walker, Barbara. *The Art of the Turkish Tale.* Texas Tech University Press, 1990.

Walker, Warren, and Ahmet Uysal. *Tales Alive in Turkey.* Harvard University Press, 1966.

Wallace, Ernest, and E. Adamson Hoebel. *The Comanches: Lords of the South Plains.* University of Oklahoma Press, 1952.

Wallace, Martin. *Celtic Saints.* The Appletree Press, 2007.

Weaver, Zofia. "An Extraordinary Clairvoyant and an Extraordinary Policeman." White Crow Books website, accessed January 6, 2024.

Westropp, Thomas J. "A Folklore Survey of County Clare (concluded)," *Folklore* 23, no. 2 (1912): 204–15.

White, William. *A Picture of Pioneer Times in California: Illustrated with Anecdotes and Stories Taken from Real Life.* W. M. Hinton & Co., 1881.

Whitney, Orson. "A Terrible Ordeal," In *Helpful Visions,* 9–22. Faith-Promoting Series 14.

Whitten, Norman. *Sacha Runa: Ethnicity and Adaptation of Ecuadorian Jungle Quichua.* Urbana: University of Illinois Press, 1976.

Wilby, Emma. *Cunning Folk and Familiar Spirits: Shamanistic Visionary Traditions in Early Modern British Witchcraft and Magic.* Sussex Academic Press, 2005.

Wilby, Emma. *The Visions of Isobel Gowdie: Magic, Witchcraft and Dark Shamanism in Seventeenth-Century Scotland.* Sussex Academic Press, 2010.

Wilhelm, Richard, ed; Martens, Frederick, trans. *The Chinese Fairy Book*. Frederick A. Stokes Company Publishers, 1921.

Willard, Park. "Paviotso Shamanism." *American Anthropologist* 36, no. 1 (1934): 98–113.

Williams, Francis. *Orokaiva Magic*. Clarendon Press, 1969.

Williams, Francis. *The Social Life and Ceremonial Life of the Elema*. Clarendon Press, 1969.

Wilson, Richard. *The Lost Literature of Medieval England*. Philosophical Library Inc., 1952.

Windham, Joan. *Sixty Saints for Boys*. Christian Classics, 1990.

Wissler, Clark, and D. C. Ducall. *Mythology of the Blackfoot Indians*. Anthropological Papers of the American Museum of Natural History. Trustees of the Museum, 1908.

Yoder, Don. *Discovering American Folklife: Studies in Ethnic, Religious, and Regional Culture*. UMI Research Press, 1990.

Yuchi, Nina Jun. "Mutual Dreaming: Rest as Political Resistance and Temporal Lucidity." Futuress.org, October 18, 2021.

Ziolkowski, Jan M. *Reading the Juggler of Notre Dame: Medieval Miracles and Modern Remakings*. Open Book Publishers, 2022.

Zosimus. *The History of Count Zosimus*. J. Davis, 1814.

Index

Aboriginal community, 13–14, 33, 218
Acts of Sylvester, 188–89
African tales, 136, 166
al-Farid, Umar Ibn, 67
Al Hasan, 90
Allred, Grover, 138
al-Misri, Dhu'l-Nun, 225
Amphiarus, 39
angel visitations, 38, 103, 120, 159, 183, 186
animals, 46–47
Anthony, John, 164
Apparitions (Green and Mc Creery), 132
Apparitions at the Moment of Death (Bourke), 111–12, 143–44
Arapaho Indians, 124
Aristeas of Proconnesus, 132
Arnold, Dom, 105
arrivals
    animals and, 1, 5, 39, 46-47, 165, 178, 191, 194-6, 211, 220
    the dead and, 34–35
    demons and, 17
    dreams and, 23–28
    etiäinen and, 22
    of foreigners, 42–43
    forerunners and, 23
    of invaders, 43–45
    Ireland and, 30–32
    messengers, hermits, saints and, 30–32
    motifs and, 19–21
    prophecy and, 27–28
    shamans and, 33–37
    shared dreams and, 231
    symbols and, 38–42
    varsel experiences, 21–22
    voices and, 28–30
Arrowsmith, Father Edmund, 115
Arthurian legend, 59
Asclepian temples, 173–75, 178
Asclepius, 173–74, 176–77, 213
Ashmole, Elias, 107
Ashton, John, 159–60
Asmundr, 141
Aurelius, Marcus, 106
Austrian folktale, 190

Bairre, 229–30
balam, 188
Baldwin, Charles, 117
Bar Abdun, Mor Yuhanon, 36
Barasch, Marc, 184
Barat, Madeleine Sophie, 101
Baring-Gould, Sabine, 144

Barrett, William, 118–19
Batthyány, Alexander, 98, 113
Bayar Odun, 161
Beaumont, John, 15
Bede, 95, 104, 115, 119
Belasco, David, 145
Bell, Adam, 139
benandanti, 220
Benedict the Moor, 31–32, 83, 143
Bengali tales, 64
Bennett, Gillian, 22, 152
Berach, 35, 143
Berger, Hans, 51
Blackfoot Indians, 34
Boas, Franz, 9, 178
Bodding, Paul Olaf, 185
Boeldeke, Alfred, 61
Book of Jubilees, 84
Book of Lismore, 35
botanical knowledge, 191–94.
    See also healing
Bracciolini, Poggio, 154
Brinton, Daniel, 10–11, 12, 14
Brito of Columcille, 120
Buddhist tales, 40, 64, 133–34, 162, 232

Calmet, Antoine Augustin, 134
CampbellJones, Brenda, 212
Campion, Edmund, 105
Canadian tales, 11, 140, 144, 147–48, 163–64, 169
Canelos-Quichua, 218–19
Cantar de mio Cid, 104
Cardim, John, 121
Cassandra of Greek myth, 84
Catherine of Palma, 83
Centerwall, Arlene, 49–50
Chang Kuei, 134
Cherokee Indians, 192

Chevreul, Michael Eugène, 139
Chinese tales, 25, 73, 88, 134, 137–38, 148, 209–10, 230
Chi O, 114
Chippewa Indians, 195–96
Chips (medicine man), 142
Chorote Indians, 11, 188
Chulainn, Cú, 23–24
Cicero, 24–25, 58, 166
clairvoyance, ix, 5, 11, 61–62, 111
Cobbe, Frances Power, 114
Coffin, Margaret, 116–17
coincidence, healing, 194–98
Collison-Morely, Lacy, 128–29
Columba, 31, 103, 120
condenando, 130
connections, 7–8, 74, 204, 232–33
Cooper, Pepper, 80
Coos Indians, 62, 192
Copper Eskimos, 55, 155
Corbinelli, Father, 117
Corrado, Bill, 199–200
co-walkers, 31
Craig, Walter, 91
Craigie, William, 21, 48
Cree Indians, 192, 203
Creighton, Helen, 68, 81, 125, 229
crisis visions
    apparitions, 137
    the dead and, 73–74
    death, 50–51
    deathbed, 60–65
    disasters and decisions, 70–72
    dreams, 53–55
    evolutionary origin, 51
    illness, 60–65
    lost and found, 60–65
    medical, 49–50
    mystical aid, 56–57
    mystics and, 52–53, 63–65

myths and monastics, 69–70
persuasive, 52–53
prisoners and war, 57–60
psychological aspects of, 51, 52
symbolic crises, 54–56
warnings, 66–69
Crow Indians, 46
Csordas, Thomas, 201
Cuna, 61
curare, 195
Cyprian, 93–94

da Gama, Vasco, 58–59
Dale, Laura, 215–16
Dance, Daryl, 140
Daredevils of Sassoun, 59
d'Arles, Saint-Jean, 32
David (patron saint), 31
David-Neel, Alexandra, 12
Davies, Rodney, 161
dead, the
arrivals and, 34–35
coming for the dying, 94–99
crisis visions and, 73–74
healing and, 184–85
knowledge of, 99
as messengers, 94–99, 101–2
near-death awareness and, 94–99
presence among the living, 97
shared dreams and visions and, 221–25
death
the dead and, 94–99
distant visions, 50–51, 126
before dying, 111
knowledge of, 82–85, 87, 89–90
messengers of, 98, 131–37
predetermined, 85–91
premonitions of, 76–81
shared, 221–25

deathbed visions. *See also* nearing-death awareness
crisis visions, 60–65
death at a distance and, 119–22
drifters and, 122–25
at the end, 113–19
mentally ill and, 112
people around, 118
unusual phenomena and, 110–12
view from the peak, 112–13
de Benneville Keim, Susanna, 67
de Carvalho, Joao Fernandes, 203
Declan, 73
Dee, John, 60
Defoe, Daniel, 72
Deirdre, 41
De Moltke, Marshal, 124
Dene Indians, 7, 193, 196
Densmore, Frances, 195–96
Dentan, Robert, 45
de Peyer, Janine, 50
De Santo, Nina, 132–33
Destruction of Da Derga's Hostel, The, 28
DeVita, Philip, 8–9
Dickens, Charles, 5
Diego, Juan, 180
disinterested shades, 137–40
"Doctor Dick," 155
Dodds, Eric, 24
Donahoe, James, 216–17
doppeltraume, 213
Dorsey, George, 79
dreams
arrivals and, 23–28
in classical tales, 38–42
connections in, 232–33
crisis, 53–55
danger of belief in, 71
double, 212–14, 233

Easter Island peoples and, 11
foreshadowing from, 14–16
healing, 182–84, 206–7
incubation, 173, 174
in locating treasure, 148–49
lucid, 216–17
meshing, 214–16
nearing-death awareness, 90–91
prophetic, 223
shamans and, 11
shared, 206–34
treasure and, 148–49, 160–61
trinkets and baubles, 169–70
varsel experiences and, 21–22
dream space, sharing, 217–19
"dream telepathy," 211
"dream trackers," 43
Drusus, Nero Claudius, 102
Duke Henry II, 143
Dunlap, Bessie, 159
Dunstan (bishop), 102–3
Duong Duc, Cong, 88

Ea-Bani, 86
Eady, George, 21
"Early Life of Hasan Bey, The," 59
Easter Island peoples, 11
Edmundson, William, 69
Edwards, Peter, 46
Egyptian tales, 169, 179, 225
Eisenbud, Jule, 211
Elsaesser, Evelyn, 131, 139, 161, 164, 225
Enkidu, 28
Ethelred (king of Wessex), 47
etiäinen, 22
Evans-Pritchard, Edward, 165–66, 184
Exton-Smith, Arthur, 77, 78, 80
extrasensory phenomena and capacities, 2, 5, 6, 236

fairies, 152, 168, 179–80, 188
fate, accepting, 81–85
fetches, 138
feyness, 123
Filipino tales, 153–54, 203
Fintan, 89–90
Fiore, Edith, 204–5
"Fisherman and His Friend, The," 33
Fitzsimon, Henry, 30
Flammarion, Camille, 50
Flower, Michael, 92–93
forerunners, 23, 81, 144
Fox, Oliver, 221
Frankl, Viktor, 75–76
Freuchen, Peter, 7
Freud, Sigmund, 51
Fridolin of Säckingen, 162
Funk, Isaac, 124–25

Gambacorta, Clare, 120
Ganna (Fijian), 115–16
Garrett, Eileen, 68–69
Genko Shakusho, 40
Geoffrey, Dennis, 65–66
"Goddess Itu, The," 64
Golomb, Louis, 14–15
Graham Scott, Gini, 216
Greek tales, 38–39, 64–65, 84, 129, 141–42, 148, 170, 181, 206
Green, Lawrence George, 12, 57, 166
Grey, Margot, 183, 199
guardian spirits, 33
Guatemalan tale, 127
Guggenheims, 152
Gyoki (priest), 162

Handsome Boy, 44–45, 167
Handy, Craighill, 12–13, 185
Hankey, Rosalie, 154–55
Haraldsson, Erlendur, 103–4, 112, 116

Hasilbacker, Hans, 90
Hastings, Elizabeth, 96
Havasupai Indians, 10, 54
Hawaiian tale, 69
healing
  about, 172–73
  ancient, 173–76
  ceremonies, 185
  coincidence and, 194–98
  "curing by recital" and, 187
  the dead and, 184–85
  divine assistance in, 180–82
  dreams, 182–84
  extraterrestrials and, 204
  fairies and, 179–80, 188
  gifts from the gods, 176–84
  health near death and, 198–201
  locations of, 187–91
  medicines, 186–87, 190
  mystics and, 37–38
  placebo, belief, and truth and, 201–4
  plant wisdom and, 191
  sacred, 172–205
  saints and, 186–87
  shamans and, 177–79, 197–98
  trial and error and, 194–98
  visitations and, 37–38
Healing Dreams (Barasch), 184
Herbert, Edward, 76
Herdt, Gilbert, 44
Hermes, 181
Hichens, Mary, 70
hidden/lost items
  about, 146–47
  angels and, 159
  anonymous messengers, 166–68
  bodies, 162–66
  dreams and, 148–49, 160–61
  lore, 151–54
  messenger saints, 158–61

people, 157
trances and, 154–55
treasure and troves, 147, 158
trinkets and baubles, 168–70
in walls, 149–51
Hill-Tout, Charles, 7
Ho'-ho the Buzzard, 10
Holzer, Hans, 72, 199–200
Horus, 169–70
Hsuan-tsung, 148
Hubert (bishop), 108
Hufford, David, x–xi
Hugh of Lincoln, 120–21, 144
Huichol Indians, 62, 63, 220
Humphreys, Chris, 19
Hungarian tales, 22, 134, 224
Hutchinson, Horace, 153
Hyatt, Harry, 139
Hyvarnion, 226–27

Iamos, 2, 141
Icelandic tales, 136, 140–41, 180, 219–20
Indian tales, 47, 160–61
Iraqi tales, 66, 151, 212–13
Ireland
  arrivals and, 30–32
  holy messengers, 35–36
  secret knowledge of death and, 89–90
  Ulster Cycle, 28, 41, 230
Irene of Chrysovalantou, 170
Irghalach, 89
Irish tales, 67, 70, 116, 138–39, 149, 156, 179, 207
Istikhara, 176
Italian tales, 149–50, 154, 220–21
"Ivan the Peasant's Son and the Thumb-Sized Man," 54–55

Jackowski, Krzysztof, 164
Jackson, Jean, 111

Jacobs, Melville, 62
Jacobson, Nils-Olof, 18, 52
James and Marian (martyrs), 222
Japanese tales, 25, 36–37, 57, 64, 87–88, 133, 169, 174, 232
Jataka, 64
Jelalu-'d-Din, Arif, 100
Jenness, Diamond, 155
Jizo (bodhisattva), 36
John (Acts of John), 28–29, 38
Jones, Louis, 151–52
Jonsson, Olof, 18–19
Joseph of Cupertino, 121
Judah the Pious, 13
Jun Yuchi, Nina, 216

Kachhawa, Indubala, 99
Kalmus, Eleanor, 119
Kamanga, 184
Keeney, Bradford, 8
Khuedios, 26
Kibariun, 27
Kimball, David Patten, 106
Kirk, Robert, 31
Knop, Thorhall, 74
knowledge
　botanical, 191–94
　the dead and, 99
　of death, 82–85, 87, 89–90
　old knowing and, 108–9
　secret, 105–8
　of treasure, 147–51
Korean tales, 129, 136, 185
Kostka, Stanislaus, 82
Kwakitutl Indians, 9, 178

Lang, Andrew, 170
Laubscher, Barend, 155–56
Leach, Maria, 61, 140
Leiter, David, 19–20

Leland, Charles, 8–9, 149
Lenape Indians, 54, 157, 163
Li, Lillian, 137
Liu Qingsong, 88
Livy (Titus Livius), 209
Long, Jeffrey, 200
Lourenco, Gaspar, 82
love, in shared dreams, 226–28
lucid dreaming, 216–17
Luck, Georg, 53
Lusiads, The, 58–59

Macarius, 36
Maedoc, Cain, 31
Magallón, Linda Lane, 215, 227
Mahaprabhu, Chaitanya, 37
Maldanado, Juan, 87
Maliseet Indians, 191–92
Maoris, 40–41, 96, 139–40
Marcianus, 175
Mark the Evangelist, 71
Mary of Saint Peter, 122
Mathews, Janet, 13–14
Maximinus of Micy, 176
Maya, 127–28, 137, 164, 177–78, 186, 188
Maybruck, Patricia, 228
Mayer, Elizabeth Lloyd, 157
medieval mind, 81–82
Menippus, 135
Menominee Indians, 167, 178
"mental derangements," 16
Meseguer, Pedro, 110–11
meshing dreams, 214–16
messengers
　anonymous, 166–68
　arrivals and, 30
　common, 101–5
　crisis visions, 67
　of death, 98, 131–37

holy, 35–37
message of, 145
Metamorphoses, 189, 213, 222
Mexican tales, 62–63, 131, 148, 176
Meyner (priest), 119
Micmac Indians, 28, 42, 44, 65
Mikhailovich, Alexei, 28
Miller, Elmer, 7–8
Misra, 27
"moccasin telegraph," 6
Mochuda, 41
Moda, 168
Modoc Indians, 65, 69
Mohawk Indians, 44
Molandssveen, Gudbrand, 21
Molton, R. H., 18
Mongolian tale, 40
Monroe, James (president), 223
Moody, Raymond, 225
Muircheartach Ua Briain (king), 89
Munei, 42–43
Myers, Frederic, 20
mystics
  crisis visions and, 56–57, 63–65
  death before dying and, 111
  distant crisis visions, 52–53
  forewarned, 107–8
  healing and, 37–38
  nearing-death awareness and, 100–101

Narby, Jeremy, 196–97
Navaho Indians, 79
near-death experiences
  healing and, 200–201
  healing gifts and, 199–200
  Pliny the Elder, 156
  research and, 202
  shared death experience and, 225, 234
  time granted to stay and, 88
  White Bull and, 198

nearing-death awareness
  accepting fate and, 81–85
  African, 78–81
  in both worlds and, 99–101
  the dead and, 94–99
  decisions and departures and, 106–7
  knowledge of death and, 82–85, 87
  life prolonged and, 107–8
  medical, 76–78
  Native American, 78–81
  phenomena, 75–76
  predetermined death and, 85–91
  shared dreams and visions and, 221–25
  symbols and dreams, 90–91
  taste of heaven and, 101
neuroscience, 1–2
Newfoundland tale, 125
New Mexican tales, 9, 33–34, 102, 130, 142, 148, 155
Ngeh, Joseph, 77–78
Nicetius, 100

O'Duivna, Dermott, 32
Ojibway Indians, 175, 177, 192, 195
One Thousand and One Nights, 135–36
Onondaga Indians, 65
Orokaiva people, 223
Osis, Karlis, 103–4, 112, 116

Pa Abdul, 167
Pal, Dharm, 66
Palestinian tales, 96, 184
Panchatantra, 27
Papuan tales, 40, 44, 129, 169–70, 223
Parintintin Indians, 56
Parmensis, Gaius Cassius, 103
Passport to Magonia (Vallée), 204
Pawnee Indians, 10, 167, 192
Peak in Darien experiences, 111, 113, 114. *See also* deathbed visions

Pearson, Patricia, 124
Peruvian tales, 60–61, 62–63, 130, 178
Peter the Fuller, 163
Petit du Noyer, Anne-Marguerite, 75
Phantasms of the Living, 29, 231
Phillip (king of Macedonia), 84–85
Phillips, John Hunter, 77
Pima Indians, 142
"Pitch Woman," 62
placebos, 203
plant wisdom, 191–94. *See also* healing
  sacred, 220
Pliny, 58, 87, 156
Plutarch, 44, 86, 94, 156, 181
Podmore, Frank, 68
Polynesians, 6, 12, 80, 129, 160
"Poor Widow's Son, The," 16
Porter, Anna Maria, 138
Portuguese tales, 67, 135
precognition, as battle strategy, 43–45
Primitive Medicine (Sigerist), 197
prophecy, 23, 27–28, 85, 108
Ptolemy, 190
Pueblo Indians, 142

Quakers, 130–31

Rainwater, Pearl, 22
Ramsay, Sterling, 147–48
Rand, Silas, 65
Red Owl, Benjamin, 131
reflexes, 31
Reichard, Gladys Amanda, 79
relics, 32, 74, 115, 158, 163, 170
revelations, coordinated, 209–10
revenants
  about, 128, 129
  as death messengers, 131–37
  in the family, 130–31

psychokinetic interactions, 145
  in writings, 128–29
Rhine, Louisa, 13, 60, 68
Rhine Feather, Sally, 57, 151, 165
Richard of Ingworth, 70–71
Richet, Charles, 96
Ring, Kenneth, 199
Rogers, Louis, 153, 229
Róheim, Géza, 233
Romanes, George, 66
Romanian tales, 65
Rose, Ronald, 33
Roseman, Marina, 193–94
Rougemont, Claire, 149
Rufus, Haterius, 86
Rumi, xi, 37, 158
Russian tales, 135, 143

Sabine, William, 21
Sadeta, 186
Saga of Hromund Greipsson, 90
Saint Brigid, 231
Saint Francis of Assisi, 105, 186
Saint Gobhan, 212
Saint Hedwig, 83
Saint Lawrence, 93
Saint Lebuin, 158
Saint Leo, 95
Saint Maximus, 93
Saint-Paul-de-Narbonne, 108
saints. *See also specific saints*
  arrivals and, 36, 48
  healing and, 186–87
  Irish, 12, 30–32, 73
  messenger, 158–61
  miracles and, 14–15
  nearing-death awareness and,
    92–94, 97, 107
Sambia, 44, 220
Samuelson, R. C. A., 57

Sartori, Penny, 106, 200–201
Savage, Minot, 34, 97–98, 119–20
Savage, William, 23
Scabby-One, 11
Scandinavian tales, 141, 150, 165, 214
Schwab, George, 79, 80
Scottish tales, 64, 72, 139, 183, 222, 223–24
Secunda, Brant, 63
Sejarah Melayu, 37
Seneca Indian tales, 9–10, 59
Serabian, Mariam, 151
Serrano, General, 117
Servilius Damocrates, 181, 182
Seton, Ernest Thompson, 107
Shahnameh, 92
shamans. *See also specific shamans*
  about, 2
  arrivals and, 33–37
  clairvoyance, 11
  death before dying and, 111
  dreaming and, 11
  as healers, 199
  healing and, 177–79, 197–98
  precognition of enemies coming, 43
  in shared spaces, 220–21
  shared visions of battles and, 219–20
shared death, 221–25
shared dreams and visions
  about, 206–8
  of battles, 219–20
  coordinated revelations, 209–10
  the dead and, 221–25
  double dreams and, 212–14
  dreamtime connections, 232–33
  holy ground and, 210–11
  as inspiration for action, 210–11
  love, 226–28
  mysterious meetings, 231
  shared bonds and, 212
treasure, 229–30
unannounced arrivals, 231
understanding within dream and, 213
visionaries in, 220–21
visionary spaces, 217–19
warnings of danger, 230
Sharp, Henry, 193
Shaw, Rosalind, 13
Sheldrake, Rupert, 46, 47
Shirokogorov, Sergei, 14
Shiva, Vandana, 23
Shoshone Indians, 43, 79, 167, 195, 203, 218
Shushan, Gregory, ix–xii
Sibundoy, 8, 194
Singh, Truong, 55
Sison, Josephina, 203
Sitwell, Osbert, 4–5
sleep paralysis, xi
Socrates, 222
Sosipatra, 52–53, 56, 72
Spanish tales, 83, 117, 150
Spencer, John, 18
Steiger, Brad, 143
Steller, Georg Wilhelm, 227
Story of the Unlucky Shoayb, 25
Story of Little Mouk, The, 168
Story of the Finding of Cashel, The, 39
Sturlunga, 39–40
Summers, Montague, 134
Sutter, Virginia, 124
symbolic crises, 54–57
symbols
  arrivals and, 38–42
  nearing-death awareness and, 90–91
Syriac Chronicle, 210

Takakuraji, Kumano, 37
Tanna people, 167
Taylor, Steve, 83–84
Tedlock, Barbara, 102, 142, 177, 179

telepathy, ix, 5, 13, 51, 57, 111
Temiar people, 193–94
Temne, 13, 79, 176
Temne diviners, 13
Terror that Comes in the Night, The, (Hufford), xi
Thai tales, 193
Theobald III, 131–32
Theophanes the Confessor, 32
"Three Brothers and the Hand of Fate," 190
tietäjä, 63
Tikhon of Zadonsk, 84
Toelken Barre, 6–7, 17
Tomasa, Machi, 178
tombs, 73, 158, 161, 176
Torralva, Eugenio, 150
totems, 33–34, 40
trances, hidden/lost items and, 154–55
treasure
  buried, 156
  dreams and, 148–49, 160–61
  knowledge of, 147–51
  lore, 151–54
  shared, 229–30
  Sicilians and Italians and, 152
  tombs and, 158
  in walls, 149–51
trial and error, healing, 194–98
Tuckett, Ivor Lloyd, 122
Tukano, 111, 178–79, 196
Tungus, 14, 218
Turner, Edith, 34–35
Two Brides, The, 209–10

Ullman, Montague, 215–16
Ulster Cycle, 28, 41, 230

Valesius, 181–82
Van Bronkhorst, Jeanne, 77

vardogers, ix, 5, 6, 18, 47–48. *See also* arrivals
varsel experiences, 21–22
veridical experiences, 45
Vietnamese tales, 224
Virtanen, Leea, 22
"vision of the night," 36
visitations, 37–38
voices, 67–68, 174, 179
Voragine, De, 56–57

wafts, 123
Wakelbura, 40
Waldron, George, 17, 33
Warcollier, René, 118
Warner, Carol, 182–83
warnings, 66–69, 204, 230
Wells, Michael, 29
Westropp, Thomas Johnson, 149
Wilbarger, Josiah, 35, 54
Wilby, Emma, 208, 212, 215, 228
Wilson, Harry, 159
Wilson, Judith, 98
Wolf-Man, 187–88
wraiths, 128, 129, 140–45
Wyandot Indians, 45–46, 65

yaa phu book ("medicine revealed by a spirit"), 185
Yámana, 219
Yao-Moi, 169
Yoder, Don, 67
Yu Huang, 38
Yurok Indians, 123

Zangi, Nur al-din, 73
Zulu tale, 53–54
Zuni Indians, 102, 142–43